D1289029

BLESSED
TO BE A
BLESSING

SACRED CIRCLE TIME FOR YOUNG CHILDREN

BY LEANNE HADLEY

DISCIPLESHIP
RESOURCES

ISBN 978-0-88177-786-4

Library of Congress Number 2016950118

DR786

DEDICATION

I would like to dedicate this book to Dr. Patty Lindau, who invited and encouraged me to think more deeply about the spiritual lives of young children and to Deb Walker and the staff and volunteers of First United Methodist Church, Colorado Springs, who were so open to trying a new spiritual approach with the little ones in our care. Thank you to Albie, Allison, Alyssa, Amanda, Amanda D., Bonnie, Brandy, Cathy, Constance, Darla, Diana, Elizabeth, Joyanne, Katrina, Kiersten, Lindsey, Lisa, Marianne, Meghan, Mena, Morgan, Tamara, Tamarisk, Trish, Pam, Paula, Sharon, Stephanie. You women not only blessed the children you worked with, you blessed my life! I am honored to be in ministry to young children with you. You are a blessing!

And . . . a special thank you to Jerome Goodley for loving children, listening, and always challenging me to do my best for God.

And . . . thank you to Melanie Gordon for listening, being honest, and inviting me to share my gifts. This would not have been written without her encouragement!

CONTENTS

CONTENTS

Contents

FOREWORD

In a world filled with distractions, our children thirst for the "living God" (Ps. 42:2) and for ways to deepen their connection with God through practices and rituals. Children around the world engage differently with their surroundings. Some of our children grow up in communities where they feel valued, while other children are barely noticed and abused. From the research of Sofia Cavalletti, Jerome Berryman, Sonja Stewart, and many others, we understand that all children are born with an innate sense of God's presence. As people who care for children, we know that all children deserve to be nurtured in a way that helps them grow in faith.

I first met my friend Leanne Hadley in 2008, when she graciously welcomed me to observe and understand her ministry with hurting children in Colorado Springs, Colorado. During that week I read her dissertation and knew immediately that her work and research with thousands of children allowed her truly to connect with the spiritual needs of children. There was something refreshing about her emphasis on the relational piece of spiritual formation. In *Blessed to Be a Blessing*, children are offered the space to deepen their relationship with God and others using a model that is flexible enough to use in a weekday preschool ministry setting, in the home, during weeknight programming, and in camp and retreat settings, while sharing stories of our faith using everyday objects.

Over the years, I have been honored to share in ministry with Leanne on meeting the spiritual needs of our children in various ways. Leanne is definitely the Mary to my Martha. While I naturally look at how we prepare for the Lord in a practical way, she reminds me of the importance of time spent at the feet of our Lord. Choosing the "better part" (Luke 10:42) shines through in her ministry, illustrating for children's ministers the importance of time apart for ministry leaders.

I am blessed to call Leanne my friend and colleague. Your life will be blessed as you engage with children through the experiences in this resource, and the children whom you love and serve will know they are a blessing.

Melanie C. Gordon
Director, Ministry with Children
Discipleship Ministries of The United Methodist Church

PREFACE

Blessed to Be a Blessing: Sacred Circle Time for Young Children

While I was serving at First United Methodist Church, Colorado Springs, I hired a new preschool director, Dr. Patty Lindau. Patty understands young children better than anyone I have ever met. During her first few weeks of being part of our children's ministry staff, Patty asked, "What are you doing with the children in preschool as far as Christian education?"

I explained that I met with the children once a month and led them through Bible story time. She asked, "Is that what you think is best for young children?"

That was the beginning of an intense time of learning about the unique personalities of young children. I had worked with children of all ages (birth through sixth grade) for my entire career; but to be honest, most of what I had created and written for children was designed for older children. And then the teachers or I would modify the curriculum and lessons to make them appropriate for younger children.

Patty's questions helped me realize that I had never designed anything specifically for young children. So I started hanging out with our young children. I sat with them during their daily circle times at the preschool and watched as they delighted in learning the days of the week during calendar circle time, exploring the weather and trying to guess what color the water might turn during science circle time, and listening intently during story circle time.

I started attending the young children's classes during Sunday school and watched as they prayed and interacted with their teachers. I was amazed at the deep and rich relationships these children had developed with one another and with their teachers.

After lots of watching, lots of questions for Patty, and lots of prayer, I wondered if I could develop a spiritual experience for young children that incorporated the learning from my doctorate work and from my work with children for thirty years. I wanted it specifically for the young children in our congregation.

I decided that since preschool and kindergarten teachers use "circle times," my new time with children would follow their lead, becoming a circle time for story and prayer. As a result, this time with young children is called Sacred Circle Time, and it is fashioned after the circle times used regularly in schools and preschools with young children.

I also decided that my once-a-month time with all the children together was not the best way to help young children learn. These little ones learn best in small, intimate circles where they feel secure, have mastery over the routine, and have relationships with the leader. So instead of meeting monthly with all the children for a big worship experience, I committed to meeting monthly with each class and then invited the teachers in each classroom to begin using "Sacred Circle Time" each day.

At first, there was some resistance. The teachers were not sure that they had time to add another circle time to their already busy days in addition to the regular Sunday school curriculum. They were also unsure that they should be offering a sacred experience for children. It was one thing to tell a story and do a craft, but leading young children into sacred experiences with God and blessing them each day felt like the work a pastor should be doing.

However, these women were willing to try, so together we began using this method. Before long, we realized that it was a powerful tool. It was powerful for the children and for us as well. In this fifteen-minute experience, we were rediscovering God, and the children were growing in their faith right before our eyes!

It is this simple and powerful *Sacred Circle Time* that I would like to offer to you to use with the young children in your life . . . at church, in the preschool, at home, and wherever young children gather.

I offer two formats. The basic format is for you to use in addition to the regular curriculum you are currently using. The extended format can be used for special times where you would like to offer a spiritual experience for your young children and have a longer time slot to fill.

I know this might feel different from the formats we usually use with young children, but I am inviting you to try it. I believe that you will find that it is a simple and powerful tool to bring young children into deeper relationships with God.

Leanne Hadley

Section One

. . . .

Sacred Circle Time for Young Children

Chapter One

Blessed to Be a Blessing

A Christlike Understanding of Young Children

*People were bringing little children to him in order that he might touch them;
and the disciples spoke sternly to them. But when Jesus saw this, he was indig-
nant and said to them, "Let the little children come to me; do not stop them;
for it is to such as these that the kingdom of God belongs. Truly I tell you, who-
ever does not receive the kingdom of God as a little child will never enter it."
And he took them up in his arms, laid his hands on them, and blessed them.*

(MARK 10:13-16, NRSV)

Jesus loved children. When we read the stories that tell of Jesus and children, there
is no doubt that he loved them. We might assume, then, that most people during the
time of Jesus loved and appreciated children as well; but when we look closely at history, we discover that the people at the time of Jesus were divided in their opinion of
the worth and value of children.

The Greeks and Romans did not hold children in high regard. Fathers could, and
regularly did, remove children from the house and refuse any further care for them.

This practice was called *exposure* and was an accepted practice of the time. Children were seen as unintelligent and useless until they could contribute physically or academically to society.

In stark contrast to the Greco-Roman view of children, the Jewish community, of which Jesus was part, valued children and saw them as the greatest blessing God could bestow. Abraham and Sarah, Isaac and Rebekah, Hanna and Elkanah, Elizabeth and Zechariah all lived in shame because they were barren until God gave them a child. Children were a gift, a blessing, and a cause for great celebration.

Even though the Jewish community viewed children as a blessing, the Greco-Roman view of children had its influence. Because of the occupation of their lands, Jewish people often found themselves struggling with their religious views and the more popular views of the society in which they lived. This is evidenced in the Bible story of the children who were brought by their parents to be blessed by Jesus. The disciples tried to turn them away, saying that Jesus did not have time for children. Even among the closest followers of Jesus, children were considered a problem, a burden, and less important than the adults. They lived in the tension between what their Jewish faith taught them and what they were exposed to in their secular, daily life.

Jesus, however, made it clear that children were important. He sternly told his disciples to "Let the children come," and then told them that unless they turned and became like children, they would never enter the kingdom. Jesus clearly respected children and made time for them. He not only told the disciples how important children were, he lifted them up as examples to be followed and learned from. Jesus reinforced his words with his actions by taking children into his arms and blessing them, one at a time. At that time in history, when the influence of the Greco-Roman world was so powerful, Jesus stayed true to his belief that children are a blessing.

I find myself wondering if our view of children is that of the Greco-Roman world or a Christian one. Although we give lip service about the value of children, the lack of school funding, the shortage in humanitarian aid to children and families, rising poverty and abuse rates, the lack of medical and psychological care for children worldwide, low wages for those who work with children, the exploitation of children in the sex trade industry, and the unabashed onslaught of media and advertising directed at children as consumers makes me wonder which worldview of children we have accepted and practice today.

Perhaps our world today is not that different from the ancient world when it comes to how people regard children. That is why our work with children is so important, and I thank you for stepping up to do it!

Sacred Circle Time is more than a new curriculum or activity for young children. It is a reminder that children are a gift from God. Children matter. They deserve our time and attention. They are deeply loved by God . . . they are our blessings!

Sacred Circle Time is a time set apart for children and for us, the adults in their lives, to sit together, wonder together, learn Bible stories together, and pray together. In the process, the children will be reminded and assured that they are a blessing and we, the adults, will be reminded of the blessing children are to our lives as teachers and examples.

The Importance of Relationships

As I write the lessons and organize them into a format that I hope you find useful, I am aware that the most important components of Sacred Circle Time are the relationships that are built. Sacred Circle Time is a time where adults and children begin to live out what Christ did when the children were brought to him. Even though the Bible does not give much detail about those events, those of us who work with children know that when Jesus looked into children's eyes, took them into his arms and on his lap, he was smiling and enjoying their presence. And you know that they were smiling back at him, hugging him, talking out of turn, and doing whatever it took to get his attention. After all, that is what children do when adults pay authentic attention to them. Even the most timid children try to make subtle eye contact and move a tiny bit closer.

Sacred Circle Time is a time to appreciate children. There is a playful and warm quality to the serious work we are doing together. I encourage you, as you use this material, to remember that the format is important because it provides structure and direction, but the true work of reminding children that they are a gift and a blessing will happen as you authentically treasure them for the gifts they are. They will do what all young children do: They will speak out of turn, lose focus, go off on tangents that have nothing to do with the story. As you gently help them refocus, you will impress upon them what a blessing they are!

Young children are not yet capable of understanding the theology of the church or the intricacies of the stories of our faith; but they can understand that there is a God who wants a relationship with them, who is calling them to become followers, and who blesses them and delights in them. The goal of Sacred Circle Time is to create spaces where young children can experience God's presence, begin to understand what a blessing they are to God and to others, so that the journey to a faith-filled life begins.

The Importance of Blessings

> *Now the* LORD *said to Abram, "Go from your country and your kindred and your father's house to the land that I will show you. I will make of you a great nation, and I will bless you, and make your name great, so that you will be a blessing."*
>
> (GENESIS 12:1-2, NRSV)

God appears to Abram and tells him that if he follows God, and God alone, Abram's descendants will become a great nation. Abram was faithful and did as God asked. And God was faithful to Abram and gave him more descendants than stars in the sky. We are the descendants of Abram. We are the blessed ones called to be a blessing for others. Being blessed by God and understanding that God called him to be a blessing to others was the first step for Abram. God began a relationship with Abram by telling him he was blessed to be a blessing to others.

Is it any wonder then that Jesus simply blessed the children who were brought to him? These children were much too young to understand the concept of a messiah, or who it was that their parents had brought to see. So Jesus, rather than trying to explain to them who he was, simply blessed them and made them aware of his love for them through his touch, warmth, and presence. Jesus, as God had done with Abram, began his relationship with children by blessing them.

Sacred Circle Time is a time set apart for you to bless the children in your lives. You will bless them in three ways:

1. You will delight in them, and, through your actions, they will know that they are a blessing.
2. You will spend time with them, hearing Bible stories and praying, so you will bless them with the word and presence of God, Jesus, and the Holy Spirit.
3. You will formally bless them at the end of your time together. Just as God blessed Abram and just as Jesus blessed the children who were brought to him, you will have the opportunity to bless each child after each session. Blessings are a special time when you look into children's eyes and tell them that they are a blessing to God.

The idea of blessing is the central concept of this program. Abram was blessed by God and became a blessing. We are his children, the result of the original blessing handed down throughout the history of the Bible. Jesus blessed the children who were brought to him. The blessing of God is a gift, and it is a gift that transforms us. When we realize that we are blessed, we cannot help but bless others. Children are a blessing, and they will bless many others, including you. As you create this climate of blessings for children, be aware that you will be blessed in return. In this circle of blessings, we, the adults and the children, will become what we are called to be: children of Abram, who follow Jesus Christ and bless the world.

Chapter Two

. . . .

Young Children
Are Spiritual People

They Are a Blessing!

This book begins with the assumption that children are spiritual beings who have a relationship with God. It presents a model, designed for children's specific needs, to bring them closer to God, Jesus, and the Holy Spirit long before they can understand theology, the nature of a savior, the need for forgiveness, or the complexities of trying to live a life of faith in our world today. I begin with the core belief that children are born spiritual and that our task, as the adults in their lives, is to help them recognize and strengthen their relationship with God, Christ, and the Holy Spirit.

Before we get into the nuts and bolts of Sacred Circle Time, I want to tell you about some of the children I have been privileged to meet as I used this model in my own congregation. Sacred Circle Time is one of my most favorite times. Teachers also report that Sacred Circle Time is a highlight in the time they spend with children. The children love this special time, and we were blessed to watch them grow in their spirituality and faith as a result of it.

Our Tiniest Children . . .

When we first began using Sacred Circle Time in our Sunday school and weekday pre-school, we were not certain that our tiniest children (10-18 months) were old enough to participate in such a structured time of worship. But we soon found out that they were. When the teacher or I would bring out the Sacred Circle basket, the children would start excitedly shouting, "Sacwred Ciwrlcle Time!" These little ones, who could not even pronounce the R's in their words, knew it was time for a special time of wonder, story, and blessing. They would watch as the wonder item was shared, listen to the story, spend time in quiet, and then begin to stick out their little hands, anticipating the blessing they would receive.

SAM . . .

Sam was a four-year-old who had been diagnosed with autism. His mother was a loving mom who was very involved in Sam's life and believed that he would do best in a preschool with non-autistic children rather than a special needs preschool. She wanted him to attend a Christian preschool where he would learn the stories of Jesus. The preschool director, Patty, and I had a long discussion about whether we were equipped to have an autistic child in our small preschool, but we decided that, since there were no special needs Christian preschools in our community, we would let him attend for a trial period.

Sam was a very sweet child and did well at our school. However, during daily Sacred Circle Time, he would often talk when the others were being quiet, didn't answer questions during the wonder time, and seemed indifferent to the entire process. He also had some sensory issues and would not let us touch him, so we were never able to give him a formal blessing. One day, I was blessing each child, and as I arrived at Sam, he stuck his hand out to receive a blessing. For the first time since he had been in the preschool class, he allowed me to look him in the eyes and bless him. From then on, whenever I would walk down the hallway, he would run over and hold out his hand for me to bless. He began allowing his teacher to bless him as well. His mother told us that he had started blessing her at home. On the closing day of school, during the final *Sacred Circle Time*, Sam stood up and moved me out of the way. He began, one at a time to bless each child in the circle. Sam had been blessed, and he became a blessing to those in his class. His teacher, his mother, and I dissolved into tears!

LILLY . . .

Lilly was a little three-year-old girl who attended our weekday preschool. Her parents, like many who brought their children to the preschool, were not as interested in having a Christian education for their children as they were in having a preschool with an excellent reputation. Lilly's father and mother had decided to bring her up without any formal Christian education because they did not want to "cram religion down her throat." When her father heard that Lilly would be participating in Sacred Circle Time each day, he was very upset and met with me, demanding that Lilly be allowed to play rather than participate. I asked him to come and see the exercise and then decide. He did not, but his wife did; and she felt comfortable with it, so they decided to leave Lilly in our program until Christmas break. Then they planned to move her to a secular preschool.

About a month later, I was called to the preschool director's office. Lilly's dad was demanding to see me immediately. I went downstairs, filled with anxiety because I assumed he was once again going to express his desire for his daughter to be exempt from participating in Sacred Circle Time. I could tell, as soon as I saw him, that he was emotional.

He said, "Remember how I came into to see you and asked you to allow my daughter not to participate in the Sacred Circle Time? Well, I know she has and today, she dumped out my best aftershave bottle and filled it with water." He paused for a long time as I tried to figure what the dumping out of his aftershave had to do with my Sacred Circle Time. And then he continued, "Well, she filled the bottle with water and then came to me, took my hand, and made a cross on it. Is that what a blessing is?"

I told him that it was. All he could say through his tears was, "Thank you." The little girl stayed at our preschool until she started public kindergarten.

Visiting Company . . .

A colleague of mine recently started blessing her children at the end of class. She called to tell me that one child's mother had called her to share a story. The family had company visiting for dinner. As one of their visitors, a woman, was leaving, the four-year-old took the woman's hand and, using her small finger, slowly traced a cross on it. The woman said, "What is she doing to me?" The little girl's mother replied, "I think she just blessed you."

Theresa . . .

Theresa is a young mom, and, like most young parents today, she is very busy. She works, runs her children to all of their afterschool activities, and brings them to church regularly. She was one of the parents who asked me if I would help her family create a family ritual at home. I suggested the Sacred Circle Time model that we used with her young daughters at Sunday school. So she got a basket and, while she had great intentions, she never quite found a good time to begin using it. One day, her five-year-old daughter saw the basket. She carried it to the center of the floor and invited her mommy and brother to sit down in a circle. Then she performed the opening ritual, told them a story, and blessed her mother and brother. From then on, she led her family in Sacred Circle Time each evening.

Sacred Circle Time is a simple process. Do not assume that because it is simple, it is not effective. It has been carefully created to use with young children and, as such, it is age-appropriate and child friendly. Jesus, when children were brought to him, did not begin explaining theology to them or ask them to memorize Scripture passages. He blessed them. He understood the nature of children and met them *where they were* on their faith journey. Sacred Circle Time does the same. It brings children into the presence of Christ. In the process, they grow in their love, desire, and joy for God.

At the beginning of the church year, I wanted the young children of my Sunday school to learn about the history of our church, to know that it was a United Methodist Church, and to understand that they were United Methodist children. I told them all about John Wesley and the circuit riders. I showed them the sign on the front of the church that said, "First United Methodist Church." I showed them that the cross and flame symbol of The United Methodist Church could be found on the welcome desk and on the red pew hymnals. At the end of the weeks we had spent learning about the United Methodist Church, I decided to share what we had been learning with the congregation. So I gathered the children down front for the Children's Sermon Time, and I shared with the adults all the fun ways we had been learning about what it means to be United Methodist. And then I turned to the children and said, "Okay, now let's review. What are you?" I expected them to give me the correct answer, which was, "We are United Methodists." But to my surprise, they all yelled in unison, "We are a blessing!" Indeed, they were! The entire congregation clapped. I decided not to remind them that they are also United Methodists.

Although Sacred Circle Time was developed in a United Methodist Church, it is not exclusively a United Methodist model. It can be used with young children in a variety of Christian settings. As the story above illustrates, children at this age are not ready to understand denominational affiliation any more than they can understand complex theology. Young children are spiritual beings. Sacred Circle Time is the first step on a young child's lifelong journey of experiencing God through wonder, story, and prayer. God chose to bless Abraham (Abram) as he began his journey; Jesus blessed the children who were brought to him; and during Sacred Circle Time, you will bless the children in your congregation. They will, in return, bless you! We are all, young and old, blessed to become blessings!

Chapter Three

. . . .

The Spiritual Life
of Young Children

Young children are capable of deeply spiritual experiences. At the same time, they are certainly not adults and do not experience God in the same manner and with the same intellectual capacities as adults. One of the reasons the spiritual life of young children has been misunderstood is that we have assumed that the best way to help young children find God is by beginning with adult spiritual practices and theologies and then simplifying them down to the level of children. In reality, the practices were over their heads and too advanced, so, it appeared that children were incapable of developing a relationship with God, Christ, and the Holy Spirit until they were older. Rather than look deeply at what was being offered to the young child, many people simply accepted that young children were incapable of having spiritual experiences.

Thankfully, pioneers such as Maria Montessori, Carl Rogers, Rebecca Nye, and Jerome Berryman questioned this assumption and encouraged those of us working with children to look at the young child with fresh eyes and new expectations. The assumptions of the past claiming that young children were incapable of a relationship with God are simply wrong. Young children are uniquely spiritual. Rather than using simplified adult theology and lessons, we must begin by understanding the true nature of the young child.

Who Are Young Children?

Scientists tell us that the brain of the young child is a busy place. As young children explore the world around them, their brains are forming important channels of information. This time of discovery is critical to the way young children will view the world around them and will shape their capacity to relate to others and learn and grow intellectually and emotionally. For young children, worship must create a space where they can be exactly who they are. By creating this worship space, we will help them grow emotionally, physically, and spiritually.

(1) Young children love to explore.

Children of this age are tactile learners. They need to touch, feel, taste, and look closely at the world around them. They marvel at the colors, textures, sizes, and edges of everything they see. To understand this, take a walk with young children. They stop every few steps because they see something exciting . . . a leaf, a bug, a sidewalk crack, and they bend down to explore it more closely. They want to touch it, pick it up, hold it, and they are delighted to share it with you saying. "Lookie what I found!" Exploring is an important time for young children. The more they explore, the better their brains form.

(2) Young children love to play.

When we hear that children love to play, we assume it will be free time using toys and games. Certainly, children need lots of free-play time, but "play" in Sacred Circle Time means something more expansive. It includes times of wonder, allowing children to use their imaginations and pretend. For example, in play during Sacred Circle Time, children might pretend that a button is Baby Moses and that a ribbon is the River Nile. Guessing what is inside a small box is play. Pretending that a sheet is an ocean and shaking it makes it become the sea of Galilee is play. Play is fun and silly; and it is, at the same time, the work of children. It is how they contemplate the world around them. Play with another person, such as a leader, also allows a special bond to happen between a child and an adult. Sacred Circle Time has a playful element to it that must not be confused with wasting time or a lack of seriousness about bringing children into the presence of God. Play is an important element of our time with children.

(3) Young children are trying to figure out the world around them.

Watching children try to put simple puzzles together illustrates this point. Children do not want adults to help as they try to figure out how the pieces of a puzzle fit together. Sometimes, they give up and throw the pieces on the floor and then, moments later, resume trying again. Young childhood is not a time of *getting the correct answer* as quickly as possible. Rather, it is a time of learning that life has lots of pieces and that the struggle to figure them out is often more important than finishing.

The *world* is a puzzle for young children, and they are fascinated by it! Everything is a new adventure, a mystery, and a fun discovery. How the weather, days of the week, time, and seasons fit together and flow are all new. The relationships between people such as mommies to daddies and children to parents are new to children. Children are just learning that teachers are to be listened to and that friends are fun. As they explore the world, children attempt to put things in order and to understand the relationships among things.

Sacred Circle Time introduces children, not only to new relationships with their teachers and friends, but also to the relationship between themselves and God, the Bible characters, and the relationships of God in Trinity.

(4) Young children enjoy learning language.

Young children are learning to talk. Long before they understand the meaning of words, they are fascinated with the sounds and expressions that they hear around them. Eventually, they begin to understand the meaning of those sounds and begin using them. The other day, my four-year-old grandson used the word "amazing" for the first time in the right context! We were both delighted!

Sacred Circle Time introduces new words to children that they might hear only at church, such as: Trinity, Bible, blessing, angel, Bible characters' names, and the seasons of the liturgical year. The children may not understand what these words mean at the time of their introduction, but in the same way that they learn language in the secular world, they will learn the language of the church. It is not critical that the children understand every word being introduced. The important thing is that they hear these words over and over. Eventually the words will begin to make sense to the children. Enjoy teaching new words to the children. Let them play with and practice making new sounds and pronouncing new words. They will enjoy this, and you will be delighted as they experiment with the new words and eventually begin to understand and use them.

(5) *Young children want mastery over their environments.*

"I want to do it myself!" and "I can do it . . . I am big now" are some of the most repeated phrases of young children. These little ones have no idea that they are still little, and they long to gain mastery over their surroundings. They need structure, routine, and practice so that they can achieve a sense of control over the environment around them. Sacred Circle Time uses the same outline each week. Instead of this becoming boring or too routine to young children, it allows them to relax and gain mastery over what to do and when. Within this predictable structure, they are freed to focus on the story and object for the day, while at the same time, experiencing a sense of control. The routine becomes a place where they can explore and participate without feeling confused, uncertain, or anxious.

(6) *Young children are learning about self-control, following directions, listening, and waiting their turn.*

Since young children are such tactile learners, and since everything in the world is new and exciting to them, and since their energy knows no bounds, they are often impulsive. They stand up when they are supposed to be sitting; they talk out of turn; they change the subject when you least expect it; and it can become frustrating.

Patience and repetition will help these little ones focus, listen, and learn. But remember, at the same time they are learning to control themselves, you are teaching them about relationships. We want these children to experience church as a special place where people are kind, caring, and loving. Helping children to learn to sit, listen, and follow directions must be approached gently and done with a great deal of patience. Becoming frustrated or angry will only make children more anxious and fidgety. Over time, the structure of Sacred Circle Time will help children learn the routine and relax into learning. In the meantime, gentle reminders and a kind touch on the back or leg will help children refocus during the circle time. While children learn to be still and listen, be patient and unhurried. Your attitude will teach them as much as the lesson will.

(7) Young children are developing a sense of who they are.

Young children are, in many ways, emotional sponges. They are soaking up information and trying to make sense of the emotions that swirl around and inside them. They are also trying to understand the cause and effect of their own actions and the actions of others. Young childhood is an emotionally vulnerable time. It is easy for children to wrongly interpret a situation as being their fault or believe that their actions caused them to become unloved because of tension or stress unrelated to them or their behavior. They might say hurtful things or even push or hit someone, not out of malice, but because they do not yet understand the implications of behavior and are not old enough to manage their emotions.

During this emotionally vulnerable time, young children are taking in the world around them. Based on what is mirrored back to them, lifelong messages will take shape inside them. Am I a good boy or girl? Do others like to play with me? Am I special? Am I smart? Am I stupid? Am I worthless? Is my skin a pretty color? Does anyone love me?

For healthy spiritual formation, children need to know that they are special, unique, loved, valued, and respected. When the adults around them communicate this message to them, they are better able to accept the love and grace of God later in life. Sacred Circle Time allows interplay between adults and children. As the children speak and are listened to, as they play and wonder together with the leader, and as the individual blessing is given to each child, an atmosphere is created where children are made aware that they matter, are unique, and are special in their own right.

Each element of Sacred Circle Time was created to meet the unique needs and personalities of young children. The lessons, timing, simplicity, and rhythm of the sessions help children strengthen their relationship to God, Jesus, and the Holy Spirit as they use exploration, play, and creativity. The structured format allows children to master their surroundings, hear Bible stories, and be exposed to the language of the church. They begin to reflect, process, pray, and become aware that they are special, unique, and a blessing!

. . . .

The Nuts and Bolts of Sacred Circle Time

Chapter Four

The Model of Sacred Circle Time

Sacred Circle Time uses the three parts of the Trinity as the basic format. **God, the Creator,** is a time set aside for wonder, imagination, and play. **God, the Son,** is a time set aside for hearing the stories of Jesus and the stories Jesus heard from the Old Testament as a child. **God, the Holy Spirit,** is a time set aside for the children to experience God through prayer and stillness.

There are two forms of the model, depending on the available time and the ages of the children.

The basic model, and the simplest, takes ten to fifteen minutes. It may be used in a church setting as an additional component to the regular Sunday school or children's worship curriculum. And it can add a spiritual time to evening nurseries and dinners where a formal curriculum or no curriculum is currently being used.

It may be used in preschool or daycare as a circle time, in addition to the regular circle times, such as science and story circle times, and it may also be easily used at home by parents, grandparents, and with home-schooled young children.

The basic model may be used by children of all ages, but for the very young (12-36 months), I suggest using this model, and not the extended format, because very young children simply cannot focus on the same thing for more than about fifteen minutes. Moving into the Trinity Stations can also be difficult for this age group. It is better to spend fifteen minutes in a focused time together rather than forty minutes if the children appear uncomfortable, confused, or stressed. Remember, this model trusts that God will speak to the children through wonder, story, and prayer; and God can do that in an instant. Longer times of learning do not always equate deep experiences with God.

The extended model, which can be used with children of all ages, but is best suited for children over three years, includes the basic model with expanded centers to allow the children additional time to process and reflect. It is designed to last forty minutes. For hour-long programs, it allows forty minutes of structure with twenty minutes set aside for free play and a snack. Although young children are often left in a nursery or Sunday school class for an hour, they do not have the attention spans to focus on the same story for the entire time. It's important to include free-play and snack time.

The extended form may be used at special times such as Advent and Lent, in a parents' day out, an afterschool Wednesday night program, during vacation Bible school, and in conjunction with adult learning opportunities such as Bible studies and weekday classes.

Sacred Circle Time is also designed to be used outside the church walls. It can easily be implemented at outreach programs in parks or apartment complexes, with children during mission trips, by chaplains at hospitals, and wherever children are present.

This is intended to be a *low-cost program*. The supplies needed for Sacred Circle Time are items you should already have on hand. This program is intentionally designed to be used wherever young children are found, regardless of the size of the program or available resources. The sooner young children realize that God is part of their lives and begin connecting with God, the better. We pray that Sacred Circle Time makes our time spent with young children easy, affordable, fun, and spiritually enriching.

And, especially for you . . .

One of the best parts of working with young children is that we adults read and ponder the Bible along with them. More than once, adults have told me that they learned Bible stories, not from attending Bible studies for adults, but through teaching them to their own children or to the children at church. Working with young children gives us a built-in structure for Bible study. With this in mind, I have included the entire Scripture passage, even though the story we share with young children is an abbreviated, child-friendly version. I have also included some brief "About . . ." sections before each liturgical season and as part of each individual lesson. These are to help you better understand the story that you are going to share with the young children. You do not need to share the "about" information with the children. These are included for you . . . to help you better understand the context of the Bible story.

I invite you, as you begin to prepare for the upcoming lesson each week, to read the entire Scripture and the "About" sections and then pause for a few moments to allow the story to speak to you. Don't over-analyze the story; just sit and be in the presence of God. Ponder the story, wonder about it, and grow to love it. The better you know, love, and want to share the story, the easier time you will have sharing it with the children. Plus, God speaks to all of us through the Bible. Teaching children the stories allows God to speak to you as well as to the children.

Chapter Five

Creating the Sacred Space

Creating a sacred space is the first step into inviting young children into a holy experience with God. Without using lots of directions, we gently invite them to join us in something important. Instead of using words to describe what will happen, we sit down with a basket that will hold all the things we will use to create a sacred space so that we can spend time in wonder, hearing the Bible story, praying together, and blessing one another. Slowly and with intention, we lay out a cloth to make room for the Trinity objects. As we take out each symbolic object, we acknowledge that God is the Creator, the Son, and the Holy Spirit. Although young children will not understand the theology of the Trinity yet, they are being introduced to the triune God and to one of the foundational doctrines of the church. It is not the objects that create the space. It is our attitude and reverence for God as we recall that God is Creator, Christ, and Holy Spirit that conveys to the children the importance of this sacred time.

In referring to the Trinity, I have chosen to use the word "Creator" rather than "Father." While Father is a beautiful description of God, I believe that Creator better describes the awe and wonder of God that Sacred Circle Time has been designed to capture. Plus, studies have shown that using male terms exclusively to describe God can prevent children without males in their life or who live with abusive men from developing a healthy image of God. Creator is gender neutral. If, in your tradition, it is important to use the word "Father," it may be substituted for "Creator." However, if you do not have a strong theological reason to use male imagery for God, I encourage you to use the term "Creator." It might feel odd at first because we are so used to male imagery for God, but after saying "Creator" a few times, I think you will find that it is a powerful image and better suited for young children.

Since one of the goals of Sacred Circle Time is to be low cost and easy to use in a variety of settings, you will probably have everything you need for the basic set-up and for the lessons. If not, the items could be donated. Items that need to be purchased, such as the Sacred Circle basket and Trinity symbols, should be inexpensive and will be used over and over again.

Please note: If you do not have exactly what is listed for any given lesson, feel free to be creative and substitute something you have rather than buy something new.

What You Will Need for the Basic Format

The Sacred Circle Time Basket: This basket will need to be easy to carry, yet large enough to hold your Sacred Circle Time symbols and cloth, Bible, and object for the day. A medium-sized picnic basket with a handle is great.

The Sacred Circle Time Sacred Space Cloth: This is a small piece of material that will be unfolded and placed in the center of the children who will be seated in a circle. It may be any color and should be about 12 by 12 inches. It could be a handkerchief, bandana, or any non-fraying cloth. A large placemat also works well.

The Sacred Circle Time Symbols: The symbols will be placed, one at a time, on the sacred cloth, creating the Trinity. You will need (1) a small globe symbolizing God, the Creator. This could be a purchased small globe, a painted ball, or a homemade clay globe; (2) a cross symbolizing God, the Son (can stand on its own or lie down). This could be purchased or made from sticks tied or glued together; (3) a small bell or chime to symbolize God, the Holy Spirit.

A Bible: Any Bible will be fine. It will not be read from. Instead, the lesson will be marked and shown to the children so that they understand that all of the stories told come from this holy book.

Optional: A small unbreakable bottle to hold water or oil for the blessing. You may also use a small ChapStick®. If you prefer not to use the water or oil, you may simply create the blessing using your finger.

In addition to the items above, each lesson has an additional object that will be added to your basket. This item will change each week, depending on the story that is shared.

What You Will Need for the Extended Format

For the extended format, you will need the Sacred Circle basket and all the things listed above. The extended format allows time for the children to move into Trinity Stations (reflection centers) following the Sacred Circle Time. You will need supplies for three reflection centers based on the Trinity that provide the children time to spend in reflection, wonder, and prayer.

The three stations provide space for reflection for children of different personality types:

God, the Creator (Wonder) Station: Some children reflect through touch and creating. These are the hands-on kids and often the ones who have a difficult time sitting still. They like to touch, feel, create, and make their "own" things. This is a good station for these children, as they can explore in an unstructured, creative way.

God, the Son (Story) Station: Some children reflect through play. These are usually the children who enjoy the story part of Sacred Circle Time the best. They are often children who ask lots of questions about what comes next in the story. They listen and answer the questions quickly, and then ask to hear the same story over and over. This center allows them the free time to reenact the story and think about what happened.

The Holy Spirit (Prayer) Center: Some children like to reflect quietly. These tend to be children who are on the quieter side in general and who sometimes get overwhelmed by large-group activity and noise. This center gives them a quiet place to reflect.

It is important to allow children to choose the stations and to allow them to move freely among them. The descriptions of the type of children who might be attracted to the stations listed above are general. Many factors will affect which station children will choose. They might choose a station because a friend has chosen it. They might choose a station based on the "extra" suggested item that is there for the week. And they might choose a station depending on their mood for the day.

There is no "right or wrong" station. Children should choose the station that appeals to them. A teacher or preschool director should take the children to each station each week so that the children have time to decide where they feel they can best process and reflect on the lesson for the day. Once they take the time to look at each of the stations, they can usually choose which one appeals to them for the day.

The time allotted for the Trinity Stations is intentionally very short. These are designed to help young children who have short attention spans reflect on what they have learned. If the time in the stations is expanded much beyond five minutes, they will forget the story as their play and creativity naturally expands.

Some children will want to move from station to station. Most children will stay in their station for the entire five minutes, but if they choose to change stations, that is fine. However, if they are running from station to station frantically, this means that the station choices are overwhelming them. It is the role of the helpers to gently invite them to calm down and spend this time reflecting. On the other hand, there might be children who cannot decide upon a station. These children often stand very still and do not know where to go. Choosing sometimes overwhelms young children, especially those who tend to be perfectionists. Again, it is role of helpers to gently lead children to a Trinity Station and assure them that Scared Circle Time will happen every week and they can spend time in all of the stations eventually. It will do no good to keep asking children who are overwhelmed to decide. Gently, help them begin to process. Otherwise, they will spend the entire reflection time deciding and then feel bad because they did not participate in the Trinity Stations.

Sacred Circle Time Supplies

Supplies You Will Need for Both Formats

The Sacred Circle basket

Sacred Space Cloth

Symbols for Creator (globe), Christ (cross), and Holy Spirit (bell or chimes)

A Bible marked to the passage you will be studying

Small, unbreakable bottle to hold water or oil for the blessing.

A journal page (one per child)

Crayons and/or markers

The Additional Trinity Station Supplies

Suggested supplies are listed below. Additional suggestions will be made with each lesson. However, use your imagination and the things you already have to create these spaces. The importance of these stations is not what supplies are in them, but rather that the supplies can be used to invite the children to reflect through touch, exploration, and play. This is how young children reflect and process. The more options they have, the better.

God, the Creator (Wonder) Station

- A bowl of water and small cups
- Beans and or seeds in a large plastic container
- Clay and sand
- Spices in small containers to smell
- Magnifying glass
- Mirror
- Plants and leaves
- Crystal prisms

God, the Son (Story) Station

- Children's Bibles
- Bibles with pictures
- Lego® sets
- Blocks
- Dolls dressed up as Bible characters
- Puppets
- Costumes and cloth to create costumes
- Simple props such as broom, table, chairs, rocking horse, old boxes of different sizes

God, the Holy Spirit (Prayer) Station

FOR QUIET REFLECTION:

- Electric candles
- Crosses of all sizes and types

- Icons
- Pictures
- A mirror
- Material and boxes to create altars

FOR ART AND MUSICAL PRAYER:

- Paper
- Crayons
- Scissors
- Magazines
- Glue
- Markers
- Sequins, buttons, etc. for decorating
- CD player and several selections of music
- Rubber bands and boxes
- Tubes for blowing
- Simple stringed instruments or chimes or bells
- Buckets for drumming

Chapter Six

. . . .

Recruiting the Leaders

Since young children are so active and filled with wonder, the more people you have to help focus and direct their energy, the better. Young children do not need punishment or even correction. Their energy is part of their *being*, and it does not need to be squelched. We want to do all we can to draw young children into the story and invite them to focus on Sacred Circle Time. Adults should be recruited who understand the personalities of young children, enjoy this age group, and can engage with them and delight in them. Young children need to be invited to explore, wonder, and engage. There is a fluid sense to working with them. I often describe it as keeping *kittens in a box*. Have you ever tried to keep tiny kittens in a box when they are constantly trying to climb out? Working with young children is like that! They are active, easily distracted, and everything is new! I find that some of my most talented teachers are those who can work with this age group! The teacher must be able to focus on presenting the lesson, and—at the same time—enjoy the children.

In the **Basic Sacred Circle Time model**, there should be a leader and at least two other adults. That way, the leader can focus on presenting the lesson, while the other adults can help invite the children to listen and be still. If a child leaves the space or needs to go to the bathroom, one adult can work with that child while the other stays with the group, and the leader is free to continue leading and focusing on the lesson.

Remember that inviting children to focus is not done through correcting them. Rather, the leader's interest in and focus on the lesson will draw the children into the story. The adults model attention by focusing on the Sacred Time themselves and by delighting in the answers and reactions of the children.

In the **Extended Sacred Circle Time format**, it is best to have a leader and three other adults. During the Extended Sacred Circle Time, the adults will be involved, just as they are during the Basic Sacred Circle Time. However, in the extended format, after the Basic Sacred Circle Time is presented, the children will move into their Trinity Stations to spend time in play, reflection, and processing time. It would be ideal to have an adult at each of the stations to play along with the children and model the kinds of things the children might do at each station. They will also help the children stay focused and intervene when conflict between children occurs. Young children are learning to share, play together, and work together. As they learn these new skills, they naturally become anxious; conflict easily arises. It is a good idea to have an adult in close proximity so that as soon as the children begin to become anxious or conflict begins, the adult quietly, and without many words, redirects the children and makes sure they have what they need to use in their processing time. The more adults you have, the fewer words will be needed as the children are gently guided into times of reflection, play, and processing.

As you recruit leaders to work with young children, you will want to find people who:

- delight in young children.
- are patient and respectful of children.
- believe that young children are capable of having a relationship with God.
- are willing to model focused behavior rather than correct or scold children.
- understand the personalities of young children and have the energy to keep up with them. (This has nothing to do with chronological age, but more to do with attitude.)
- are good storytellers and have engaging personalities.

- understand the importance of play and are willing to play along with the children rather than simply watch them.

Some questions you might ask as you recruit leaders are:

- Tell me what you know about young children.

  A person who really enjoys this age group will light up and smile as he or she describes young children.
- Tell me about the last time you played with a young child. What did you do?

  People who enjoy this age group will tell you of playing peek-a-boo, building blocks, swinging, and so on. It does not matter what they did with the children. You are watching to see if they had a good time interacting with children.
- What would you do when a child becomes disruptive during Sacred Circle Time?

  Remember that the idea of redirection is not familiar to some people. Many people accept that correction is the proper reaction. Ideally, people will name redirection. If they do not, follow up with a brief description of redirection. If people react positively, they are trainable; but if they think it is a ridiculous idea, or begin talking about the "good old days" when children behaved, they might work better with another age group.
- What is your favorite book to read to children?

  Asking someone to name his or her favorite Bible story can be intimidating. This question is designed to determine whether this person likes reading to and telling stories to children. Telling stories in an engaging manner is central to Sacred Circle Time.
- Tell me about a young child who was or is part of your life.

  A person who enjoys this age group will tell of a child and smile and become animated and excited as he or she talks. The person might also become sad because he or she misses a child who lives far away or show empathy for a child who is facing difficulty. You will be able to discern if a person loves children by the respectful, caring tone he or she shows. If the person appears harsh, he or she might be better suited serving another age group.

A WORD ABOUT SAFETY

In addition to finding the right people to work with young children, it is critical—as it is when working with people of all ages—to make sure the space is physically and emotionally safe. Young children are completely dependent on the adults who care for them to make sure that they do not become harmed in any way while in our care.

The room or space where the Sacred Circle Time happens needs to be safe. There are easy-to-find checklists on the web. You might want to print one out and then carefully go over the room to make sure that electrical outlets are covered, paint is not chipping on windows, and that any cleaning supplies and toxic materials are put out of reach. Follow a checklist. You might even crawl around on the floor, so that your eyes will be at the eye level of a young child to notice anything that you might have missed while standing upright. Do weekly each time you leave and enter the space because things often get moved around by others sharing your space or by those who clean the space.

Emotional safety is as important as physical safety. Because young children are often limited in their language skills, it makes it difficult for them to understand safety and to report any abuse against them. In the UMC and most other denominations, there are stringent programs designed to make sure that children are safe. These programs include, at a minimum, requiring two people to be with the children at all times, background checks, references checked and files kept and updated regularly for all volunteer and paid staff. While these may seem over-reactive or like extra work, studies have proven that such measures are deterrents for pedophiles who might volunteer or apply for a job to gain access to children. Such policies are also designed to protect adults against any false accusations made against them. Making the space safe takes extra time and effort, and it is worth it! Please do not forget that safety is the most basic and first step in caring for children.

WHERE TO BEGIN WITH RECRUITMENT

When finding the best people to work with young children, we often find ourselves frustrated. Rarely do people volunteer to help. Many times, when we approach people we feel might be a great fit, they tell us "no," or give us a laundry list of reasons they can't help us.

To recruit the best people for Sacred Circle Time, begin by telling stories. The actual stories I included earlier on pages 24–26 were designed to inspire you and others as well. Tell them, share them, publish them and invite people who find them inspiring to join you as your congregation, preschool, daycare, or mission trip begins creating your own sacred spaces where *your* young children will also experience God.

Tell *your* stories to everyone you know. Invite people to come and witness for themselves how powerful the Sacred Circle Time is. And if they do not come, invite them again . . . over and over. Once people see for themselves just how powerfully God, Christ, and the Holy Spirit are present during Sacred Circle Time, you will have no trouble recruiting volunteers.

Tell your stories, and then invite, invite, invite!

The Sacred Circle Time Lessons

Now that you have read this far in the book, I hope you have a good understanding of the nature of young children and a basic understanding of the way Sacred Circle Time allows these precious little ones to experience God. I hope you have gathered your supplies and designed your space. Now, the fun begins: the actual lessons for the Sacred Circle Time.

This book contains 52 lessons that follow the church calendar. The church calendar begins with Advent each year, and our lessons do as well. It is not important that you begin in Advent or that you use all 52 lessons. You may begin using Sacred Circle Time any time and pick and choose the lessons that best meet your needs.

Each section begins with a brief description of the church season and contains lessons appropriate for use during that season. The supplies needed and step-by-step instructions for both the basic and extended formats are included in each lesson.

Practice a couple of times before you present to the children. You want to be as familiar with the material as possible so that you can stay focused, fully present, and non-anxious when the young children are there with you. There is no right or wrong way to do this. Let your personality shine through, relax, and enjoy being with these little ones.

You have stepped up as a person who wants to bring the love of God to young children. In accepting this role, you are following in the steps of Jesus who valued, respected, and blessed children. So remember, above all else, that you are a blessing!

Sacred Circle Time Lessons

About the Season of Advent

The word *Advent* is derived from Latin and means "to come." Advent is a time set aside by the church to prepare ourselves for the arrival of Christmas, the day when we celebrate the birth of Jesus. There are many traditions associated with Advent. The early church spent time in Advent in fasting, prayer, and trying to purify their hearts and lives of sin.

With the passing of time, Advent has morphed into a more joyful time where we prepare for the coming of Jesus with the joy we experience in much the same way we anticipate the birth of a child, grandchild, or friend's child. It has a festive and happy mood. We decorate, sing, anticipate, and wait for the arrival of the baby Jesus.

Advent for young children should reflect joy and happiness. One of the challenges during Advent is that children will be extra energetic as they anticipate Christmas. They are just learning about holiday traditions such as Santa and giving and receiving gifts. They are also eating lots of sugar-filled treats that they might not normally eat, and their regular schedules are disrupted as they have special programs at daycare and school. They are excited about their relatives who will soon be visiting. They feel, and are animated by, the excitement and stress of those around them.

As we experience God with them during Sacred Circle Time, we should enter the time knowing that being still and listening is especially difficult during Advent. Rather than correct or lecture the children, we need to focus deeply on what we are doing. We will need to arrive early so that everything is set up and we are relaxed as the children arrive. We will need to slow down a bit more than usual, try to be fully present, and model focusing on the story. This sounds easy, but we, like the children are excited, overwhelmed, have been eating poorly, and our sleep schedules are off. We are having the same struggles as the children. So be kind to yourself and to the children and trust that God will speak, even when it is nearly impossible to find the quiet and stillness we desire and need.

Advent 1

Story: Gabriel Visits Mary

Text: Luke 1:26-38, NRSV

THE BIRTH OF JESUS FORETOLD

In the sixth month the angel Gabriel was sent by God to a town in Galilee called Nazareth, to a virgin engaged to a man whose name was Joseph, of the house of David. The virgin's name was Mary. And he came to her and said, "Greetings, favored one! The Lord is with you." But she was much perplexed by his words and pondered what sort of greeting this might be. The angel said to her, "Do not be afraid, Mary, for you have found favor with God. And now, you will conceive in your womb and bear a son, and you will name him Jesus. He will be great, and will be called the Son of the Most High, and the Lord God will give to him the throne of his ancestor David. He will reign over the house of Jacob forever, and of his kingdom there will be no end." Mary said to the angel, "How can this be, since I am a virgin?" The angel said to her, "The Holy Spirit will come upon you, and the power of the Most High will overshadow you; therefore the child to be born will be holy; he will be called Son of God. And now, your relative Elizabeth in her old age has also conceived a son; and this is the sixth month for her who was said to be barren. For nothing will be impossible with God." Then Mary said, "Here am I, the servant of the Lord; let it be with me according to your word." Then the angel departed from her.

About the text: The Hebrew word for *angel* means *messenger* and was usually associated with a message originating with God and being delivered by a supernatural being. While we often see angels depicted as women or children in liturgical art, this angel is masculine. Gabriel is a male angel sent with a very important message for Mary. Angels were one way that God communicated with people throughout the Bible. They often brought messages aimed at helping people, and they often brought other helpful things such as food or encouragement for someone in need.

Sacred Circle Time Focus: We will focus on angels as those who bring messages to people, and we will focus specifically on Gabriel, who brought a very special message from God to Mary.

Sacred Circle Time Basic Format

Sacred Circle basket and contents:

- Sacred space cloth
- Symbols for Creator (globe), Christ (cross), and Holy Spirit (bell or chimes)
- Small, unbreakable bottle to hold water or oil for the blessing.
- A journal page (one per child)
- Crayons and/or markers
- Bible bookmarked at Luke 1:26-28
- Focused Objects from the Bible story: Three things we use to communicate with others. Some suggestions are a simple can to be used as a drum; a candle to indicate the way people used to make smoke signals; paper and pen or pencil; a cell phone; email message.

The Lesson

Gathering

Sit down and place the sacred basket in front of you.

Pause so that the children notice it and begin to come closer.

Invite them to form a circle.

Sit quietly until they settle in and are quiet.

Say: "It is time for Sacred Circle Time. I am so glad that you are here today. I love learning our stories and experiencing God with you."

Creating the Sacred Space

Say: "First, we create our sacred space."

Slowly lay out the sacred cloth.

Slowly lift the globe (symbol of God, the Creator) and hold it at the eye level of the children. Say: "This is our symbol for God, the Creator." Carefully lay it on the sacred cloth. *(Pause.)*

Slowly lift the cross (symbol of God, the Son). Say: "This is our symbol for God, the Son." Carefully lay it on the sacred cloth. (*Pause.*)

Slowly lift the bell (symbol of God, the Holy Spirit). Say: "This is our symbol of God, the Holy Spirit." Carefully lay it on the sacred cloth. (*Pause.*)

Point to each symbol and say: "So we have God, the Creator; God, the Son; and God, the Holy Spirit. (*Pause.*) Our sacred space is ready. We are ready to begin our Sacred Circle Time together."

God, the Creator (A Time to Wonder)

Show. Have all the objects—A can to be used as a drum; a candle; paper and pen or pencil; a cell phone; email message—covered or in a bag or basket. Pull the items out, one at a time, and let the children look at them, touch them, and pass them around. Do not tell them what they are. Just let them wonder about them.

Ask: "What do you think each of these is for?" Let them guess. They will probably know what the phone is, but you will need to explain some of the items, such as a drum being a way to communicate with others when danger arrived or when it was time to go to a celebration.

Say: "Each of these is a way that people communicate with one another. Let's all say that word together." (*Say "communicate" slowly and have them repeat it.*)

"If you call your mommy, you are *communicating* with her.

"If you write your daddy or grandma a letter, you are *communicating* with them.

"When people send smoke up in the sky, they are *communicating* that something wonderful has happened!

"When people need to *communicate*, and they have to send out a message really far, they might beat a drum. That is *communication*.

"Let's say the word again . . . *communication*.

"What do you use when you communicate? Do you use any of these things?" Let them respond and prompt them to think of things such as a hug is communication, a smile is communication, drawing a picture for someone is communication, cuddling is communication, dancing together is communication, playing together and sharing is communication.

God, the Son (Telling the Story)

Say: "In our story for today, which is found in (*open the Bible*) Luke, chapter one, verses 26-38, God communicated with a woman named Mary. And do you know how God communicated? God sent an angel named Gabriel to communicate a very special message to Mary. Do you know what the message was? (*Pause and let them share.*)

"The message that God asked Gabriel to communicate to Mary was that she was going to be a mommy. And do you know who her baby was going to be? Jesus. The angel Gabriel brought that very special message to Mary from God. She was going to be the mommy of Jesus."

God, the Holy Spirit (Quiet and Prayer Time)

Say: "It is now time to pray. If you could communicate with anyone right now, who would it be? I am going to pass the phone (*or you can use any of the objects*) around, and when it is your turn to hold it, I want you to tell us who you would like to communicate with right now." *(Pass the phone and have each child share.)*

Say: "Now shut your eyes. Imagine that the person you just told us about is standing with you and God. In your mind, see yourself and God and the person you told us about all standing together." *(Give them a few seconds of silence.)*

Pray: "God, please be close to all of us and those we love. In the name of Christ, we pray. Amen."

(If using the extended Sacred Circle Time, stop here.)

A Time of Blessing

Explain: "The symbol for the story today is an angel because God sent an angel to communicate to Mary that she was going to be the mommy of Baby Jesus.

Ask: "Where would you like your blessing today?" *(Let the children tell you.)*

Make the symbol as you look into each child's eyes.

Say: "Thank you for being here today and spending time experiencing God with me. You are a blessing!"

Closing Time

Slowly put each Trinity symbol away.

Say: "And now we are finished with our Sacred Circle Time. We put away our symbol for God, the Creator. We put away our symbol for God, the Son. And we put away our symbol for God, the Holy Spirit.

Then quietly and gently put the sacred cloth away.

Conclude: "And we are all done with our Sacred Circle time. You did a great job. Yay!" Clap and celebrate a job well done.

Extended Format

(*10 minutes*) Begin with free-play time. Greet the children warmly and let them get used to the space. Have something in the free-play space for them to play with. Rotate each week:

Week One: Paper and crayons, markers, or paint.

Week Two: Clay, wire, pipe cleaners and beads, and tools to work the clay.

Week Three: Things to build with: blocks, Legos®, cans, boxes, or flat stones.

Week Four: Things that make noise.

(*3 minutes*) Transition time. Let the children know that it is almost Sacred Circle Time.

Say: "It is almost our Sacred Circle Time. I cannot wait to have sacred time with you today. Will you start to finish up? Then come join me for our special, holy time together."

Sit down in the Sacred Circle Time space and place your sacred basket in front of you.

(*10 minutes*) Sacred Circle Time (*Basic Format*)—Use the Sacred Circle Basic Format, but do not include the blessing or closing.

(*10 minutes*) Trinity Stations

Explain the Trinity Stations procedure for new children and for those who might forget from time to time.

Walk with the children to the Trinity Stations and show them what they can do in the stations, but do not let them start until they have seen all three stations.

Tell the children that after the Trinity Stations, they will spend five minutes in quiet time thinking about the story and the activities they have completed. They will then return to the Sacred Circle Time space to draw pictures and talk about their activities.

Station One: God, the Creator (Wonder) Station

Walk with the children to station one and show them what they can do here. In addition to the suggested supplies (page 469), you might want to add the communication tools that you used for the "God, the Creator (Wonder)" time from the Sacred Story Time Circle.

Station Two: God, the Son (Story) Station

Walk with the children to station two and show them what they can do here. In addition to the suggested supplies (page 469), you might want to include angel wings or halos.

Station Three: God, the Holy Spirit (Prayer) Station

Walk with the children to station three and show them what they can do here. In addition to the suggested supplies (page 469), you might want to add some stationery and envelopes. If you have parents' email addresses, you might provide a computer and volunteer to help the children email their parents.

Begin Quiet Time

Say: "Let's begin five minutes of thinking about the story and how Gabriel communicated God's message to Mary that she was going to be the mommy of Jesus.

After five minutes, I will invite you, one at a time, to come to the Sacred Circle Time space and draw what you did or thought about, so we can all share together."

(*2-minute transition time*) Start laying paper in the circle and laying out the crayons and other materials. Invite the children, one at a time, to come and draw what they did, thought about, or experienced.

(*10 minutes*) **Journal and Share Time**

Let the children draw and journal as they gather. As most of the children finish, have them begin to share. Tell them that listening to one another is important.

Say: "Thank you for spending time with me in the Trinity Stations. I cannot wait to hear what you experienced today. Who would like to share?" (Give each child time to talk, and you should talk as well.)

Place their activities in individual folders; or if they are to take the folders home, place them behind them so they will not be distracted. This will keep you from having to correct the children's behavior.

10 minutes (*snack or toy time*)

A Time of Blessing

Say, "The symbol from today's story is an angel because the Angel Gabriel visited Mary."

Say: "Where would you like your blessing today? I am going to make the angel on your _____ (*whatever part they choose*)."

Make the symbol as you look into each child's eyes.

Say: "Thank you for being here today and spending time experiencing God with me. You are a blessing!"

Closing Time

Slowly put each Trinity symbol away.

Say: "And now we are finished with our Sacred Circle Time. We put away our symbol for God, the Creator. We put away our symbol for God, the Son. And we put away our symbol for God, the Holy Spirit."

Then quietly and gently put the sacred cloth away.

Conclude: "And we are all done with our Sacred Circle time. You did a great job. Yay!" Clap and celebrate a job well done.

Advent 2

Story: Mary Visits Elizabeth

Text: Luke 1:39-56, NRSV

In those days Mary set out and went with haste to a Judean town in the hill country, where she entered the house of Zechariah and greeted Elizabeth. When Elizabeth heard Mary's greeting, the child leaped in her womb. And Elizabeth was filled with the Holy Spirit and exclaimed with a loud cry, "Blessed are you among women, and blessed is the fruit of your womb. And why has this happened to me, that the mother of my Lord comes to me? For as soon as I heard the sound of your greeting, the child in my womb leaped for joy. And blessed is she who believed that there would be a fulfillment of what was spoken to her by the Lord."

Mary's Song of Praise

And Mary said,
"My soul magnifies the Lord,
    and my spirit rejoices in God my Savior,
for he has looked with favor on the lowliness of his servant.
    Surely, from now on all generations will call me blessed;
for the Mighty One has done great things for me,

and holy is his name.
His mercy is for those who fear him
   from generation to generation.
He has shown strength with his arm;
   he has scattered the proud in the thoughts of their hearts.
He has brought down the powerful from their thrones,
   and lifted up the lowly;
he has filled the hungry with good things,
   and sent the rich away empty.
He has helped his servant Israel,
   in remembrance of his mercy,
according to the promise he made to our ancestors,
   to Abraham and to his descendants forever."
And Mary remained with her about three months and then returned to her home.

About the text: After the Angel Gabriel left, Mary must have felt overwhelmed, alone, and very frightened. Perhaps that is why Gabriel had shared with her that a sign of the truth of his message from God would be that Elizabeth, Mary's cousin, was going to have a baby as well. So, after Gabriel leaves, Mary sets out to visit Elizabeth for two reasons: to make sure that what the angel told her was the truth and that she was not hallucinating, and because her cousin's home would give her a respite away from her own community as well as provide emotional support. She is so relieved when she arrives and discovers that the message is true and that her cousin believes her story that she begins to sing. And the song she sings is one of most beautiful songs ever recorded in the Bible. It is song of great hope and joy.

The Sacred Circle Time Focus: We will learn this story and then experience singing as a way of praying to and being with God.

Sacred Circle Time Basic Format

Sacred Circle basket and contents:

- The sacred cloth along with the Creator (globe), Christ (cross) and Holy Spirit (bell or chime) objects
- Small, unbreakable bottle to hold water or oil for the blessing.
- A journal page (one per child)
- Crayons and/or markers
- A Bible bookmarked at Luke 1:39-56.
- Focused objects from the Bible story: A blank sheet of paper and marker; a hymnal or songbook or paper with the notes of a song written on it.

The Lesson

Gathering

Sit down and place the sacred basket in front of you.

Pause so that the children notice it and begin to come closer.

Invite them to form a circle.

Sit quietly until they settle in and are quiet.

Say: "It is time for Sacred Circle Time. I am so glad that you are here today. I love learning our stories and experiencing God with you."

Creating the Sacred Space

Say: "First, we create our sacred space."

Slowly lay out the sacred cloth.

Slowly lift the globe (symbol of God, the Creator) and hold it at the eye level of the children. Say: "This is our symbol for God, the Creator." Carefully lay it on the sacred cloth. *(Pause.)*

Slowly lift the cross (symbol of God, the Son). Say: "This is our symbol for God, the Son." Carefully lay it on the sacred cloth. (*Pause.*)

Slowly lift the bell (symbol of God, the Holy Spirit). Say: "This is our symbol of God, the Holy Spirit." Carefully lay it on the sacred cloth. (*Pause.*)

Point to each symbol and say: "So we have God, the Creator; God, the Son; and God, the Holy Spirit. (*Pause.*) Our sacred space is ready. We are ready to begin our Sacred Circle Time together."

God, the Creator (A Time to Wonder)

Show. (*Hold up the blank sheet of paper so the children can see it.*)

Say: "When we write words, we use our letters and make words. So I will use a (*make a C*). What letter is that? (*Let them guess.*) Now I will add an (*make an A*). What letter is that? (*Let them guess.*) Now I will add a (*make a T*). What letter is that? (*Let them guess.*) And when I put all of these letters together, it spells a word. Does anyone know the word? (*Let them guess.*) The word is CAT! We made a word using our letters."

Get out the sheet music and show them the notes. Ask: "What do you think this is?" (*Let them guess.*) "It is how we read music. When we write stories, we use our letters and words, like we did for the word CAT. But when we write music, we use notes. The notes go up, and the notes go down; and they help us know what to sing. See how the notes go up and down? You say up or down when I point to a note." (*Point to each note and let the children say up and down.*)

"Notes make songs. I am going to hum a song and see if you can guess what it is."

Hum two or three songs. You can use songs familiar to the children in your group such as "Twinkle, Twinkle Little Star" or a Christmas song. Beware: If you mention Santa, they will all want to tell you what they want for Christmas! Hum the song and let them try and guess it. Then sing it with them.

Say: "Songs are so much fun!"

God, the Son (Telling the Story)

Say: "In our story today, which is found in (*open the Bible*), Luke, chapter one, verses 39-56, Mary has just been told by the Angel Gabriel that she is going to be the mommy of Jesus; and she is scared! She has never been a mommy before, and it is a very big and important job. So she goes to visit her cousin, Elizabeth. Elizabeth is so happy to see Mary, and she gives her a big hug. Mary knows that everything is going to be all right now. Elizabeth made her feel better. So do you know what Mary did? She sang a song! She was so happy to be with her cousin and to know that everything was going to be okay that she sang a song! And do you know who she sang to? God! She sang a song to God! It was a prayer song; and in it, she thanked God for choosing her to be a mommy. She wasn't scared any more, and she sang a prayer song to God."

God, the Holy Spirit (Quiet and Prayer Time)

Say: "It is now time for us to pray. And for our prayer time, I want to teach you a song."

Teach them this simple song sung to the tune of "Twinkle, Twinkle Little Star," or make one up on your own with a tune more familiar to your children.

God I love you and I know that you love me, love me so.

Joy, joy, joy, joy, happiness,

Joy, joy, joy, joy happiness.

God I love you and I know that you love me, love me so.

Say: "Now that you know the song, let's sing it as a prayer song, just like Mary did when she sang her prayer song to God."

Sing the song once or twice.

Pray: "God, please help us remember that you love us and care for us every day! In the name of Christ, we pray. Amen."

(If using the extended Sacred Circle Time, stop here.)

A Time of Blessing

Say: "The symbol for the story today is a music note because we use music notes to write songs for people to sing. Mary sang a prayer song, and so did you. Any time you want to pray to God, you can sing a song. You can sing one you know or make one up!"

Ask the children where they would like to receive their blessing and bless them. Be sure to maintain eye contact. Say: "Thank you for being here today and spending time experiencing God with me. You are a blessing!"

Closing Time

Slowly put each Trinity symbol away.

Say: "And now we are finished with our Sacred Circle Time. We put away our symbol for God, the Creator. We put away our symbol for God, the Son. And we put away our symbol for God, the Holy Spirit."

Then quietly and gently put the sacred cloth away.

Conclude: "And we are all done with our Sacred Circle time. You did a great job. Yay!" Clap and celebrate a job well done.

Extended Format

(10 minutes) Free-Play Time. Greet the children warmly and let them get used to the space. Have something in the free-play space for them to play with. Rotate each week:

Week One: Paper and crayons, markers, or paint.

Week Two: Clay, wire, pipe cleaners and beads, and tools to work the clay.

Week Three: Things to build with: Blocks, Legos®, cans, boxes, flat stones.

Week Four: Things that make noise.

(3 minutes) Transition time. Let the children know that it is almost Sacred Circle Time. Say: "It is almost our Sacred Circle Time. I cannot wait to have sacred time with you today. Will you start to finish up? Then come join me for our special, holy time together."

Sit down in the Sacred Circle Time space and place your sacred basket in front of you.

(10 minutes) Sacred Circle Time (*Basic format*)
Use the Sacred Circle Basic Format, but do not include the blessing or closing.

(10 minutes) Trinity Stations
Explain the Trinity Stations procedure for new children and for those who might forget from time to time.

Walk with the children to the Trinity Stations and show them what they can do there, but do not let them start until they have seen all three stations.

Tell the children that after the Trinity Stations, they will spend five minutes in quiet time thinking about the story and the activities they have completed. They will then return to the Sacred Circle Time space to draw pictures and talk about their activities.

Station One: God, the Creator (Wonder) Station

Walk with the children to station one and show them what they can do here. In addition to the suggested supplies (page 469), you might want to add some things to make musical instruments. Cardboard with rubber bands to stretch over it makes a great instrument. Use old coffee cans or Pringles® cans as containers and let the children put different objects in them to make different sounds.

Station Two: God, the Son (Story) Station

Walk with the children to station two and show them what they can do here. In addition to the suggested supplies (page 469), include books with pictures of people singing and playing instruments.

Station Three: God, the Holy Spirit (Prayer) Station

Walk with the children to station three and show them what they can do here. In addition to the suggested supplies (page 469), add some musical instruments that play chords easily, quiet chimes, or a rain stick.

Begin Quiet Time

Have five minutes to allow the children to ponder the story about Mary visiting her cousin and singing a special prayer song. Then invite them to the Sacred Circle Time space to draw what they did or thought about.

(*2-minute transition time*) Start laying paper in the circle and laying out the crayons and other materials. Invite the children, one at a time, to come and draw what they did, thought about, or experienced.

(*10 minutes*) **Journal and Share Time**

Let the children draw and journal as they gather. When most of the children have finished, let them begin to share. Remind them that listening to one another is important.

Say: "Thank you for spending time with me in the Trinity Stations. I cannot wait to hear what you experienced today. Who would like to share? (Give each child a time to talk, and you should talk as well.)

Place their activities in individual folders; or if they are to take them home, place them behind them so they will not be distracted. This will keep you from having to correct anyone.

10 minutes (snack or toy time)

A Time of Blessing

Explain: "The symbol for the story today is a music note, because we use music notes to write songs for people to sing. Mary sang a prayer song, and so did you. Any time you want to pray to God, you can sing a song. You can sing one you know or make one up all by yourself!"

Ask: "Where would you like your blessing today?" (*Let them tell you.*)

As you look into each child's eyes, make the music note.

Say: "Thank you for being here today and spending time experiencing God with me. You are a blessing!"

Closing Time

Slowly put each Trinity symbol away.

Say: "And now we are finished with our Sacred Circle Time. We put away our symbol for God, the Creator. We put away our symbol for God, the Son. And we put away our symbol for God, the Holy Spirit."

Then quietly and gently put the sacred cloth away.

Conclude: "And we are all done with our Sacred Circle time. You did a great job. Yay!" Clap and celebrate a job well done.

Advent 3

Story: Joseph Has a Dream

Text: Matthew 1:18-24, NRSV

Now the birth of Jesus the Messiah took place in this way. When his mother Mary had been engaged to Joseph, but before they lived together, she was found to be with child from the Holy Spirit. Her husband Joseph, being a righteous man and unwilling to expose her to public disgrace, planned to dismiss her quietly. But just when he had resolved to do this, an angel of the Lord appeared to him in a dream and said, "Joseph, son of David, do not be afraid to take Mary as your wife, for the child conceived in her is from the Holy Spirit. She will bear a son, and you are to name him Jesus, for he will save his people from their sins." All this took place to fulfill what had been spoken by the Lord through the prophet:

"Look, the virgin shall conceive and bear a son,
   and they shall name him Emmanuel,"

which means, "God is with us." When Joseph awoke from sleep, he did as the angel of the Lord commanded him; he took her as his wife, but had no marital relations with her until she had borne a son; and he named him Jesus.

About the text: This text reminds the reader that the one who was called to give birth to the long-awaited Messiah was to be a virgin. Mary is a virgin who is betrothed to Joseph. In Jewish law, a betrothal was a legal agreement where the promised woman belonged to the man to whom she was betrothed. Mary's pregnancy, if not from God, would indicate that she had been unfaithful to Joseph and would have broken the betrothal agreement. The punishment for such a breech of contract was death. Joseph had the right to drag her into the streets and have the mob kill her, probably, by stoning her to death. However, even before his dream, he had decided to leave her quietly. By doing so, he would be sparing her life. He was a good man.

In Joseph's dream, the Angel Gabriel, the same angel who appeared to Mary, tells Joseph that the baby is from God, that Mary is telling the truth, and that he is to take her as his wife. Again, Joseph is a good man. He does as the angel asks him to do. I am sure people talked and gossiped. I am sure he and Mary were shunned. Still, he remained a good man who did what God asked him to do. Mary had no choice, but Joseph did. In stepping up and caring for Mary and the baby in her womb, Joseph provides an excellent role model for all who feel called by God to perform a difficult task.

The Sacred Circle Time Focus: We will focus on the people in the lives of the children who take care of them and thank God for them.

Sacred Circle Time Basic Format

Sacred Circle basket and contents:

- The sacred cloth along with the Creator (globe), Christ (cross) and Holy Spirit (bell or chime) objects
- Small, unbreakable bottle to hold water or oil for the blessing
- A journal page (one per child)
- Crayons and/or markers
- A Bible with the page marked to Matthew 1:18-24
- Focused Objects from the Bible story:
    Three things that symbolize what children need. Some suggestions are:
    ○ Food of some kind

○ A small house
○ A piece of clothing
○ A hidden heart . . . made of paper or clay or other material.

The Lesson

Gathering

Sit down and place the sacred basket in front of you.

Pause so that the children notice it and begin to come closer.

Invite them to form a circle.

Sit quietly until they settle in and are quiet.

Say: "It is time for Sacred Circle Time. I am so glad that you are here today. I love learning our stories and experiencing God with you."

Creating the Sacred Space

Say: "First, we create our sacred space."

Slowly lay out the sacred cloth.

Slowly lift the globe (symbol of God, the Creator) and hold it at the eye level of the children. Say: "This is our symbol for God, the Creator." Carefully lay it on the sacred cloth. (*Pause.*)

Slowly lift the cross (symbol of God, the Son). Say: "This is our symbol for God, the Son." Carefully lay it on the sacred cloth. (*Pause.*)

Slowly lift the bell (symbol of God, the Holy Spirit). Say: "This is our symbol of God, the Holy Spirit." Carefully lay it on the sacred cloth. (*Pause.*)

Point to each symbol and say: "So we have God, the Creator; God, the Son; and God, the Holy Spirit. (*Pause.*) Our sacred space is ready. We are ready to begin our Sacred Circle Time together."

God, the Creator (A Time to Wonder)

Show. (*Show the children the house.*)

Ask: "What is this?" (*Let them respond.*) "Did you know that we all need shelter like a home? Why?" (*Let them tell you.*)

Ask: "What is this?" (*Show them the food.*) "Did you know that we all need food? Why?" (*Let them tell you. Then, show them the clothing.*)

Ask: "Did you know we all need clothes to wear. Why?" (*Let them tell you.*)

"What else do we need?" (*Let them share. Do not correct them by saying things such as "Well, we don't need toys . . . we want them." Just let them share.*) "So we need things like a home and shelter, clothes, and food. But you are kids. Who gets these things for you? Who takes care of you?" (*Let them tell you.*)

God, the Son (Telling the Story)

Say: "In our story for today, which is found in (*open the Bible*) Matthew, chapter 1, verses 18-24, Joseph finds out that he is going to be the daddy of Jesus. Do you know who the mommy of Jesus was going to be?" (*Let them respond.*)

Say: "Mary was going to be the mommy, and Joseph was going to be the daddy. Joseph had a big job and so did Mary, because they had to care for Baby Jesus. And you know, it would be hard for Mary to care for him by herself.

"God wanted Joseph to help Mary take care of Baby Jesus, so God sent an angel to communicate with Joseph that God wanted Joseph to be the daddy of Jesus. Joseph was asleep and had a dream. In the dream, the Angel Gabriel told Joseph to take care of Mary and Jesus. And when Joseph woke up, he did! He took very good care of Mary and Jesus. He made sure they had shelter and a home. He worked hard so they could have food and clothes. And Mary worked hard too. They made sure Jesus had the things he needed.

"They made sure he had (*lift up the house*) shelter and a house. They made sure he had (*lift up the food*) food to eat. They made sure he had (*lift up the cloth*) clothes to wear that would keep him warm. They gave him a home, food, and clothes. Do you know why they gave these things to him? Because (*show them the heart*) they loved him."

God, the Holy Spirit (Quiet and Prayer Time)

Say: "It is now time to pray. Mary and Joseph cared for Jesus because they loved him so much! Who loves you and takes care of you? I am going to pass this heart to each of you, and I want you to share the names of the people who love and take care of you."

Pass the heart to the children and let them share the names of those who love them and care for them. Do not rush this or cut them off. They need to begin to realize that they have many people who love them.

Pray: "God, thank you for all the people who care for us and love us. In the name of Jesus, we pray. Amen."

(If using the extended Sacred Circle Time, stop here.)

A Time of Blessing

Explain, "The symbol for the story today is a heart because Joseph and Mary loved Jesus so much. You, like Jesus, have people who love and care for you."

Ask: "Where would you like your blessing today?"

(*Let them tell you.*)

(*Make the symbol and look the children in their eyes.*)

Say: "Thank you for being here today and spending time experiencing God with me. You are a blessing!"

Closing Time

Slowly put each Trinity symbol away.

Say: "And now we are finished with our Sacred Circle Time. We put away our symbol for God, the Creator. We put away our symbol for God, the Son. And we put away our symbol for God, the Holy Spirit.

Then quietly and gently put the sacred cloth away.

Conclude: "And we are all done with our Sacred Circle time. You did a great job. Yay!" Clap and celebrate a job well done.

Extended Format

(*10 minutes*) Begin with free-play time. Greet the children warmly and let them get used to the space. Have something in the free-play space for them to play with. Rotate each week:

Week One: Paper and crayons, markers, or paint.

Week Two: Clay, wire, pipe cleaners and beads, and tools to work the clay.

Week Three: Things to build with: blocks, Legos®, cans, boxes, or flat stones.

Week Four: Things that make noise.

(*3 minutes*) Transition time. Let the children know that it is almost Sacred Circle Time. Say: "It is almost our Sacred Circle Time. I cannot wait to have sacred time with you today. Will you start to finish up? Then come join me for our special, holy time together."

Sit down in the Sacred Circle Time space and place your sacred basket in front of you.

(*10 minutes*) **Sacred Circle Time** (*Basic Format*)—Use the Sacred Circle Basic Format, but do not include the blessing or closing.

(*10 minutes*) **Trinity Stations**

Explain the Trinity Stations procedure for new children and for those who might forget from time to time.

Walk with the children to Trinity Stations and show them what they can do in each station, but do not let them start until they have seen all three stations.

Tell the children that after the Trinity Stations, they will spend five minutes in quiet time thinking about the story and the activities they have completed. They will then return to the Sacred Circle Time space to draw pictures and talk about their activities.

Station One: God, the Creator (Wonder) Station

Walk with the children to station one and show them what they can do here. In addition to the suggested supplies (page 469), you might want to add different food types and outfits and old clothes.

Station Two: God, the Son (Story) Station

Walk with the children to station two and show them what they can do here.

In addition to the suggested supplies (page 469), you might want to include baby dolls and doll-care items such as bottles, diapers, dishes, and spoons.

Station Three: God, the Holy Spirit (Prayer) Station

Walk with the children to station three and show them what they can do here. In addition to the suggested supplies (page 469), you might want to add some heart-shaped cookie cutters and rolling pins so the children can make heart shapes out of clay.

Begin Quiet Time

Say: "Let's begin five minutes of thinking about the story and how Mary and Joseph cared for and loved Jesus. And then, after the time is over, I will invite you, one at a time, to come to the Sacred Circle Time space and draw what you did or thought about so we can all share together."

(*2-minute transition time*) Start laying paper in the circle and laying out the crayons and other materials. Invite the children, one at a time, to come and draw what they did, thought about, or experienced.

(*10 minutes*) **Journal and Share Time**

Let the children draw and journal as they gather. As most of the children finish, have them begin to share. Emphasize that listening to one another is important.

Say: "Thank you for spending time with me in the Trinity Stations. I cannot wait to see what you experienced today. Who would like to share?" (Give each child time to talk, and you should talk as well.)

Place their activities in individual folders; or if they are to take the folders home, place them behind them so they will not be distracted. This will keep you from having to correct the children's behavior.

10 minutes (snack or toy time)

A Time of Blessing

Explain: "The symbol for the story today is a heart because Joseph and Mary loved Jesus so much. You, like Jesus, have people who love and care for you."

Ask: "Where would you like your blessing today?" (*Let them tell you.*) As you look into each child's eyes, make the symbol.

Say: "Thank you for being here today and spending time experiencing God with me. You are a blessing!"

Closing Time

Slowly put each Trinity symbol away.

Say: "And now we are finished with our Sacred Circle Time. We put away our symbol for God, the Creator. We put away our symbol for God, the Son. And we put away our symbol for God, the Holy Spirit."

Then quietly and gently put the sacred cloth away.

Conclude: "And we are all done with our Sacred Circle time. You did a great job. Yay!" Clap and celebrate a job well done.

Advent 4

Story: The Journey to Bethlehem

Text: Luke 2:1-5, NRSV

In those days a decree went out from Emperor Augustus that all the world should be registered. This was the first registration and was taken while Quirinius was governor of Syria. All went to their own towns to be registered. Joseph also went from the town of Nazareth in Galilee to Judea, to the city of David called Bethlehem, because he was descended from the house and family of David. He went to be registered with Mary, to whom he was engaged and who was expecting a child.

About the text: Whenever the Bible mentions people being counted, it is a heads up that some kind of oppression is happening. Kings and people in powerful positions counted people to determine how much money it was possible to raise through taxing them. The money did not go to make life better for those being taxed, but to support the often extravagant and sinful lives of the government officials. The story of Mary and Joseph traveling to their hometown to be counted is another time in the history of the Jewish people where they were being unfairly taxed, ruled over, and exploited. Mary and Joseph did not go on a vacation from Nazareth to Bethlehem. Instead, they were forced on an oppressive journey. This story provides a wonderful backdrop for the next one. For in the midst of one king trying to expand his kingdom on the backs of the poor, a new King will be born who will establish a new kingdom, where the poor will be cared for, rather than exploited.

The Sacred Circle Time Focus: We will explore the difficulty of the journey, how difficult it was to find a place to stay, and the beauty of hospitality.

Sacred Circle Time Basic Format

Sacred Circle basket and contents:

- Sacred space cloth
- Symbols for Creator (globe), Christ (cross), and Holy Spirit (bell or chimes)
- Small, unbreakable bottle to hold water or oil for the blessing.
- A journal page (one per child)
- Crayons and/or markers
- A Bible with the page marked to Luke 2:1-5
- Focused Objects from the Bible Story: Take a very long piece of yarn or string and make a web out of it all over the room. Wrap it around chairs, lamps, the bookcase, and other furniture. Place one end in the Bible to mark the passage and tie a picture or drawing of a stable on the other end. Hide the stable and manger and make sure the children cannot see them.

The Lesson

Gathering

Sit down and place the sacred basket in front of you.

Pause so that the children notice it and begin to come closer.

Invite them to form a circle.

Sit quietly until they settle in and are quiet.

Say: "It is time for Sacred Circle Time. I am so glad that you are here today. I love learning our stories and experiencing God with you."

Creating the Sacred Space

Say: "First, we create our sacred space."

Slowly lay out the sacred cloth.

Slowly lift the globe (symbol of God, the Creator) and hold it at the eye level of the children. Say: "This is our symbol for God, the Creator." Carefully lay it on the sacred cloth. *(Pause.)*

Slowly lift the cross (symbol of God, the Son). Say: "This is our symbol for God, the Son." Carefully lay it on the sacred cloth. *(Pause.)*

Slowly lift the bell (symbol of God, the Holy Spirit). Say: "This is our symbol of God, the Holy Spirit." Carefully lay it on the sacred cloth. *(Pause.)*

Point to each symbol and say: "So we have God, the Creator; God, the Son; and God, the Holy Spirit. *(Pause.)* Our sacred space is ready. We are ready to begin our Sacred Circle Time together."

God, the Creator (A Time to Wonder)

Sit quietly and ask the children to look around the room and notice if anything seems different. *(They will notice the string or yarn.)*

Say: "You are so observant! And you are correct. There is string stretching all over our classroom. Why do you think it is here?" *(Let them respond.)*

Ask: "If we followed the string, what do you think we would find on the other end?" *(Let them respond.)*

God, the Son (Telling the Story)

Say: "Well, in our story today, which is found in *(open the Bible)* Luke, chapter 2, verses 1-5, Mary and Joseph find out that a ruler, sort of like a mean king, named Caesar Augustus, is ordering everyone to go on a journey so that he can count them and take their money away from them. And poor Mary is going to have a baby, and it will be a very long, difficult journey for her. They have to go all the way from Nazareth, where they live, to Bethlehem; and it is a long journey! But at the end of the journey, they find something wonderful. And that is what is on the end of this string.

"Are you ready to take a journey with me and discover the wonderful thing Mary and Joseph found at the end of their long journey?

"Let's stand up and go on a journey together. Let's follow the string. I will go first: you follow me."

Start following the string and then stop.

Say: "It was such a long and difficult journey for Mary and Joseph. It was hot." (*Pretend to be hot and wipe sweat off your brow.*)

Say: "Let me see you pretend to be hot like Mary and Joseph were."

(*Everyone pretends.*)

Say: "Let's continue our long and difficult journey." (*Move along the string and stop.*)

Say: "And poor Mary and Joseph: They were hot, and they were also hungry and thirsty." (*Pretend to be hot, hungry, and thirsty.*)

Say: "Let me see you pretend to be hot, and now hungry and thirsty."

(*Let them pretend.*)

Say: "Poor Mary and Joseph. They had a long and difficult journey."

(*Move along the string some more.*)

Say: "Poor Mary and Joseph. They had a long and difficult journey. They were hot and hungry and thirsty and so, so tired!" (*Pretend to be hot, hungry, thirsty, and tired.*)

Say: "Let me see you pretend to be hot, hungry, thirsty, and tired."

(*Let them pretend.*)

Say: "Poor Mary and Joseph. They had a long and difficult journey. And when they finally got to Bethlehem, they were hot, hungry, and thirsty; and they could not find a place to sleep. Mary was about to have the baby, and they needed a place to stay. So they kept looking." (*Move along the string and stop.*)

Say: "They asked at the first place, 'Do you have a place for us to stay? We are hot, hungry, thirsty, and tired; and Mary is about to have the baby. We need to find a place to stay.' But the innkeeper said, 'I don't have a place for you. Go away!' Poor Mary and Joseph! They had a long and difficult journey." (*Move along the string and stop.*)

Say: "They asked at the second place, 'Do you have a place for us to stay? We are hot, hungry, thirsty, and tired; and Mary is about to have the baby. We need to find a place to stay.' But the innkeeper said, 'I don't have a place for you. Go away!' Poor Mary and Joseph! They had a long and difficult journey." (*Move along the string and stop.*)

Say: "Poor Mary and Joseph. They were hot, hungry, thirsty, and tired; and they could not find a place to stay. Poor Mary and Joseph!" (*Move along to the end of the string, but do not show them the stable yet.*)

Say: "And then, finally, poor Mary and Joseph were so hot, so hungry, so thirsty, and so tired; and they were worried that they would never find a place to stay. They asked one last time, 'Do you have a place for us to stay? We are hot, hungry, thirsty, and tired; and Mary is about to have the baby. We need to find a place to stay. And the innkeeper said, 'I have a place for you!' " (*Pull out the stable.*)

Say: "Mary and Joseph's long and difficult journey was finally over. They found a place to stay!! This is a stable. It was a place where animals were kept. It was not a house. It was not a nice clean motel. But it was warm and dry, and it was a place, finally, to stay!" (*Everyone cheers and returns to the Sacred Circle space.*)

God, the Holy Spirit (Quiet and Prayer Time)

Say: "It is now time to pray. Mary and Joseph had a long journey. Finally, someone was nice to them and gave them a place to stay. Can you think of a time when someone was kind to you? I am going to pass this stable around; and when it is your turn, you can share a time when someone was nice to you." (*Let them pass the stable and share.*)

Pray: "God, thank you for the nice innkeeper who gave Mary and Joseph a place to stay and rest in after their long and difficult journey. And thank you for all the people who are nice to us. In the name of Jesus, we pray. Amen."

(If using the extended Sacred Circle Time, stop here.)

A Time of Blessing

Say, "The symbol for the story today is a stable because someone was very nice to Mary and Joseph and gave them a stable to stay and rest in after their journey."

Say: "Where would you like your blessing today?" (*Let them tell you*).

As you look into each child's eyes, make the symbol.

Say: "Thank you for being here today and spending time experiencing God with me. You are a blessing!"

Closing Time

Slowly put each Trinity symbol away.

Say: "And now we are finished with our Sacred Circle Time. We put away our symbol for God, the Creator. We put away our symbol for God, the Son. And we put away our symbol for God, the Holy Spirit."

Then quietly and gently put the sacred cloth away.

Conclude: "And we are all done with our Sacred Circle time. You did a great job. Yay!" Clap and celebrate a job well done.

Extended Format

(*10 minutes*) Begin with free-play time. Greet the children warmly and let them get used to the space. Have something in the free-play space for them to play with. Rotate each week:

Week One: Paper and crayons, markers, or paint.

Week Two: Clay, wire, pipe cleaners and beads, and tools to work the clay.

Week Three: Things to build with: blocks, Legos®, cans, boxes, or flat stones.

Week Four: Things that make noise.

(*3 minutes*) Transition time. Let the children know that it is almost Sacred Circle Time. Say: "It is almost our Sacred Circle Time. I cannot wait to have sacred time with you today. Will you start to finish up? Then come join me for our special, holy time together."

Sit down in the Sacred Circle Time space and place your sacred basket in front of you.

(*10 minutes*) **Sacred Circle Time** (*Basic format*)—Use the Sacred Circle Basic Format, but do not include the blessing or closing.

(*10 minutes*) **Trinity Stations**

Explain the Trinity Stations procedure for new children and for those who might forget from time to time.

Walk with the children to Trinity Stations and show them what they can do there, but do not let them start until they have seen all three stations.

Tell the children that after the Trinity Stations, they will spend five minutes in quiet time thinking about the story and the activities they have completed. They will then return to the Sacred Circle Time space to draw pictures and talk about their activities.

Station One: God, the Creator (Wonder) Station

Walk with the children to station one and show them what they can do here.

In addition to the regular supplies (page 469), you might want to add animal pelts or different stuffed animals and explain that the stable had animals in it.

Station Two: God, the Son (Story) Station

Walk with the children to station two and show them what they can do here.

In addition to the regular supplies (page 469), you might want to include some nativity sets with stables for the children to play with or a big box to be used as a stable.

Station Three: God, the Holy Spirit (Prayer) Station

Walk with the children to station three and show them what they can do here.

In addition to the regular supplies (page 469), you might want to add some pillows for resting—as Mary and Joseph did after their long journey.

Begin Quiet Time

Say: "Let's begin five minutes of thinking about the story and Mary and Joseph's long journey. Let's also think about how kind the person was who gave them a stable to stay and rest in. And then, after the time is over, I will invite you, one at a time, to come to the Sacred Circle Time space and draw what you did or thought about, so we can all share together."

(*2-minute transition time*) Start laying paper in the circle and laying out the crayons and other materials. Invite the children, one at a time, to come and draw what they did, thought about, or experienced.

(*10 minutes*) **Journal and Share Time**

Let them draw and journal as they gather. When most of the children have finished, let them begin to share. Remind them that listening to one another is important.

Say: "Thank you for spending time with me in the Trinity Stations. I cannot wait to hear what you experienced today. Who would like to share?" (Give each child a time to talk, and you should talk as well.)

Place their activities in individual folders; or if they are to take the folders home, place them behind them so they will not be distracted. This will keep you from having to correct the children's behavior.

10 minutes (snack or toy time)

A Time of Blessing

Explain, "The symbol for the story today is a stable because someone was very nice to Mary and Joseph and gave them a stable to stay and rest in after their journey."

Say: "Where would you like your blessing today?" (*Let them tell you.*)

Make the symbol as you look into each child's eyes.

Say: "Thank you for being here today and spending time experiencing God with me. You are a blessing!"

Closing Time

Slowly put each Trinity symbol away.

Say: "And now we are finished with our Sacred Circle Time. We put away our symbol for God, the Creator. We put away our symbol for God, the Son. And we put away our symbol for God, the Holy Spirit."

Then quietly and gently put the sacred cloth away.

Conclude: "And we are all done with our Sacred Circle time. You did a great job. Yay!" Clap and celebrate a job well done.

About the Twelve Days of Christmas (Christmas Through Epiphany)

Celebrating the birth of Christ began formally in the fourth century. No one knows the actual birth date of Jesus, but the early church began to gather for a mass (worship service) on December 25, the date chosen to be a yearly celebration of his birth. So the mass for Christ, The Christ-mass, soon became known as Christmas; and Christians still gather to celebrate it each year.

Because the birth of Jesus is such a special day, it was decided to celebrate it as a season rather than a single day. So twelve days were set apart to be a time of celebration. The Christmas celebration is not just one day, but twelve days!

The Christmas Season lasts from Christmas morning until the celebration of Epiphany. When we have an *epiphany*, we see things in a new way. The word *epiphany* is used to describe the insight that the wise men had when they saw the star in the sky after the birth of Jesus. To most people, the star was simply a star, but to those who were very wise and lived in the East, it was an epiphany, a sign that something amazing had occurred. They followed the star; and it led them to Jesus, God incarnate, the

Savior, the promised Messiah. God had done a new thing, and the world was about to change!

Epiphany is the Sunday when we celebrate the arrival of the wise men from the East. It is the last day of the Christmas Season. The star is a perfect symbol for Epiphany, not only because a star led the wise men to the Christ child, but because it reminds us that while Christmas has ended, the light of Jesus continues to shine in the darkness.

The twelve days of Christmas can help young children experience the joy of Christmas. Before Christmas Day, children have so much activity and are inundated with the more secular side of the holiday, such as pictures with Santa, anticipating receiving gifts, food, and parties. The twelve days of Christmas are a quieter time when schedules get back to normal and when children are better able to listen, be present, and process the gift of the Christ child.

Many times, we, who work with children, are tired after Christmas; but try not to let the fatigue you feel stop you from allowing the children to experience the birth of Jesus during these twelve days. Some of the best insights and reflections will happen during these days. Let's not waste or overlook them.

Christmas Sunday

Story: Baby Jesus is Born

Text: Luke 2:6-7, NRSV

> While they were there, the time came for her to deliver her child. And she gave birth to her firstborn son and wrapped him in bands of cloth, and laid him in a manger, because there was no place for them in the inn.

About the text: The use of swaddling cloths to wrap Baby Jesus in had nothing to do with the fact that Mary and Joseph were probably poor. They probably did not have much money, but that is not the reason that Jesus was wrapped in swaddling cloths. It was a common practice for babies in biblical times. Babies were wrapped in swaddling cloths for the same reason we swaddle our newborn babies today. It makes a newborn, who is used to being in the safety of the womb, feel secure and safe. Plus, swaddling prevents the baby from experiencing the sensation of falling as it drifts off to sleep.

Wrapping Baby Jesus in swaddling cloths was a loving act by his parents, Mary and Joseph, to make sure he felt safe and secure during his first few hours and days on the earth. The power of this act of kindness compared with the real danger the family faced makes it even more tender and precious.

The Sacred Circle Time Focus: We will focus on the care that Mary and Joseph gave to Baby Jesus and compare it to the care the children receive from their parents.

Sacred Circle Time Basic Format

Sacred Circle basket and contents:

- Sacred space cloth
- Symbols for Creator (globe), Christ (cross), and Holy Spirit (bell or chimes)
- Small, unbreakable bottle to hold water or oil for the blessing
- A journal page (one per child)
- Crayons and/or markers
- A Bible with the page marked to Luke 2:6-7
- Focused objects from the Bible story: A baby doll and strips of torn cloth

The Lesson

Gathering

Sit down and place the sacred basket in front of you.

Pause so that the children notice it and begin to come closer.

Invite them to form a circle.

Sit quietly until they settle in and are quiet.

Say: "It is time for Sacred Circle Time. I am so glad that you are here today. I love learning our stories and experiencing God with you."

Creating the Sacred Space

Say: "First, we create our sacred space."

Slowly lay out the sacred cloth.

Slowly lift the globe (symbol of God, the Creator) and hold it at the eye level of the children. Say: "This is our symbol for God, the Creator." Carefully lay it on the sacred cloth. (Pause.)

Slowly lift the cross (symbol of God, the Son). Say: "This is our symbol for God, the Son." Carefully lay it on the sacred cloth. (Pause.)

Slowly lift the bell (symbol of God, the Holy Spirit). Say: "This is our symbol of God, the Holy Spirit." Carefully lay it on the sacred cloth. (*Pause.*)

Point to each symbol and say: "So we have God, the Creator; God, the Son; and God, the Holy Spirit. (*Pause.*) Our sacred space is ready. We are ready to begin our Sacred Circle Time together."

God, the Creator (A Time to Wonder)

Say: "This is my baby." (*Pretend that a baby doll is real. Rock it, kiss it, and hold it lovingly; and then pretend that the baby is cold.*)

Say: "My baby is cold. What can I use to wrap my baby in?"

(*Let the children respond.*)

Ask: "What should I use?" (*Let them respond.*)

Say: "All I have is some strips of cloth. Do you think this will work?" (*Let them respond and invite them to try to wrap the baby with them.*)

God, the Son (Telling the Story)

Say: "You remember the story of Mary and Joseph? The Angel Gabriel told Mary that she was going to have a baby, Jesus. And the same angel told Joseph that he was to become the daddy of Baby Jesus, and Joseph took good care of Mary and the baby.

"And they went on a very long journey from Nazareth to Bethlehem because the king was going to make them pay money to him. And it was so crowded in Bethlehem that they could not find a place to stay. But one innkeeper was very kind to them and let them sleep in the stable with the animals. And it was in that stable with all of those animals that Baby Jesus was born.

"Mary and Joseph wanted him to feel warm and secure and loved. In those days, people did not wrap babies in blankets to make them warm and secure. Your mommy and daddy wrapped you in a blanket to help you stay warm and make you feel all snug and safe. But Jesus was born a long time ago; and in that time, they did not use blankets. They used swaddling cloths. These are swaddling cloths like they used for Baby

Jesus." (*Carefully and very lovingly and slowly, wrap the baby doll in the cloth bands. Begin rocking the baby doll as if it were real. Keep rocking the baby doll as you speak to the children.*)

Say: "Mary and Joseph loved little Baby Jesus so much that they wrapped him in swaddling cloths to keep him warm and secure. You were wrapped in a blanket when you were tiny because you are loved. Just like Mary and Joseph loved their baby, you are loved."

God, the Holy Spirit (Quiet and Prayer Time)

Say: "It is now time to pray. For our prayer, I am going to pass this baby around three times. It is a symbol of love. The first time we pass the baby, think of someone who loves you. You can say the name out loud or just sit in quiet with the baby." (*Pass the baby. If the children get silly, simply take the baby, love on it, and give it back. Do not correct or lecture; just model!*)

Say: "Now, I am going to pass the baby around a second time. This time, think of someone you love. You can say the name out loud or simply sit in quiet and think of the person." (*Pass the baby again.*)

Say: "Now I am going to pass the baby a third time. This time, try to feel God's love. God loves you very much and holds you and me just as a loving mommy and daddy hold their baby. This time, let's pass the baby in silence. (*Pass the baby a third time.*)

Pray: "God, please be close to all of us and those we love. And thank you for loving us. In the name of Christ, we pray. Amen."

(If using the extended Sacred Circle Time, stop here.)

A Time of Blessing

Explain: "The symbol for the story today is a heart as a symbol of love."

Ask: "Where would you like your blessing today?" (*Let the children tell you.*)

As you look into each child's eyes, make the symbol of the heart.

Say: "Thank you for being here today and spending time experiencing God with me. You are a blessing!"

Closing Time

Slowly put each Trinity symbol away.

Say: "And now we are finished with our Sacred Circle Time. We put away our symbol for God, the Creator. We put away our symbol for God, the Son. And we put away our symbol for God, the Holy Spirit."

Then quietly and gently put the sacred cloth away.

Conclude: "And we are all done with our Sacred Circle time. You did a great job. Yay!" Clap and celebrate a job well done.

Extended Format *(10 minutes)*

Begin with free-play time. Greet the children warmly and let them get used to the space. Have something in the free-play space for them to play with. Rotate each week:

Week One: Paper and crayons, markers, or paint.

Week Two: Clay, wire, pipe cleaners and beads, and tools to work with clay.

Week Three: Things to build with: Blocks, Legos®, cans, boxes, flat stones.

Week Four: Things that make noise.

(*3 minutes*) Transition time. Let the children know that it is almost Sacred Circle Time. Say: "It is almost our Sacred Circle Time. I cannot wait to have sacred time with you today. Will you start to finish up? Then come join me for our special, holy time together."

Sit down in the Sacred Circle Time space and place your sacred basket in front of you.

(*10 minutes*) **Sacred Circle Time** (*Basic format*)—Use the Sacred Circle Basic Format, but do not include the blessing or closing.

(*10 minutes*) **Trinity Stations**

Explain the Trinity Stations procedure for new children and for those who might forget from time to time.

Walk with the children to the Trinity Stations and show them what they can do there, but do not let them start until they have seen all three stations.

Tell the children that after the Trinity Stations, they will spend five minutes in quiet time thinking about the story and the activities they have completed. They will then return to the Sacred Circle Time space to draw pictures and talk about their activities.

Station One: God, the Creator (Wonder) Station

Walk with the children to station one and show them what they can do here.

In addition to the regular supplies (page 469), you might want to add a few baby dolls and swaddling cloth materials and blankets and encourage the children to try to wrap the babies themselves.

Station Two: God, the Son (Story) Station

Walk with the children to station two and show them what they can do here.

In addition to the regular supplies (page 469), you might want to include story picture books of Christmas or a few nativity sets for the children to act out the story.

Station Three: God, the Holy Spirit (Prayer) Station

Walk with the children to station three and show them what they can do here.

In addition to the regular supplies (page 469), you might also want to add some different hearts made of various materials that will help children reflect on love.

Begin Quiet Time

Say: "Let's begin five minutes of thinking about the story and how Mary and Joseph showed that they loved Baby Jesus by wrapping him in swaddling cloths. And then, after the time is over, I will invite you, one at a time, to come to the Sacred Circle Time space and draw what you did or thought about so we can all share together."

(*2-minute transition time*) Start laying paper in the circle and laying out the crayons and other materials. Invite the children, one at a time, to come and draw what they did, thought about, or experienced.

(*10 minutes*) **Journal and Share Time**

Let the children draw and journal as they gather. When most of the children have finished, let them begin to share. Tell them that listening to one another is important.

Say: "Thank you for spending time with me in the Trinity Stations. I cannot wait to hear what you experienced today. Who would like to share?" (Give each child time to talk; you should talk as well.)

Place their activities in individual folders; or if they are to take the folders home, place them behind them so they will not be distracted. This will keep you from having to correct the children's behavior.

10 minutes (snack or toy time)

A Time of Blessing

Explain: "The symbol for the story today is a heart as a symbol of love."

Ask: "Where would you like your blessing today?" (*Let them tell you*).

As you look into each child's eyes, make the heart symbol.

Say: "Thank you for being here today and spending time experiencing God with me. You are a blessing!"

Closing Time

Slowly put each Trinity symbol away.

Say: "And now we are finished with our Sacred Circle Time. We put away our symbol for God, the Creator. We put away our symbol for God, the Son. And we put away our symbol for God, the Holy Spirit."

Then quietly and gently put the sacred cloth away.

Conclude: "And we are all done with our Sacred Circle time. You did a great job. Yay!" Clap and celebrate a job well done.

Epiphany Sunday

Story: The Wise People Visit Baby Jesus

Text: Matthew 2:1-12, NRSV

In the time of King Herod, after Jesus was born in Bethlehem of Judea, wise men from the East came to Jerusalem, asking, "Where is the child who has been born king of the Jews? For we observed his star at its rising, and have come to pay him homage." When King Herod heard this, he was frightened, and all Jerusalem with him; and calling together all the chief priests and scribes of the people, he inquired of them where the Messiah was to be born. They told him, "In Bethlehem of Judea; for so it has been written by the prophet:

'And you, Bethlehem, in the land of Judah,
> are by no means least among the rulers of Judah;
for from you shall come a ruler
> who is to shepherd my people Israel.'"

Then Herod secretly called for the wise men and learned from them the exact time when the star had appeared. Then he sent them to Bethlehem, saying, "Go and search diligently for the child; and when you have found him, bring me word so that I may also go and pay him homage." When they had heard the king, they set out; and there, ahead of them, went the star that they had seen at its rising, until it stopped over the place where the child was. When they saw that the star had stopped, they were overwhelmed with joy. On entering the house, they saw the child with Mary his mother; and they knelt down and paid him homage. Then, opening their treasure chests, they offered him gifts of gold, frankincense, and myrrh. And having been warned in a dream not to return to Herod, they left for their own country by another road.

About the text: This text is a favorite one of theologians, artists, musicians, and poets who have spent countless hours and years trying to figure out who these wise men truly were and what the significance in the gifts they brought to the baby and his family represented. Buddhists claim that they might have been from the Buddhist tradition, seeking out a new incarnation of the Buddha. There have been some scholars who believe these wise men were Zoroastrians. But in truth, we do not know how many there were, what their religious background was, or what political or spiritual significance their gifts had.

What we do know about this text is that these wise men saw a star or some kind of amazing event in space and followed it. When the star appeared, they had an "epiphany" and connected the star to the birth of someone special. So they followed the star and discovered the Christ child and his family.

The wise men knew that the Christ child was special because his birth had triggered some kind of change in the heavens. Even though we do not know exactly who they thought had been born, or why they chose to bring the gifts they did, we know that they realized the special nature of Jesus. He was a very special baby.

The Sacred Circle Time Focus: We will focus on the fact that the wise men knew that Jesus was special. We will also stress that we are special too.

Sacred Circle Time Basic Format

Sacred Circle basket and contents:

- Sacred space cloth
- Symbols for Creator (globe), Christ (cross), and Holy Spirit (bell or chimes)

- Small, unbreakable bottle to hold water or oil for the blessing
- A journal page (one per child)
- Crayons and/or markers
- A Bible with the page marked to Matthew 2:1-12
- Focused objects from the Bible story:
    - Something gold (It does not have to real gold . . . a chain, some shiny paper, a brass candlestick, etc.)
    - Two things that smell yummy (spices, fruit, perfume sprayed on a cotton ball or cloth, oil of some kind, etc.)
    - A covered box or basket to put the items in.

The Lesson

Gathering

Sit down and place the sacred basket in front of you.

Pause so that the children notice it and begin to come closer.

Invite them to form a circle.

Sit quietly until they settle in and are quiet.

Say: "It is time for Sacred Circle Time. I am so glad that you are here today. I love learning our stories and experiencing God with you."

Creating the Sacred Space

Say: "First, we create our sacred space."

Slowly lay out the sacred cloth.

Slowly lift the globe (symbol of God, the Creator) and hold it at the eye level of the children. Say: "This is our symbol for God, the Creator." Carefully lay it on the sacred cloth. (Pause.)

Slowly lift the cross (symbol of God, the Son). Say: "This is our symbol for God, the Son." Carefully lay it on the sacred cloth. (Pause.)

Slowly lift the bell (symbol of God, the Holy Spirit). Say: "This is our symbol of God, the Holy Spirit." Carefully lay it on the sacred cloth. (*Pause.*)

Point to each symbol and say: "So we have God, the Creator; God, the Son; and God, the Holy Spirit. (*Pause.*) Our sacred space is ready. We are ready to begin our Sacred Circle Time together."

God, the Creator (A Time to Wonder)

Get out the covered basket or box with the items in it and say nothing. Let the children have time to wonder about what is inside.

Ask: "What do you think I have in this basket (or box)?" Let the children guess. After they give each answer, say, "Good Guess!" Let all the children have one or two turns guessing what you have. Do not show them.

God, the Son (Telling the Story)

Say: "Well, in our story today, which is found in (*open the Bible*) Matthew, chapter two, verses 1-12, Baby Jesus was born. When he was born, God placed a very special star in the sky. Lots of people saw that star, but they still did not think anything special had happened. But the wise men in the far away East, saw that star; and do you know what they thought?" (*Let the children answer.*)

Say: "They thought, 'Wow, that star is amazing and special! Something amazing and special has happened. We had better follow it and find out what has happened that is so amazing and special.' So they traveled a very long way, following the star. And do you know where that star led them?" (*Let them guess.*)

"To baby Jesus and his family. And when they got there, the star was shining right over the place where Jesus was. They knew then that the Baby Jesus was amazing and special! And they gave him gifts, and that is what I have in my basket today."

(*Open the basket or uncover it.*)

Say: "In this basket I have the gifts the wise men gave to baby Jesus. First (*take out the gold*), they gave him gold. Then (*take out one of the good-smelling things*), they gave him the gift of myrrh, which smelled very good and (take out the other good-smelling thing) frankincense, which also smelled very good. They gave the baby three very wonderful gifts; gold, frankincense, and myrrh. And do you know why they gave these wonderful gifts to Baby Jesus?" (*Let the children respond.*)

Say: "Because they knew that he was a special and amazing baby! And he *was* amazing and special . . . they were correct!"

God, the Holy Spirit (Quiet and Prayer Time)

Say: "It is now time to pray. You know Jesus was amazing and special. The wise men knew it. Do you know what I know? That Jesus was amazing and special, and so are you! I am going to pass this basket filled with the wonderful gifts that the wise men gave to Jesus; and when the basket comes to you, I want you to hold it and tell me what is amazing and special about you."

Pass the basket and let each child say what is amazing about himself or herself. Respond with, "You are amazing and special!" If a child cannot think of anything, you should prompt him or her. However, whatever the children say should be honored. Do not correct them or try to make what they share sound deeper or better.

Pray: "God, we are all special to you. May we never forget that! In the name of Christ, we pray. Amen."

(If using the extended Sacred Circle Time, stop here.)

A Time of Blessing

Explain: "The symbol for the story today is a star because the wise men followed a star to find the amazing and special Baby Jesus."

Ask: "Where would you like your blessing today?" (*Let them tell you.*)

As you look into each child's eyes, make the symbol.

Say: "Thank you for being here today and spending time experiencing God with me. You are amazing and special! You are a blessing!"

Closing Time

Slowly put each Trinity symbol away.

Say: "And now we are finished with our Sacred Circle Time. We put away our symbol for God, the Creator. We put away our symbol for God, the Son. And we put away our symbol for God, the Holy Spirit."

Then quietly and gently put the sacred cloth away.

Conclude: "And we are all done with our Sacred Circle time. You did a great job. Yay!" Clap and celebrate a job well done.

Extended Format

(*10 minutes*) Begin with free-play time. Greet the children warmly and let them get used to the space. Have something in the free-play space for them to play with. Rotate each week:

Week One: Paper and crayons, markers, or paint.

Week Two: Clay, wire, pipe cleaners and beads, and tools to work the clay.

Week Three: Things to build with: blocks, Legos®, cans, boxes, or flat stones.

Week Four: Things that make noise.

(*3 minutes*) Transition time. Let the children know that it is almost Sacred Circle Time. Say: "It is almost our Sacred Circle Time. I cannot wait to have sacred time with you today. Will you start to finish up? Then come join me for our special, holy time together."

Sit down in the Sacred Circle Time space and place your sacred basket in front of you.

(*10 minutes*) **Sacred Circle Time** (*Basic format*)—Use the Sacred Circle Basic Format, but do not include the blessing or closing.

(*10 minutes*) **Trinity Stations**

Explain the Trinity Stations procedure for new children and for those who might forget from time to time. Walk with the children to the Trinity Stations and show them what they can do there, but do not let them start until they have seen all three stations.

Tell the children that after the Trinity Stations, they will spend five minutes in quiet time thinking about the story and the activities they have completed. They will then return to the Sacred Circle Time space to draw pictures and talk about their activities.

Station One: God, the Creator (Wonder) Station

Walk with the children to station one and show them what they can do here. In addition to the suggested supplies (page 469), you might want to add some glow-in-the-dark stars, flashlights, and a big box to put them in where it will be dark.

Station Two: God, the Son (Story) Station

Walk with the children to station two and show them what they can do here. In addition to the suggested supplies (page 469), you might want to include some Epiphany storybooks or crowns, so that the children can dress up like the wise men.

Station Three: God, the Holy Spirit (Prayer) Station

Walk with the children to station three and show them what they can do here.

In addition to the suggested supplies (page 469), you might want to add some stars of different sizes and black paper to glue them on or trace them with yellow crayons to make a night sky.

Begin Quiet Time

Say: "Let's begin five minutes of thinking about the story and how the wise men saw a star and followed it to the very special Baby Jesus. And then, after the time is over, I will invite you, one at a time, to come to the Sacred Circle Time space and draw what you did or thought about so we can all share together."

(*2-minute transition time*)—Place paper in the circle and lay out the crayons and other materials. Invite the children, one at a time, to come and draw what they did, thought about, or experienced.

(*10 minutes*) **Journal and Share Time**

Let the children draw and journal as they gather. As most of the children finish, have them begin to share. Explain that listening to one another is important.

Say: "Thank you for spending time with me in the Trinity Stations. I cannot wait to hear what you experienced today. Who would like to share?" (*Give each child time to talk, and you should talk as well.*)

Place their activities in individual folders; or if they are to take the folders home, place them behind them so they will not be distracted. This will keep you from having to correct the children's behavior.

10 minutes (snack or toy time)

A Time of Blessing

Explain: "The symbol for the story today is a star because the wise men followed a star to find the amazing and special Baby Jesus."

Ask: "Where would you like your blessing today?" (*Let them tell you.*)

As you look into each child's eyes, make the symbol.

Say: "Thank you for being here today and spending time experiencing God with me. You are amazing and special! You are a blessing!"

Closing Time

Slowly put each Trinity symbol away.

Say: "And now we are finished with our Sacred Circle Time. We put away our symbol for God, the Creator. We put away our symbol for God, the Son. And we put away our symbol for God, the Holy Spirit."

Then quietly and gently put the sacred cloth away.

Conclude: "And we are all done with our Sacred Circle time. You did a great job. Yay!" Clap and celebrate a job well done.

About Special Sundays
of the Church Year

As I explained earlier, this program follows the church calendar. The seasons of Advent, Christmas, and Lent through Pentecost, highlight the main events in the life of Jesus. During the season of Ordinary Time, many more stories from the life of Jesus are told and remembered. They vary from year to year, depending on which cycle (there are three different ones) the church is using that particular year. However, there are a few Sundays that almost stand alone in the church calendar. These days highlight specific stories or theological concepts about Jesus. I call these the *Special Sundays,* and they are listed below. The dates of them vary each year.

These stories are important to the church because they highlight certain theological truths about Jesus, and they are important to teach to young children because the terms such as baptism, Trinity, and Christ the King will be foundational to their faith systems as they mature. Our task is not to explain theological concepts to them while they are still young, but to introduce and familiarize them with the terms that they will more fully understand as they mature and grow.

Special Sunday:
Baptism of the Lord

Story: Jesus is Baptized

Text: Mark 1:9-11, NRSV

> In those days Jesus came from Nazareth of Galilee and was baptized
> by John in the Jordan. And just as he was coming up out of the water,
> he saw the heavens torn apart and the Spirit descending like a dove on
> him. And a voice came from heaven, "You are my Son, the Beloved;
> with you I am well pleased."

About the text: The baptism of Jesus is mentioned in all three of the synoptic gospels, Matthew, Mark, and Luke. It is an important story because it describes a universal sacrament of the church today. There are a variety of beliefs about how, when, and exactly what baptism means and does for the person receiving it. There are also differing opinions about the age a person should be when receiving baptism. While these are important theological debates, they are things that need to be talked about, debated, and articulated by adults. In teaching children about the baptism of Jesus, we need to be sensitive that some of the children have been baptized, some have not, and that the decision about when and how a child will be baptized often lies in the hands of their parents.

I have chosen to use the Mark passage because it is the simplest form of the story. It states that Jesus was baptized and that in that moment God announced him as special.

Since baptism is a difficult concept for adults, let alone preschoolers, to understand, in telling this story to preschoolers, I believe we should leave the theological portion out, focusing on what happened on the day Jesus was baptized and begin to associate the word "baptism" with an important event and being a special child of God.

The Sacred Circle Time Focus: We will focus on the story of Jesus' baptism and that children are very special to God.

Sacred Circle Time Basic Format

Sacred Circle basket and contents:

- Sacred space cloth
- Symbols for Creator (globe), Christ (cross), and Holy Spirit (bell or chimes)
- Small, unbreakable bottle to hold water or oil for the blessing
- A journal page (one per child)
- Crayons and/or markers
- A Bible with the page marked to Mark 1:9-11
- Focused objects from the Bible story: A pitcher or jar of water and a large bowl

The Lesson

Gathering

Sit down and place the sacred basket in front of you.

Pause so that the children notice it and begin to come closer.

Invite them to form a circle.

Sit quietly until they settle in and are quiet.

Say: "It is time for Sacred Circle Time. I am so glad that you are here today. I love learning our stories and experiencing God with you."

Creating the Sacred Space

Say: "First, we create our sacred space."

Slowly lay out the sacred cloth.

Slowly lift the globe (symbol of God, the Creator) and hold it at the eye level of the children. Say: "This is our symbol for God, the Creator." Carefully lay it on the sacred cloth. (*Pause.*)

Slowly lift the cross (symbol of God, the Son). Say: "This is our symbol for God, the Son." Carefully lay it on the sacred cloth. (*Pause.*)

Slowly lift the bell (symbol of God, the Holy Spirit). Say: "This is our symbol of God, the Holy Spirit." Carefully lay it on the sacred cloth. (*Pause.*)

Point to each symbol and say: "So we have God, the Creator; God, the Son; and God, the Holy Spirit. (*Pause.*) Our sacred space is ready. We are ready to begin our Sacred Circle Time together."

God, the Creator (A Time to Wonder)

Place the bowl and pitcher of water in front of you. Ask: "Do you know what I have in my pitcher?" (*They will say water.*)

Say: "You are correct! I have a pitcher of water. Water is very important. What kinds of things can we do with water?"

Let them list things such as bathe in it, drink it, play in it, swim, make mud with it, clean our cuts with it so we don't get infections. Some children will even know that "babies grow in water in a mommy's tummy before being born."

Explain: "There are so many things that water is used for. It is very important."

God, the Son (Telling the Story)

Say: "In our story for today, which is found in (*open the Bible*) Mark, chapter one, verses 9-11, water is used for a very special purpose. You know Jesus needed water like we all do. He took a bath in water. He played in water. He drank water. He needed water to clean his cuts when he hurt himself. He went on a boat on water. He went fishing in water. He even walked on top of water once. But today, water was used for something very important." (*Pour the water into the bowl as you talk.*)

Say: "Jesus was a baby, and then a child like you are, and then a teen; and when he was a grown-up man, he decided to start telling people about God. And one of the first things he did was to go to the river, and his cousin John baptized him."

(*Begin to dip your hand into the bowl of water.*) "Jesus went to the river, and there he got into the water, and John baptized him. And when John helped Jesus get all wet in the water, something amazing happened. Do you know what happened?" (*Let them guess.*)

Say: "After Jesus was baptized by John, the sky opened up and God, the Holy Spirit (*make a dove using your two hands; thumbs together for the bird's body and your fingers as the wings*), came down. It looked like a dove, and it came down from heaven all the way to the water (*bring your hands in the dove shape all the way down to the water*); and people heard God say, 'This is my beloved, my very special son.' And everyone knew that Jesus was very special. And he is very special!" (*Repeat the story so that the children can really listen to it this time.*)

God, the Holy Spirit (Quiet and Prayer Time)

Say: "It is now time to pray. At his baptism, Jesus knew he was special. And you are special too. For our prayer time, I am going to have each of you move close to the bowl, and you can touch the water. When you do, we will all say, 'You (*Name of child*) are special.'" (*Have the children—one at a time—place their hands in the bowl of water and be told that they are special.*)

Pray: "God, please help us to remember that you know us and love us very much. We are very special to you. In the name of Christ, we pray. Amen."

(If using the extended Sacred Circle Time, stop here.)

A Time of Blessing

Explain, "The symbol for the story today is a dove, because the spirit of God, who told the people that Jesus was special, looked like a dove."

Ask, "Where would you like your blessing today?" (*Let them tell you.*)

As you look into each child's eyes, make the symbol.

Say: "Thank you for being here today and spending time experiencing God with me. You are a blessing!"

Closing Time

Slowly put each Trinity symbol away.

Say: "And now we are finished with our Sacred Circle Time. We put away our symbol for God, the Creator. We put away our symbol for God, the Son. And we put away our symbol for God, the Holy Spirit."

Then quietly and gently put the sacred cloth away.

Conclude: "And we are all done with our Sacred Circle time. You did a great job. Yay!" Clap and celebrate a job well done.

Extended Format

(*10 minutes*) Begin with free-play time. Greet the children warmly and let them get used to the space. Have something in the free-play space for them to play with. Rotate each week:

Week One: Paper and crayons, markers, or paint.

Week Two: Clay, wire, pipe cleaners and beads, and tools to work with clay.

Week Three: Things to build with: Blocks, Legos®, cans, boxes, flat stones.

Week Four: Things that make noise.

(*3 minutes*) Transition time. Let the children know that it is almost Sacred Circle Time.

Say: "It is almost our Sacred Circle Time. I cannot wait to have sacred time with you today. Will you start to finish up? Then come join me for our special, holy time together."

Sit down in the Sacred Circle Time space and place your sacred basket in front of you.

(*10 minutes*) **Sacred Circle Time** (*Basic format*)—Use the Sacred Circle Basic Format, but do not include the blessing or closing.

(*10 minutes*) **Trinity Stations**

Explain the Trinity Stations procedure for new children and for those who might forget from time to time.

Walk with the children to Trinity Stations and show them what they can do there, but do not let them start until they have seen all three stations.

Tell the children that after the Trinity Stations, they will spend five minutes in quiet time thinking about the story and the activities they have completed. They will then return to the Sacred Circle Time space to draw pictures and talk about their activities.

Station One: God, the Creator (Wonder) Station

Walk with the children to station one and show them what they can do here. In addition to the suggested supplies (page 469), you might want to add the bowl of water and some small cups from God, the Creator/Wonder time from the Sacred Story Circle, so the children can spend time playing in water.

Station Two: God, the Son (Story) Station

Walk with the children to station two and show them what they can do here. In addition to the suggested supplies (page 469), you might want to include a doll dressed as Jesus, a plastic or paper dove, and water in which to baptize Jesus.

Station Three: God, the Holy Spirit (Prayer) Station

Walk with the children to station three and show them what they can do here. In addition to the suggested supplies (page 469), you might want to add some bottles filled with water and colored oil for children to sit and reflect with.

Begin Quiet Time

Say: "Let's begin five minutes of thinking about the story and how Jesus was baptized in the river and God's spirit came down and announced that Jesus was special.

And then, after the time is over, I will invite you, one at a time, to come to the Sacred Circle Time space and draw what you did or thought about so we can all share together."

(*2-minute transition time*) Start laying paper in the circle and laying out the crayons and other materials. Invite the children, one-at-a-time, to come and draw what they did, thought about, or experienced.

(*10 minutes*) Journal and Share Time

Let the children draw and journal as they gather. As most of the children finish, have them begin to share. Tell them that listening to one another is important.

Say: "Thank you for spending time with me in the Trinity Stations. I cannot wait to hear what you experienced today. Who would like to share? (Give each child time to talk, and you should talk as well.)

Place their activities in individual folders; or if they are to take the folders home, place them behind them so they will not be distracted. This will keep you from having to correct the children's behavior.

10 minutes (snack or toy time)

A Time of Blessing

Explain: "The symbol for the story today is a dove because the spirit of God, who told the people that Jesus was special, looked like a dove."

Say: "Where would you like your blessing today?" (*Let them tell you.*)

As you look into each child's eyes, make the symbol.

Say: "Thank you for being here today and spending time experiencing God with me. You are a blessing!"

Closing Time

Slowly put each Trinity symbol away.

Say: "And now we are finished with our Sacred Circle Time. We put away our symbol for God, the Creator. We put away our symbol for God, the Son. And we put away our symbol for God, the Holy Spirit."

Then quietly and gently put the sacred cloth away.

Conclude: "And we are all done with our Sacred Circle time. You did a great job. Yay!" Clap and celebrate a job well done.

Special Sunday: Trinity Sunday

Story: Great Commission of Jesus

Text: Matthew 28:18-20, NRSV

> And Jesus came and said to them, "All authority in heaven and on earth has been given to me. Go therefore and make disciples of all nations, baptizing them in the name of the Father and of the Son and of the Holy Spirit, and teaching them to obey everything that I have commanded you. And remember, I am with you always, to the end of the age."

About the text: In this story, Jesus is about to ascend into heaven after having spent the past fifty days appearing to the disciples as a resurrected Christ. As he prepares to leave, he speaks the words above, which are often referred to as *The Great Commission*. The Great Commission is one of the most recited passages of Scripture in the church today; and most of our evangelism, mission work, and reaching out to others has this passage at its roots.

In the Scripture, Jesus tells the disciples to go out in the name of the Father, Son, and Holy Spirit and that he will be with them . . . always and until the end of time. This passage reminds us that God is with us and that because of this, we should go out and love as he loved us! This text is used on Trinity Sunday because it is one place where Jesus uses the phrase, "in the name of the Father, Son, and Holy Spirit."

The Sacred Circle Time Focus: We will introduce the concept of the Trinity and of God's love being experienced through all three persons of the Trinity.

Sacred Circle Time Basic Format

Sacred Circle basket and contents:

- Sacred space cloth
- Symbols for Creator (globe), Christ (cross), and Holy Spirit (bell or chimes)
- Small, unbreakable bottle to hold water or oil for the blessing
- A journal page (one per child)
- Crayons and/or markers
- A Bible with the page marked to Matthew 28:18-20
- Focused objects from the Bible story: Lots of triangle-shaped objects. Look around and find things that are shaped like triangles. If you have a difficult time finding objects, you can make some from cut paper, bending wire, or pipe cleaners.

The Lesson

Gathering

Sit down and place the sacred basket in front of you.

Pause so that the children notice it and begin to come closer.

Invite them to form a circle.

Sit quietly until they settle in and are quiet.

Say: "It is time for Sacred Circle Time. I am so glad that you are here today. I love learning our stories and experiencing God with you."

Creating the Sacred Space

Say: "First, we create our sacred space."

Slowly lay out the sacred cloth.

Slowly lift the globe (symbol of God, the Creator) and hold it at the eye level of the children. Say: "This is our symbol for God, the Creator." Carefully lay it on the sacred cloth. (Pause.)

Slowly lift the cross (symbol of God, the Son). Say: "This is our symbol for God, the Son." Carefully lay it on the sacred cloth. (*Pause.*)

Slowly lift the bell (symbol of God, the Holy Spirit). Say: "This is our symbol of God, the Holy Spirit." Carefully lay it on the sacred cloth. (*Pause.*)

Point to each symbol and say: "So we have God, the Creator; God, the Son; and God, the Holy Spirit. (*Pause.*) Our sacred space is ready. We are ready to begin our Sacred Circle Time together."

God, the Creator (A Time to Wonder)

Say: "I want to show you some things I have brought with me today, and then I want you to guess what shape we will be talking about today."

Carefully lay out each triangle. The kids will get very excited and yell, "triangle." That is okay. Let them have fun.

Say: "You are correct! We are going to talk about triangles today. Before we start our story, I want you to look around the room and see if you see anything that is shaped like a triangle." (*Let them look for things shaped like a triangle.*)

God, the Son (Telling the Story)

Say: "In our story today, which is found in (*open the Bible*) Matthew, the twenty-eighth chapter, verses 18-20, Jesus names three things that we use every week in our Sacred Circle Time. Listen to me read it and see if you can hear the three things. (*Read the text.*)

Let the children try to hear what Jesus said.

Say: "Now I am going to read the story again; and this time, I will lift up the symbol we use for the three things Jesus mentions." (*Read the story again. This time, lift up the objects used in Sacred Circle Time.*)

Say: "Do you see that when we create our sacred space, I place God, the Creator (*point at it*); God, the Son (*point at it*); and God, the Holy Spirit (point at it) in a triangle? This is called the Trinity; and that word means God, the Creator; God, the

Son; and God, the Holy Spirit. Can you say *Trinity?*" (*Have them repeat it after you several times.*)

Say: "What do you think is in the center of the triangle of the Trinity?"

(*Let them guess.*)

Say: "In the center of God, the Creator; God, the Son; and God, the Holy Spirit—the Trinity—is love! This whole middle is filled with God's love! And in our story today, Jesus tells his followers to go and love others with God's love in the name of the Trinity—God, the Creator (*point to it*); God, the Son (*point to it*); and God, the Holy Spirit (*point to it*).

God, the Holy Spirit (Quiet and Prayer Time)

Say: "It is now time to pray. For our prayer time, I am going to help you form a triangle of love."

Help the children form a triangle. Do not worry if it is not exact because you do not have an odd number of children. They will know what it is.

Say: "One at a time, I want one of you to go into the center of the triangle. When you do, we will all say, 'you are loved' because the center of the Trinity is filled with God's love."

Have each child go into the center of the Trinity and have everyone say: "You are loved."

Pray: "God, please help us to know how deeply loved we are. We pray in the name of God, the Creator; God, the Son; and God, the Holy Spirit. Amen."

(*Please note: If you have only a small group of children, you can always make the Trinity shape for the prayer time out of yarn or rope laid on the floor in the shape of a triangle and have the children stand inside it, one at a time.*)

(*If using the extended Sacred Circle Time, stop here.*)

A Time of Blessing

Explain, "The symbol for the story today is a triangle because today is the day when we remember the Trinity: God, the Creator; God, the Son; and God, the Holy Spirit."

Ask: "Where would you like your blessing today?" (*Let them tell you.*)

As you look into each child's eyes, make the symbol.

Say: "Thank you for being here today and spending time experiencing God with me. You are a blessing!"

Closing Time

Slowly put each Trinity symbol away.

Say: "And now we are finished with our Sacred Circle Time. We put away our symbol for God, the Creator. We put away our symbol for God, the Son. And we put away our symbol for God, the Holy Spirit."

Then quietly and gently put the sacred cloth away.

Conclude: "And we are all done with our Sacred Circle time. You did a great job. Yay!" Clap and celebrate a job well done.

Extended Format

(*10 minutes*) Begin with free-play time. Greet the children warmly and let them get used to the space. Have something in the free-play space for them to play with. Rotate each week:

Week One: Paper and crayons, markers, or paint.

Week Two: Clay, wire, pipe cleaners and beads, and tool to work with clay.

Week Three: Things to build with: Blocks, Legos®, cans, boxes, flat stones.

Week Four: Things that make noise.

(*3 minutes*) Transition time. Let the children know that it is almost Sacred Circle Time.

Say: "It is almost our Sacred Circle Time. I cannot wait to have sacred time with you today. Will you start to finish up? Then come join me for our special, holy time together."

Sit down in the Sacred Circle Time space and place your sacred basket in front of you.

(*10 minutes*) **Sacred Circle Time** (*Basic format*)—Use the Sacred Circle Basic Format, but do not include the blessing or closing.

(*10 minutes*) **Trinity Stations**

Explain the Trinity Stations procedure for new children and for those who might forget from time to time.

Walk with the children to Trinity Stations and show them what they can do there, but do not let them start until they have seen all three stations.

Tell the children that after the Trinity Stations, they will spend five minutes in quiet time thinking about the story and the activities they have completed. They will then return to the Sacred Circle Time space to draw pictures and talk about their activities.

Station One: God, the Creator (Wonder) Station

Walk with the children to station one and show them what they can do here.

In addition to the suggested supplies (page 469), you might want to add some things like clay or wire for constructing triangles.

Station Two: God, the Son (Story) Station

Walk with the children to station two and show them what they can do here. In addition to the suggested supplies (page 469), you might include symbols of the Trinity like those you use in Sacred Circle Time.

Station Three: God, the Holy Spirit (Prayer) Station

Walk with the children to station three and show them what they can do here.

In addition to the suggested supplies (page 469), consider making a triangle out of yarn or rope on the floor. Encourage the children to sit in the middle of the triangle for prayer and contemplation.

Begin Quiet Time

Say: "Let's begin five minutes of thinking about the story and about how Jesus told people to love one another in the name of the Creator, the Son, and the Holy Spirit.

And then, after the time is over, I will invite you, one at a time, to come to the Sacred Circle Time space and draw what you did or thought about so we can all share together."

(*2-minute transition time*) Start laying paper in the circle and laying out the crayons and other materials. Invite the children, one at a time, to come and draw what they did, thought about, or experienced.

(10 minutes) **Journal and Share Time**

Let them draw and journal as they gather. When most of the children have finished, let them begin to share. Tell them that listening to one another is important.

Say: "Thank you for spending time with me in the Trinity Stations. I cannot wait to hear what you experienced today. Who would like to share?" (Give each child a time to talk, and you should talk as well.)

Place their activities in individual folders; or if they are to take the folders home, place them behind them so they will not be distracted. This will keep you from having to correct the children's behavior.

10 minutes (snack or toy time)

A Time of Blessing

Explain, "The symbol for the story today is a triangle because today is the day when we remember the Trinity: "God, the Creator; God, the Son; and God, the Holy Spirit."

Ask: "Where would you like your blessing today?" (*Let them tell you.*)

As you look into each child's eyes, make the symbol.

Say: "Thank you for being here today and spending time experiencing God with me. You are a blessing!"

Closing Time

Slowly put each Trinity symbol away.

Say: "And now we are finished with our Sacred Circle Time. We put away our symbol for God, the Creator. We put away our symbol for God, the Son. And we put away our symbol for God, the Holy Spirit."

Then quietly and gently put the sacred cloth away.

Conclude: "And we are all done with our Sacred Circle time. You did a great job. Yay!" Clap and celebrate a job well done.

Special Sunday:
Christ the King Sunday

Story: Jesus as the King

Text: Luke 1:26-33, NIV

In the sixth month of Elizabeth's pregnancy, God sent the angel Gabriel to Nazareth, a town in Galilee, to a virgin pledged to be married to a man named Joseph, a descendant of David. The virgin's name was Mary. The angel went to her and said, "Greetings, you who are highly favored! The Lord is with you."

Mary was greatly troubled at his words and wondered what kind of greeting this might be. But the angel said to her, "Do not be afraid, Mary; you have found favor with God. You will conceive and give birth to a son, and you are to call him Jesus. He will be great and will be called the Son of the Most High. The Lord God will give him the throne of his father David, and he will reign over Jacob's descendants forever; his kingdom will never end."

About the text: Christ the King Sunday is observed as the final Sunday of the liturgical year. It reminds us that Jesus is the fulfillment of God's promise to send a messiah. Jesus is the Messiah, the Savior, and the king of all kings. The other kings in the Bible came and went, but Jesus, who is now placed on the throne of heaven, is the king whose kingdom will never end.

The Sacred Circle Time Focus: We will focus on Jesus being our King and leading us with great love.

Sacred Circle Time Basic Format

Sacred Circle basket and contents:

- Sacred space cloth
- Symbols for Creator (globe), Christ (cross), and Holy Spirit (bell or chimes)
- Small, unbreakable bottle to hold water or oil for the blessing
- A journal page (one per child)
- Crayons and/or markers
- A Bible with the page marked to Luke 1:26-33
- Focused objects from the Bible story:
  - A king's crown (If you do not have one already, you can make a simple one from paper.)
  - A Scepter—Construct from a stick or wooden spoon or ruler with a diamond shape on it.
  - A heart that will cover the diamond (above on the scepter) and some tape.

The Lesson

Gathering

Sit down and place the sacred basket in front of you.

Pause so that the children notice it and begin to come closer.

Invite them to form a circle.

Sit quietly until they settle in and are quiet.

Say: "It is time for Sacred Circle Time. I am so glad that you are here today. I love learning our stories and experiencing God with you."

Creating the Sacred Space

Say: "First, we create our sacred space."

Slowly lay out the sacred cloth.

Slowly lift the globe (symbol of God, the Creator) and hold it at the eye level of the children. Say: "This is our symbol for God, the Creator." Carefully lay it on the sacred cloth. (*Pause.*)

Slowly lift the cross (symbol of God, the Son). Say: "This is our symbol for God, the Son." Carefully lay it on the sacred cloth. (*Pause.*)

Slowly lift the bell (symbol of God, the Holy Spirit). Say: "This is our symbol of God, the Holy Spirit." Carefully lay it on the sacred cloth. (*Pause.*)

Point to each symbol and say: "So we have God, the Creator; God, the Son; and God, the Holy Spirit. (*Pause.*) Our sacred space is ready. We are ready to begin our Sacred Circle Time together."

God, the Creator (A Time to Wonder)

Show the children the crown and scepter. Ask: "Who would wear this?"

They will say that the items belong to a king or queen.

Say: "You are correct. A king or queen wears a crown and carries a scepter. What is a crown made of?" (*Let them describe it as being made of gold with jewels all over it.*)

Ask: "And what is a scepter made of?" (*Let them describe it as a being made of gold and other materials.*)

Say: "You are so smart! What is a scepter for? Why does a king have one?"

(*Let them guess.*)

Say: "The crown is sort of a hat that queens and kings wear so that everyone will know they are queens or kings. And the scepter is used to hold up as a sign that everyone should follow the king or queen. When they tell people what to do, they hold up their scepter; and the people follow."

Ask the children to stand.

Say: "Let's play king or queen. I am going to choose a queen (or king). (*Place the crown on a child's head.*) The crown tells you that she/he is the queen/king. Now I am going to give her/him a scepter. (*Give the scepter to the child.*) The scepter tells you that you are supposed to follow her/him. Let's follow the queen/king."

Have the child walk, and have the others follow. Play this game several times; then have them sit back in the circle.

God, the Son (Telling the Story)

Say: "Well, in our story today, which is found in (*open the Bible*) Luke, chapter one, verses 26-33, God sends the Angel Gabriel to tell Mary that she is going to have a baby. The baby is going to be named Jesus. The angel tells Mary that Jesus will be the greatest king ever! The best king ever! The most powerful king ever! And Jesus is our king. There is only one problem. He doesn't wear a king's crown, so he doesn't look like a king. And he doesn't carry a scepter, so he doesn't make people follow him. Jesus doesn't look like a king, but he is one!" (*Pause so that they can let what you have said soak in.*)

Say: "Jesus does not have a crown and a scepter. Instead, Jesus shows us what love looks like. He is kind, gentle, and loving. Instead of *making* us follow him, he *asks* us to follow him. He leads us with love!"

Place the heart over the diamond on the scepter.

Say: "Jesus does not need a crown or a scepter. His loving heart is what makes him our king."

God, the Holy Spirit (Quiet and Prayer Time)

Say: "It is now time to pray. For our prayer time, I am going to pass this scepter of love to each one of you. When you receive the scepter, just hold it for a minute and think about what a special King of Love we have been given."

Pass the scepter around to each child.

Pray: "God, we thank you for our loving king, Jesus. May we always follow his love. In his name, we pray. Amen."

(If using the extended Sacred Circle Time, stop here.)

A Time of Blessing

Explain: "The symbol for the story today is a heart because Jesus is the king of love!"

Ask: "Where would you like your blessing today?" (*Let them tell you.*)

As you look into each child's eyes, make the symbol.

Say: "Thank you for being here today and spending time experiencing God with me. You are a blessing!"

Closing Time

Slowly put each Trinity symbol away.

Say: "And now we are finished with our Sacred Circle Time. We put away our symbol for God, the Creator. We put away our symbol for God, the Son. And we put away our symbol for God, the Holy Spirit."

Then quietly and gently put the sacred cloth away.

Conclude: "And we are all done with our Sacred Circle time. You did a great job. Yay!" Clap and celebrate a job well done.

Extended Format

(*10 minutes*) Begin with free-play time. Greet the children warmly and let them get used to the space. Have something in the free-play space for them to play with. Rotate each week:

Week One: Paper and crayons, markers, or paint.

Week Two: Clay, wire, pipe cleaners and beads, and tools to work the clay.

Week Three: Things to build with: blocks, Legos®, cans, boxes, or flat stones.

Week Four: Things that make noise.

(*3 minutes*) Transition time. Let the children know that it is almost Sacred Circle Time. Say: "It is almost our Sacred Circle Time. I cannot wait to have sacred time with you today. Will you start to finish up? Then come join me for our special, holy time together."

Sit down in the Sacred Circle Time space and place your sacred basket in front of you.

(*10 minutes*) **Sacred Circle Time** (*Basic format*)—Use the Sacred Circle Basic Format, but do not include the blessing or closing.

(*10 minutes*) **Trinity Stations**

Explain the Trinity Stations procedure for new children and for those who might forget from time to time.

Walk with the children to Trinity Stations and show them what they can do there, but do not let them start until they have seen all three stations.

Tell the children that after the Trinity Stations, they will spend five minutes in quiet time thinking about the story and the activities they have completed. They will then return to the Sacred Circle Time space to draw pictures and talk about their activities.

Station One: God, the Creator (Wonder) Station

Walk with the children to station one and show them what they can do here. In addition to the suggested supplies (page 469), you might want to add some things to make hearts or crowns to decorate with hearts.

Station Two: God, the Son (Story) Station

Walk with the children to station two and show them what they can do here. In addition to the suggested supplies (page 469), you might want to include some king and queen dress-up clothes and toys.

Station Three: God, the Holy Spirit (Prayer) Station

Walk with the children to station three and show them what they can do here. In addition to the suggested supplies (page 469), you might want to include some small plastic jewels, glue, and paper for the children to make hearts as they contemplate the story.

Begin Quiet Time

Say: "Let's begin five minutes of thinking about how Jesus is the king of love. After the time is over, I will invite you, one at a time, to come to the Sacred Circle Time space and draw what you did or thought about so we can all share together."

(*2-minute transition time*) Start laying paper in the circle and laying out the crayons and other materials. Invite the children, one at a time, to come and draw what they did, thought about, or experienced.

(*10 minutes*) **Journal and Share Time**

Let them draw and journal as they gather. As most of the children finish, have the others begin to share. Tell them that listening to one another is important.

Say: "Thank you for spending time with me in the Trinity Stations. I cannot wait to hear what you experienced today. Who would like to share?" (Give each child a time to talk, and you should talk as well.)

Place their activities in individual folders; or if they are to take the folders home, place them behind them so they will not be distracted. This will keep you from having to correct the children's behavior.

10 minutes (snack or toy time)

A Time of Blessing

Explain: "The symbol for the story today is a heart because Jesus is the king of love!"

Ask: "Where would you like your blessing today?" (*Let them tell you.*)

As you look into each child's eyes, make the symbol.

Say: "Thank you for being here today and spending time experiencing God with me. You are a blessing!"

Closing Time

Slowly put each Trinity symbol away.

Say: "And now we are finished with our Sacred Circle Time. We put away our symbol for God, the Creator. We put away our symbol for God, the Son. And we put away our symbol for God, the Holy Spirit."

Then quietly and gently put the sacred cloth away.

Conclude: "And we are all done with our Sacred Circle time. You did a great job. Yay!" Clap and celebrate a job well done.

About the Season of Lent

Lent is a time set apart by the early church as a time of reflection and purification as Christians prepare to celebrate the holiest day of the church year, Easter. The date for Easter is set each year according to the phases of the moon. As a result, the date moves from year to year. The date for Lent is then set by counting backward from Easter Sunday, forty days plus six Sundays. The first day of Lent is Ash Wednesday.

Ash Wednesday is a somber day when the church gathers to look over the past year and reflect on those habits, actions, and thoughts where we failed to be the people God calls us to be. No one lives the perfect life, so Ash Wednesday is set apart for everyone! We look back and assess where we are spiritually. On Ash Wednesday, we are reminded that we humans were created by God from dust and that one day we will return to the ground from which we came. Ashes are used as a sign of repentance for the past and as a reminder that our time on earth is limited. Because our days are short, we must do all we can in our lifetime to follow God.

Between the Ash Wednesday worship of honest reflection and Easter, many people enter a time of prayer, fasting, and other spiritual disciplines designed to bring them closer to God.

The last week of Lent is Holy Week. During that week, we remember the events leading to the death and resurrection of Christ. We begin Holy Week with Palm Sunday, where Jesus made his triumphant entrance into Jerusalem. On Maundy Thursday, we remember the Last Supper, where Jesus began the ritual of Holy Communion by sharing bread and wine with his disciples and followers. The Friday of Holy Week recalls his unjust trial and death on the cross. Saturday is often "Silent Saturday," and it is the day when we remember that he lay in the tomb for three days. Lent officially ends on Silent Saturday, and its somberness is broken by the joy of Easter.

Young children can participate in Lent. In creating experiences for them, we must remember that much of what happens during Holy Week is theological, and young children simply cannot grasp these concepts yet. We must also remember that Christ on the cross is an extremely powerful symbol and can be upsetting for sensitive young children.

Children can learn that Lent lasts forty days, that it is an important and holy time, that we pray more than usual during Lent, and that Jesus loved his disciples and loves us. Children can also begin to become familiar with practices associated with Lent such as the Last Supper, footwashing on Maundy Thursday, and the services on Palm Sunday. Most important, Lent can be an intentional time to help young children enter into prayer and experience the love of God in prayer practices.

(*Note: We will be intentionally using the cross as the symbol for blessing the children each week during Lent. This makes the cross a central part of the Sacred Circle Time and the Lenten journey.*)

Ash Wednesday

Story: Jonah and the Big Fish

Text: Jonah 3:1-10, NRSV

The word of the Lord came to Jonah a second time, saying, "Get up, go to Nineveh, that great city, and proclaim to it the message that I tell you." So Jonah set out and went to Nineveh, according to the word of the Lord. Now Nineveh was an exceedingly large city, a three days' walk across. Jonah began to go into the city, going a day's walk. And he cried out, "Forty days more, and Nineveh shall be overthrown!" And the people of Nineveh believed God; they proclaimed a fast, and everyone, great and small, put on sackcloth.

When the news reached the king of Nineveh, he rose from his throne, removed his robe, covered himself with sackcloth, and sat in ashes. Then he had a proclamation made in Nineveh: "By the decree of the king and his nobles: No human being or animal, no herd or flock, shall taste anything. They shall not feed, nor shall they drink water. Human beings and animals shall be covered with sackcloth, and they shall cry mightily to God. All shall turn from their evil ways and from the violence that is in their hands. Who knows? God may relent and change his mind; he may turn from his fierce anger, so that we do not perish."

When God saw what they did, how they turned from their evil ways, God changed his mind about the calamity that he had said he would bring upon them; and he did not do it.

About the text: This story is the first time in the Bible where people placed ashes on themselves as a sign of repentance. It has often been used as an Ash Wednesday text because it acknowledges that God forgives the wickedness of even the most sinful people—the lost people of Nineveh. Jonah being in the belly of a big fish for three days can be symbolic of the three days that Jesus was in the tomb. After three days, Jesus arose; and through him, we are saved. Jonah was in the fish for three days; when he was spit out and delivered God's message, the people of Nineveh were forgiven.

The Sacred Circle Time Focus: We will learn the story of Jonah and focus on Ash Wednesday being a day of ashes as symbols of forgiveness.

Sacred Circle Time Basic Format

Sacred Circle basket and contents:

- Sacred space cloth
- Symbols for Creator (globe), Christ (cross), and Holy Spirit (bell or chimes)
- Small, unbreakable bottle to hold water or oil for the blessing
- A journal page (one per child)
- Crayons and/or markers
- A Bible bookmarked at Jonah
- Focused objects from the Bible story: A small blanket, ashes in a small bowl or clear bag (Any ash will do.)

The Lesson

Gathering

Begin by sitting down and placing the Sacred basket in front of you. Pause so that the children notice it and begin to come closer.

Invite them to form a circle. Sit quietly until they settle in and are quiet.

Say: "It is time for Sacred Circle Time. I am so glad that you are here today. I love learning our stories and experiencing God with you."

Introducing Lent as Forty-Six Holy Days

We will be doing this ritual with the children each time we gather during Lent. It will impress on them that Lent is long time and a holy time and different from other times of the church year. Do not explain Lent. Let them learn as the weeks unfold.

Say: "Easter will be here in forty-six days. Today is Ash Wednesday, and it is the first day of forty-six holy days between now and Easter. It is forty days and six Sundays. Let's count the days by clapping forty-six times."

Have the children stand; let them count loudly while they clap. As the numbers get higher, lower your voice and the children will follow. By the time you get to forty, be whispering. Sit down during 40 through 46. After you sit, be silent for a few seconds.

Say: "Lent is a holy time of forty-six days."

Creating the Sacred Space

Say: "First, we create our sacred space."

Slowly lay out the sacred cloth.

Slowly lift the globe (symbol of God, the Creator) and hold it at the eye level of the children. Say: "This is our symbol for God, the Creator." Carefully lay it on the sacred cloth. (*Pause.*)

Slowly lift the cross (symbol of God, the Son). Say: "This is our symbol for God, the Son." Carefully lay it on the sacred cloth. (*Pause.*)

Slowly lift the bell (symbol of God, the Holy Spirit). Say: "This is our symbol of God, the Holy Spirit." Carefully lay it on the sacred cloth. (*Pause.*)

Point to each symbol and say: "So we have God, the Creator; God, the Son; and God, the Holy Spirit. (*Pause.*) Our sacred space is ready. We are ready to begin our Sacred Circle Time together."

God, the Creator (A Time to Wonder)

Fold a blanket into different shapes and animals. Have fun and remember that children have very good imaginations! Don't worry if what you fold looks like what you intend it to be. This is wonder and fun time!

God, the Son (Telling the Story)

Say: "In our story today, which is found in (*open the Bible*) Jonah, we learn the story of a man named Jonah." (*Use your two fingers, pretending that you hand is Jonah walking around on the floor*).

Say: "And God spoke to Jonah and asked Jonah to go to Nineveh, a city where the people were really mean and terrible to one another. They hit one another and yelled at one another and were mean to one another!"

Use the blanket to make the road to Nineveh by folding it into one long road.

Say: "So God asked Jonah to go down the road to Nineveh" (*Finger-walk Jonah toward Nineveh and pause.*)

Say: "But Jonah was afraid to go to Nineveh because the people who lived there were so mean! So he did not go to Nineveh. He went the other way and got onto a ship."

(*Fold the blanket into a ship.*)

Say: "And Jonah was going to go to Tarshish not Nineveh! But while he was on the ship, a big storm came." (*Shake the blanket as if it is wild sea during a storm.*)

Say: "Oh, poor Jonah was thrown overboard and just about that time . . .

(*Fold the blanket into a fish*) a big fish came along and swallowed Jonah."

(*Place finger Jonah under the blanket while the blanket is still folded like a fish.*)

Say: "And Jonah had to stay swallowed by that big fish for three days. Count with me." (*Let them count to three very slowly.*)

Say: "Day One. Day Two. Day Three. Poor Jonah was inside the belly of that fish; and he prayed to God and said, 'God, please get me out of here, and I will go to that mean city of Nineveh and do what you told me to do! I promise.' And the big fish spit Jonah out; and guess what? That fish had swum all the way to Nineveh! That big fish spat Jonah out right into the city of Nineveh. And Jonah went into the city, even though he was scared." (*Finger-walk Jonah into the center of the circle and make him shake with fear.*)

Say: "Jonah was scared and shaking because those people were so mean, and he was afraid of them! But he walked in anyway and said, 'People of Nineveh. God wants you to stop being mean!' And do you know what the people did? They rubbed ashes all over themselves. It was their way of telling God they were sorry!" (*Show the children the ashes.*)

Say: "And those mean people were sorry, and they stopped being mean! Today is Ash Wednesday. On Ash Wednesday, we can go to church and get ashes put on us. We do not rub them all over us like the people of Nineveh did. We just get them on our forehead or sometimes on our hand. But before we get our ashes, we remember something mean that we did or said, and we say we are sorry to God. And then the minister places a little tiny bit of ash on our forehead."

Place a tiny bit of ash on your own forehead. The children might laugh. That is okay; just stay focused.

Say: "Those mean people of Nineveh put ashes all over their bodies to say they were sorry to God. We put a tiny bit of ashes on ourselves on Ash Wednesday as a way to tell God we are sorry for the mean things we do. And Ash Wednesday is the first day of the forty-six days of Lent."

God, the Holy Spirit (Quiet and Prayer Time)

Say: "It is now time to pray. I am not going to put any ashes on you, but I am going to pass these around to each of you. As you hold them, I want you to think of or say out loud anything you have done that was mean or naughty. Then we will all say: 'God loves you and forgives you.'"

You should go first to model for the children that we do naughty things, and there is nothing to be embarrassed about. Pass the ashes to each child and let each share. After each child shares, have everyone say in unison, "God loves you. You are forgiven."

Pray: "God, we all do things we should not. We are all mean sometimes, and we are all naughty sometimes. Remind us that you love us and will always forgive us! In the name of Christ, we pray. Amen."

(If using the extended Sacred Circle Time, stop here.)

A Time of Blessing

Explain: "The symbol for the story today is a heart because God always loves us, even when we do mean things or naughty things, and God always forgives us!"

Ask: "Where would you like your blessing today?" (*Let them tell you.*)

As you look into each child's eyes, make the symbol.

Say: "You are loved by God always! Thank you for experiencing God with me today. You are a blessing!"

Extended Format

(*10 minutes*) Begin with free-play time. Greet the children warmly and let them get used to the space. Have something in the free-play space for them to play with. Rotate each week:

Week One: Paper and crayons, markers, or paint.

Week Two: Clay, wire, pipe cleaners and beads, and tools to work the clay.

Week Three: Things to build with: blocks, Legos®, cans, boxes, or flat stones.

Week Four: Things that make noise.

(*3 minutes*) Transition time. Let the children know that it is almost Sacred Circle Time. Say: "It is almost our Sacred Circle Time. I cannot wait to have sacred time with you today. Will you start to finish up? Then come join me for our special, holy time together."

Sit down in the Sacred Circle Time space and place your sacred basket in front of you.

(*10 minutes*) **Sacred Circle Time** (*Basic format*)—Use the Sacred Circle Basic Format, but do not include the blessing or closing.

(*10 minutes*) **Trinity Stations**

Explain the Trinity Stations procedure for new children and for those who might forget from time to time.

Walk with the children to Trinity Stations and show them what they can do there, but do not let them start until they have seen all three stations.

Tell the children that after the Trinity Stations, they will spend five minutes in quiet time thinking about the story and the activities they have completed. They will then return to the Sacred Circle Time space to draw pictures and talk about their activities.

Station One: God, the Creator (Wonder Station)

Walk with the children to station one and show them what they can do here. In addition to the suggested supplies (page 469), you might want to add some ocean materials such as fish, seaweed, saltwater. Invite the children to smell, feel, and taste these items.

Station Two: God, the Son (Story) Station

Walk with the children to station two and show them what they can do here. In addition to the suggested supplies (page 469), you might want to include a storybook of Jonah and the blanket you used to tell the story so the children can act it out.

Station Three: God, the Holy Spirit (Prayer) Station

Walk with the children to station three and show them what they can do here. In addition to the suggested supplies (page 469), you might want to add a battery-operated candle with fish symbols on it or some water and ashes (to allow the children to put ash on their hands and wash it off).

Begin Quiet Time

Say: "Let's begin five minutes of thinking about the story of Jonah being swallowed by that big fish and how the people of Nineveh rubbed ashes all over themselves to tell God that they were sorry. After the time is over, I will invite you, one at a time, to come to the Sacred Circle Time space and draw what you did or thought about so we can all share together."

(*2-minute transition time*) Start laying paper in the circle and laying out the crayons and other materials. Invite the children, one at a time, to come and draw what they did, thought about, or experienced.

(*10 minutes*) **Journal and Share Time**

Let them draw and journal as they gather. When most of the children have finished, let them begin to share. Tell them that listening to one another is important.

Say: "Thank you for spending time with me in the Trinity Stations. I cannot wait to find out what you experienced today. Who would like to share?" (Give each child time to talk, and you should talk as well.)

Place their activities in individual folders; or if they are to take the folders home, place them behind them so they will not be distracted. This will keep you from having to correct the children's behavior.

10 minutes (snack or toy time)

A Time of Blessing

Explain: "The symbol for the story today is a heart because God always loves us, even when we do mean things or naughty things; and God always forgives us!"

Ask: "Where would you like your blessing today?" (*Let them tell you.*)

As you look into each child's eyes, make the symbol.

Say: "You are loved by God always! Thank you for experiencing God with me today. You are a blessing!"

Closing Time

Slowly put each Trinity symbol away.

Say: "And now we are finished with our Sacred Circle Time. We put away our symbol for God, the Creator. We put away our symbol for God, the Son. And we put away our symbol for God, the Holy Spirit."

Then quietly and gently put the sacred cloth away.

Conclude: "And we are all done with our Sacred Circle time. You did a great job. Yay!" Clap and celebrate a job well done.

The First Sunday of Lent

Story: Jesus Prayed

Text: Matthew 6:7-13, NRSV

"When you are praying, do not heap up empty phrases as the Gentiles do; for they think that they will be heard because of their many words. Do not be like them, for your Father knows what you need before you ask him.

"Pray then in this way:

Our Father in heaven,
> hallowed be your name.
> Your kingdom come.
> Your will be done,
>> on earth as it is in heaven.
> Give us this day our daily bread.
> And forgive us our debts,
>> as we also have forgiven our debtors.
> And do not bring us to the time of trial,
>> but rescue us from the evil one.

About the Text: The Lord's Prayer is one of the most commonly memorized and used parts of Scripture. It is central because it is *the* prayer that Jesus asked his followers to pray; and it has been prayed and passed down from Jesus, through the generations of followers, to us today. It is precious to all Christian faith traditions and, as we say it, we are reminded that we are part of the body of Christ. It also reminds us that God will care for us, and we are called to provide for others.

While we might be tempted to try and have the children memorize this prayer or learn what it means, most of them are too young to grasp its meaning and will be frustrated by trying to memorize it. They will hear this prayer many times throughout their lives and will memorize it at a more age-appropriate time. For now, we want to teach them that it is a special prayer and gift from Jesus.

The Sacred Circle Time Focus: We will introduce Lent as an important holy time for prayer and introduce children to this important prayer that Jesus gave to us.

Sacred Circle Time Basic Format

Sacred Circle basket and contents:

- Sacred space cloth
- Symbols for Creator (globe), Christ (cross), and Holy Spirit (bell or chimes)
- Small, unbreakable bottle to hold water or oil for the blessing
- A journal page (one per child)
- Crayons and/or markers
- A Bible with the page marked to Matthew 6:7-13
- Focused object from the Bible story: A chain (the bigger, the better, but any chain will do. You can use one made of paper, but an actual chain is better.)

The Lesson

Gathering

Begin by sitting down and placing the Sacred basket in front of you. Pause so that the children notice it and begin to come closer.

Invite them to form a circle. Sit quietly until they settle in and are quiet.

Say: "It is time for Sacred Circle Time. I am so glad that you are here today. I love learning our stories and experiencing God with you."

Observing Lent as Forty-Six Holy Days

Say: "Lent is made up of forty-six holy days between Ash Wednesday and Easter. It is forty days and six Sundays. Let's count the days by clapping forty-six times."

Have the children stand. Let them count loudly while they clap. As the numbers get higher, lower your voice, and the children will follow. By the time you get to forty, be whispering; and then sit down during 40 through 46. After you sit, be silent for a few seconds.

Say: "Lent is a holy time of forty-six days."

Creating the Sacred Space

Say: "Now, we create our sacred space."

Slowly lay out the sacred cloth.

Slowly lift the globe (symbol of God, the Creator) and hold it at the eye level of the children. Say: "This is our symbol for God, the Creator." Carefully lay it on the sacred cloth. (*Pause.*)

Slowly lift the cross (symbol of God, the Son). Say: "This is our symbol for God, the Son." Carefully lay it on the sacred cloth. (*Pause.*)

Slowly lift the bell (symbol of God, the Holy Spirit). Say: "This is our symbol of God, the Holy Spirit." Carefully lay it on the sacred cloth. (*Pause.*)

Point to each symbol and say: "So we have God, the Creator; God, the Son; and God, the Holy Spirit. (*Pause.*) Our sacred space is ready. We are ready to begin our Sacred Circle Time together."

God, the Creator (A Time to Wonder)

Show the children the chain. Let them touch it and pass it around. If it is large, let them try to break it.

Ask: "What do we do with chains?" Encourage them to guess lots of things.

God, the Son (Telling the Story)

Say: "I am going to use this chain to help you understand what a wonderful prayer Jesus gave to his disciples a long time ago. Our story is found in (*open the Bible*) Matthew, chapter six, verses 7-13. In our story, Jesus is talking to his followers about praying. What is praying?" Encourage the children to respond.

Tell the children, "Praying is when we make time to talk to God and listen to God speak to us. Sometimes we use words when we pray. In the story, Jesus gave the disciples a word prayer. It is called the Lord's Prayer. Let me read it to you."

Read the Lord's Prayer to the children. Do not explain it. Just read it. This will help them become familiar with.

Explain: "So let's say that the Lord's Prayer started right here with Jesus."

(*Hold up the very end of the chain.*)

Say: "Jesus said the prayer, and then he taught it to the disciples." (*Touch the next link of the chain.*)

Say: "And then the followers taught others the prayer, and they taught others, and they taught others . . ." (*Touch the next link of the chain and continue until you reach the last link of the chain.*)

Say: "And now, we say this prayer. This is a long chain of the prayer being passed from person to person, and it was given to us by Jesus. This is a very special prayer!"

God, the Holy Spirit (Quiet and Prayer Time)

Say: "It is now time to pray. I am going to say this special Lord's Prayer with you. I will say one line, and you can repeat it."

> "Our Father who art in heaven (*children repeat*),
> Hallowed be thy name (children *repeat*),
> Thy Kingdom come (children *repeat*),
> Thy will be done (*children repeat*),
> On earth as it is in heaven (children *repeat*).
> Give us this day our daily bread (*children repeat*),

And forgive us out trespasses (*children repeat*),
As we forgive those (*children repeat*),
who trespass against us (*children repeat*),
And lead us not into temptation (*children repeat*),
But deliver us from evil (*children repeat*),
For thine is the kingdom (*children repeat*),
And the power (*children repeat*),
And the glory forever (*children repeat*),
Amen (*children repeat*)."

Explain: "This prayer started with Jesus, and we still say it today. Someday you will understand it and even be able to say it without even reading it. It is a precious and important prayer."

(If using the extended Sacred Circle Time, stop here)

A Time of Blessing

Explain: "The symbol for the story today is a cross because Jesus gave us this special prayer."

Ask: "Where would you like your blessing today?" (*Let them tell you.*)

As you look into each child' eyes, make the symbol.

Say: "Thank you for being here today and spending time experiencing God with me. You are a blessing!"

Closing Time

Slowly put each Trinity symbol away.

Say: "And now we are finished with our Sacred Circle Time. We put away our symbol for God, the Creator. We put away our symbol for God, the Son. And we put away our symbol for God, the Holy Spirit."

Then quietly and gently put the sacred cloth away.

Conclude: "And we are all done with our Sacred Circle time. You did a great job. Yay!" Clap and celebrate a job well done.

Extended Format

(*10 minutes*) Begin free-play time. Greet the children warmly and let them get used to the space. Have something in the free-play space for them to play with. Rotate each week:

Week One: Paper and crayons, markers, or paint.

Week Two: Clay, wire, pipe cleaners and beads, and tools to work the clay.

Week Three: Things to build with: blocks, Legos®, cans, boxes, or flat stones.

Week Four: Things that make noise.

(*3 minutes*) Transition time. Let the children know that it is almost Sacred Circle Time. Say: "It is almost our Sacred Circle Time. I cannot wait to have sacred time with you today. Will you start to finish up? Then come join me for our special, holy time together."

Sit down in the Sacred Circle Time space and place your sacred basket in front of you.

(*10 minutes*) **Sacred Circle Time** (*Basic format*)—Use the Sacred Circle Basic Format, but do not include the blessing or closing.

(*10 minutes*) **Trinity Stations**

Explain the Trinity Stations procedure for new children and for those who might forget from time to time.

Walk with the children to the Trinity Stations and show them what they can do there, but do not let them start until they have seen all three stations.

Tell the children that after the Trinity Stations, they will spend five minutes in quiet time thinking about the story and the activities they have completed. They will then return to the Sacred Circle Time space to draw pictures and talk about their activities.

Station One: God, the Creator (Wonder) Station

Walk with the children to station one and show them what they can do here. In addition to the suggested supplies (page 469), you might want to add some chains of different sizes and shapes; or provide wire so the children can make their own chains.

Station Two: God, the Son (Story) Station

Walk with the children to station two and show them what they can do here. In addition to the suggested supplies (page 469), you might want to include copies of the Lord's Prayer for the children to copy or trace.

Station Three: God, the Holy Spirit (Prayer) Station

Walk with the children to station three and show them what they can do here. In addition to the suggested supplies (page 469), you might want to add some beautiful paper on which the children may draw or write their own prayers.

Begin Quiet Time

Say: "Let's begin five minutes of thinking about the story and about the special prayer that Jesus gave to us that is still prayed by Christians today. After the time is over, I will invite you, one at a time, to come to the Sacred Circle Time space and draw what you did or thought about, so we can all share together."

(*2-minute transition time*) Start laying paper in the circle and laying out the crayons and other materials. Invite the children, one at a time, to come and draw what they did, thought about, or experienced.

(*10 minutes*) **Journal and Share Time**

Let them draw and journal as they gather. When most of the children have finished, ask them to begin to share. Tell them that listening to one another is important.

Say: "Thank you for spending time with me in the Trinity Stations. I cannot wait to see what you experienced today. Who would like to share?" (Give each child a time to talk, and you should talk as well.)

Place their activities in individual folders; or if they are to take them home, place them behind them so they will not be distracted. This will keep you from having to correct the children's behavior.

10 minutes (snack or toy time)

A Time of Blessing

Explain, "The symbol for the story today is a cross because Jesus gave us this special prayer."

Ask, "Where would you like your blessing today?" (*Let them tell you.*)

As you look into each child's eyes, make the symbol.

Say: "Thank you for being here today and spending time experiencing God with me. You are a blessing!"

Closing Time

Slowly put each Trinity symbol away.

Say: "And now we are finished with our Sacred Circle Time. We put away our symbol for God, the Creator. We put away our symbol for God, the Son. And we put away our symbol for God, the Holy Spirit."

Then quietly and gently put the sacred cloth away.

Conclude: "And we are all done with our Sacred Circle time. You did a great job. Yay!" Clap and celebrate a job well done.

The Second Sunday of Lent

Story: Jesus Prayed Alone

Text: Mark 1:35, NRSV

> In the morning, while it was still very dark, he got up and went out to
> a deserted place, and there he prayed.

About the text: To fully understand the importance of Jesus praying alone, we must look at this passage in context. Jesus is baptized and then immediately begins full-time ministry. He starts out at full force! On his first day, he preaches, calls his disciples, drives out an evil spirit, heals many people (including Simon's mother-in-law), and casts out many demons. The next morning, he gets up early, before anyone has time to ask him for a favor or a miracle, and goes alone to pray. This story reminds us that prayer time was centrally important to Jesus and the way he refilled his cup so that he had the energy to continue his ministry.

The Sacred Circle Time Focus: We will continue to emphasize Lent as an important holy time for prayer by teaching children this story. Then they will experience contemplative prayer.

Sacred Circle Time Basic Format

Sacred Circle basket and contents:

- Sacred space cloth

- Symbols for Creator (globe), Christ (cross), and Holy Spirit (bell or chimes)
- Small, unbreakable bottle to hold water or oil for the blessing
- A journal page (one per child)
- Crayons and/or markers
- A Bible bookmarked to Mark 1:35
- Focused objects from the Bible story: A bag of 33 small stones of different shapes and sizes. You may pick up any stones from the ground.

The Lesson

Gathering

Begin by sitting down and placing the sacred basket in front of you. Pause so that the children notice it and begin to come closer.

Invite them to form a circle. Sit quietly until they settle in and are quiet.

Say: "It is time for Sacred Circle Time. I am so glad that you are here today. I love learning our stories and experiencing God with you."

Observing Lent as Forty-Six Holy Days

Say: "Lent is made up of the forty-six holy days between Ash Wednesday and Easter. It is forty days and six Sundays. Let's count the days by clapping forty-six times."

Have the children stand. Let them count loudly while they clap. As the numbers get higher, lower your voice, and the children will follow. By the time you get to forty, be whispering; and sit down during 40 through 46. After you sit, be silent for a few seconds.

Say: "Lent is a holy time of forty-six days."

Creating the Sacred Space

Say: "Let's create our sacred space."

Slowly lay out the sacred cloth.

Slowly lift the globe (symbol of God, the Creator) and hold it at the eye level of the children. Say: "This is our symbol for God, the Creator." Carefully lay it on the sacred cloth. *(Pause.)*

Slowly lift the cross (symbol of God, the Son). Say: "This is our symbol for God, the Son." Carefully lay it on the sacred cloth. *(Pause.)*

Slowly lift the bell (symbol of God, the Holy Spirit). Say: "This is our symbol of God, the Holy Spirit." *(Pause.)*

Point to each symbol and say: "So we have God, the Creator; God, the Son; and God, the Holy Spirit. *(Pause.)* Our sacred space is ready. We are ready to begin our Sacred Circle Time together."

God, the Creator (A Time to Wonder)

Show the children the stones. Let them touch them, pass them around, and begin to notice all the differences in them. Children loves stones, so let them enjoy looking at them. Do not rush them. Enjoy their enthusiasm about these small gifts from God!

God, the Son (Telling the Story)

Say: "Today I want to tell you a story found in *(open the Bible)* the first chapter of Mark, verse 35. Let's pretend that this stone is Jesus. *(Place a stone in the center of the sacred circle space.)* Jesus had just started teaching people about God, and he was very busy! He preached to some people and told them about God and how much God loved them. *(Place ten stones in the center of the sacred circle.)* He found disciples who would be his students and learn all about God from him. *(Place twelve more stones into the center of the sacred circle.)* People who were very sick came to him and asked him to heal them and make them all better, and he did." *(Add ten more stones to the center.)*

Pause and take a dramatic BIG breath.

Say: "Wow! Jesus was very busy teaching people about God and making the sick people all better, wasn't he? Let's count and see how many people he helped on his first day of work." (*Let the children count along with you. This is a high number for young children to count to, and they will be amazed!*)

Say: "Wow! Jesus taught and helped so many people. He must have been really tired. So do you know what he did next? He went off all by himself (*move the Jesus stone away from the other stones*) to pray all alone. He knew praying would help him have the energy to keep going and keep helping more and more people! He helped so many people (*move the Jesus stone back to the people*), and then he would go pray alone. It was important for Jesus to pray."

God, the Holy Spirit (Quiet and Prayer Time)

Say: "It is now time to pray. In our story, Jesus went off alone to pray, so I want us to pray alone today. I would like each of you to go someplace in the room all by yourself for just a few minutes." (*Let them find a space alone.*)

Continue: "We are alone like Jesus was. Now just sit quietly with God." (*Let them sit quietly for about two minutes.*)

Say, "Thank you for praying alone like Jesus did! Let's come back to our Sacred Circle." (*Let them come back to the circle.*)

Ask: "How did it feel to pray alone?"

Encourage the children to talk about the experience, and do not correct them. For some, it will be a good experience. Others might not like being alone. Listen to their thoughts and feelings.

Say: "Praying alone is one way to pray. During our forty-six days of Lent, we are going to learn many ways to pray. We already have two ways: The Lord's Prayer that Jesus gave us where we pray with his special words and now praying alone in silence."

(If using the extended Sacred Circle Time, stop here)

A Time of Blessing

Explain: "The symbol for the story today is a cross because it is a symbol for Jesus."

Ask: "Where would you like your blessing today?" (*Let them tell you.*)

As you look into each child's eyes, make the symbol.

Say: "Thank you for being here today and spending time experiencing God with me. You are a blessing!"

Closing Time

Slowly put each Trinity symbol away.

Say: "And now we are finished with our Sacred Circle Time. We put away our symbol for God, the Creator. We put away our symbol for God, the Son. And we put away our symbol for God, the Holy Spirit."

Then quietly and gently put the sacred cloth away.

Conclude: "And we are all done with our Sacred Circle time. You did a great job. Yay!" Clap and celebrate a job well done.

Extended Format

(*10 minutes*) Begin with free-play time. Greet the children warmly and let them get used to the space. Have something in the free-play space for them to play with. Rotate each week:

Week One: Paper and crayons, markers, or paint.

Week Two: Clay, wire, pipe cleaners and beads, and tools to work the clay.

Week Three: Things to build with: blocks, Legos®, cans, boxes, or flat stones.

Week Four: Things that make noise.

(*3 minutes*) Transition Time

Let the children know that it is almost Sacred Circle Time.

Say: "It is almost our Sacred Circle Time. I cannot wait to have sacred time with you today. Will you start to finish up? Then come join me for our special, holy time together."

Sit down in the Sacred Circle Time space and place your sacred basket in front of you.

(*10 minutes*) **Sacred Circle Time** (*Basic format*)—Use the Sacred Circle Basic Format, but do not include the blessing or closing.

(*10 minutes*) **Trinity Stations**

Explain the Trinity Stations procedure for new children and for those who might forget from time to time.

Walk with the children to the Trinity Stations and show them what they can do in the stations, but do not let them start until they have seen all three stations.

Tell the children that after the Trinity Stations, they will spend five minutes in quiet time thinking about the story and the activities they have completed. They will then return to the Sacred Circle Time space to draw pictures and talk about their activities.

Station One: God, the Creator (Wonder) Station

Walk with the children to this station and show them what they can do here. In addition to the suggested supplies (page 469), you might want to add some rocks of all kinds and a few magnifying glasses so the children can explore the beauty of different rocks.

Station Two: God, the Son (Story) Station

Walk with the children to this station and show them what they can do here. In addition to the suggested supplies (page 469), you might want to include the stones from the Sacred Circle Time so the children can retell the story themselves.

Station Three: God, the Holy Spirit (Prayer) Station

Walk with the children to this station and show them what they can do here.

In addition to the suggested supplies (page 469), you might also want to have some boxes or a laundry basket available that children can sit in to create the illusion that they are praying alone.

Begin Quiet Time

Say: "Let's begin five minutes of thinking about the story of Jesus praying alone after a long day of work. After the time is over, I will invite you, one at a time, to come to the Sacred Circle Time space and draw what you did or thought about, so we can all share together."

(*2-minute transition time*) Start laying paper in the circle and laying out the crayons and other materials. Invite the children, one at a time, to come and draw what they did, thought about, or experienced.

(*10 minutes*) Journal and Share Time

Let them draw and journal as they gather. When most of the children have finished, let the children begin to share. Explain to the children that listening to one another is important.

Say: "Thank you for spending time with me in the Trinity Stations. I cannot wait to hear what you experienced today. Who would like to share?" (Give each child time to talk, and you should talk as well.)

Place their activities in individual folders; or if they are to take the folders home, place them behind them so they will not be distracted. This will keep you from having to correct the children's behavior.

10 minutes (snack or toy time)

A Time of Blessing

Explain, "The symbol for the story today is a cross because it is a symbol for Jesus."

Ask: "Where would you like your blessing today?" (*Let them tell you.*)

As you look into each child's eyes, make the symbol.

Say: "Thank you for being here today and spending time experiencing God with me. You are a blessing!"

Closing Time

Slowly put each Trinity symbol away.

Say: "And now we are finished with our Sacred Circle Time. We put away our symbol for God, the Creator. We put away our symbol for God, the Son. And we put away our symbol for God, the Holy Spirit."

Then quietly and gently put the sacred cloth away.

Conclude: "And we are all done with our Sacred Circle time. You did a great job. Yay!" Clap and celebrate a job well done.

The Third Sunday of Lent

Story: Jesus Tells Us to Pray

Text: Matthew 7:7-11, NRSV

"Ask, and it will be given you; search, and you will find; knock, and the door will be opened for you. For everyone who asks receives, and everyone who searches finds, and for everyone who knocks, the door will be opened. Is there anyone among you who, if your child asks for bread, will give a stone? Or if the child asks for a fish, will give a snake? If you then, who are evil, know how to give good gifts to your children, how much more will your Father in heaven give good things to those who ask him!

About the text: This explanation of prayer was given by Jesus during the "Sermon on the Mount," when he spoke directly to those who had chosen to follow him. Many consider this one of the most beautiful parts of Scripture because Jesus spoke so personally and intimately to the crowd. Plus, it helps clarify how we should live if we want to truly follow Jesus. The Scripture you will be using with the children is only a portion of the Sermon on The Mount, but it addresses an important point about prayer. Jesus tells us to pray without hesitation or stopping and to expect good things from God in return.

The Sacred Circle Time Focus: We will continue to emphasize Lent as an important holy time for prayer by teaching children this story and encouraging them to pray.

Sacred Circle Time Basic Format

Sacred Circle basket and contents:

- Sacred space cloth
- Symbols for Creator (globe), Christ (cross), and Holy Spirit (bell or chimes)
- Small, unbreakable bottle to hold water or oil for the blessing
- A journal page (one per child)
- Crayons and/or markers
- A Bible bookmarked to Matthew 7:7-11
- Focused objects from the Bible story: A piece of wood and three or four things to bang on it with, such as a stick, a metal or wooden spoon, and a brush of some kind

The Lesson

Gathering

Sit down and place the sacred basket in front of you.

Pause so that the children notice it and begin to come closer.

Invite them to form a circle.

Sit quietly until they settle in and are quiet.

Say: "It is time for Sacred Circle Time. I am so glad that you are here today. I love learning our stories and experiencing God with you."

Observing Lent as Forty-Six Holy Days

Say: "Lent is made up of forty-six holy days between Ash Wednesday and Easter. It is forty days and six Sundays. Let's count the days by clapping forty-six times."

Have the children stand. Let them count loudly while they clap. As the numbers get higher, lower your voice, and the children will follow. By the time you get to forty, be whispering; then sit down during 40 through 46. After you sit, be silent for a few seconds.

Say: "Lent is a holy time of forty-six days."

Creating the Sacred Space

Say: "Let's create our sacred space."

Slowly lay out the sacred cloth.

Slowly lift the globe (symbol of God, the Creator) and hold it at the eye level of the children. Say: "This is our symbol for God, the Creator." Carefully lay it on the sacred cloth. (*Pause.*)

Slowly lift the cross (symbol of God, the Son). Say: "This is our symbol for God, the Son." Carefully lay it on the sacred cloth. (*Pause.*)

Slowly lift the bell (symbol of God, the Holy Spirit). Say: "This is our symbol of God, the Holy Spirit." (*Pause.*)

Point to each symbol and say: "So we have God, the Creator; God, the Son; and God, the Holy Spirit. (*Pause.*) Our sacred space is ready. We are ready to begin our Sacred Circle Time together."

God, the Creator (A Time to Wonder)

Begin by laying the wood down in front of you on the floor. Use different objects to bang on it. Have the children listen and tell you which sound they like best.

God, the Son (Telling the Story)

Say: "Today I want to tell you a story found in (*open the Bible*) Matthew, chapter seven, verses 7-11. In our story, Jesus is sitting on a hill and lots of people are sitting around him, listening to him talk and learning from him. And he tells them lots of things about God. One of the things he tells the people is that prayer is like knocking on God's door and waiting for God to answer. So if this wood is God's door (*hold the wood up like a door*), when I pray, I am knocking on God's door." (*Using your fist, knock on the wood/door three times and wait.*)

Say: "And Jesus said that you can knock on the door as many times as you want because God loves to hear you pray! Let me show you."

"I can pray for so many things!"

Knock on the door; and at the same time, say: "God, I am sick and need to feel better. (*Knock again.*) God, I am afraid of the dark. Please help me. (*Knock again.*) God, my friend is being mean to me, and it hurts my feelings. (*Knock again.*) God, I love my mommy and daddy; thank you for giving them to me. (*Knock again.*) God, I love rainbows."

Say: "Jesus told us to knock on God's door as many times as we would like. God loves to hear us pray and never gets tired of it! You can knock on God's door by praying as often as you want."

God, the Holy Spirit (Quiet and Prayer Time)

Say: "It is now time to pray. I am going to pass this door to each of you. You can knock on it and share what you would like to pray for today."

Pass the door and let each child knock and share his or her prayer request with the group.

(If using the extended Sacred Circle Time, stop here.)

A Time of Blessing

Explain, "The symbol for the story today is a cross because it is a symbol for Jesus."

Ask: "Where would you like your blessing today?" (*Let them tell you.*)

As you look into each child's eyes, make the symbol.

Say: "Thank you for being here today and spending time experiencing God with me. You are a blessing!"

Closing Time

Slowly put each Trinity symbol away.

Say: "And now we are finished with our Sacred Circle Time. We put away our symbol for God, the Creator. We put away our symbol for God, the Son. And we put away our symbol for God, the Holy Spirit."

Then quietly and gently put the sacred cloth away.

Conclude: "And we are all done with our Sacred Circle time. You did a great job. Yay!" Clap and celebrate a job well done.

Extended Format

(*10 minutes*) Begin with free-play time. Greet the children warmly and let them get used to the space. Have something in the free-play space for them to play with. Rotate each week:

Week One: Paper and crayons, markers, or paint.

Week Two: Clay, wire, pipe cleaners and beads, and tools to work the clay.

Week Three: Things to build with: blocks, Legos®, cans, boxes, or flat stones.

Week Four: Things that make noise.

(*3 minutes*) Transition Time. Let the children know that it is almost Sacred Circle Time.

Say: "It is almost our Sacred Circle Time. I cannot wait to have sacred time with you today. Will you start to finish up? Then come join me for our special, holy time together."

Sit down in the Sacred Circle Time space and place your sacred basket in front of you.

(*10 minutes*) **Sacred Circle Time** (*Basic format*)—Use the Sacred Circle Basic Format, but do not include the blessing or closing.

(*10 minutes*) **Trinity Stations**

Explain the Trinity Stations procedure for new children and for those who might forget from time to time.

Walk with the children to the Trinity Stations and show them what they can do at the stations, but do not let them start until they have seen all three stations.

Tell the children that after the Trinity Stations, they will spend five minutes in quiet time thinking about the story and the activities they have completed. They will then return to the Sacred Circle Time space to draw pictures and talk about their activities.

Station One: God, the Creator (Wonder) Station

Walk with the children to this station and show them what they can do here. In addition to the suggested supplies (page 469), you might want to add some wood or things such as a tin can, a can with a plastic lid, a chime or a drum, and some different things for the children to hit them with to explore sounds.

Station Two: God, the Son (Story) Station

Walk with the children to this station and show them what they can do here. In addition to the suggested supplies (page 469), you might want to include a big box with a door cut in it so the children can play "knocking" and "answering."

Station Three: God, the Holy Spirit (Prayer) Station

Walk with the children to this station and show them what they can do here. In addition to the suggested supplies (page 469), you might want to add some quiet objects for the children to use to knock (pray) with, such as a very gentle chime, a small bell to ring, or water and cups.

Begin Quiet Time

Say: "Let's begin five minutes of thinking about the story of Jesus and the way he told us to pray as often and as much as we wanted. God never gets tired of our prayers.

After the five minutes is up, I will invite you, one at a time, to come to the Sacred Circle Time space to draw what you did or thought about so we can all share together."

(*2-minute transition time*) Place paper in the circle and lay out crayons and other materials. Invite the children, one at a time, to come and draw what they did, thought about, or experienced.

(*10 minutes*) Journal and Share Time

Let them draw and journal as they gather. When most of the children have finished, let them begin to share. Explain that listening to one another is important.

Say: "Thank you for spending time with me in the Trinity Stations. I cannot wait to find out what you experienced today. Who would like to share?" (Give each child a time to talk, and you should talk as well.)

Place their activities in individual folders; or if they are to take the folders home, place them behind them so the children will not be distracted. This will keep you from having to correct the children's behavior.

10 minutes (snack or toy time)

A Time of Blessing

Explain, "The symbol for the story today is a cross because it is a symbol for Jesus."

Ask: "Where would you like your blessing today?" (*Let them tell you.*)

As you look into each child's eyes, make the symbol.

Say: "Thank you for being here today and spending time experiencing God with me. You are a blessing!"

Closing Time

Slowly put each Trinity symbol away.

Say: "And now we are finished with our Sacred Circle Time. We put away our symbol for God, the Creator. We put away our symbol for God, the Son. And we put away our symbol for God, the Holy Spirit."

Then quietly and gently put the sacred cloth away.

Conclude: "And we are all done with our Sacred Circle time. You did a great job. Yay!" Clap and celebrate a job well done.

The Fourth Sunday of Lent

Story: Jesus Tells Us to Pray Together

Text: Matthew 18:19-20, NRSV

> Again, truly I tell you, if two of you agree on earth about anything you ask, it will be done for you by my Father in heaven. For where two or three are gathered in my name, I am there among them."

About the text: The context for this Scripture is not specifically about prayer, but about how to solve disputes. Jesus tells his followers that when they argue, they should gather; and in their gathering, they would find him present. Since the community of faith prays together so often, this passage has become associated with coming together whenever there is a need, not just during conflicts. The lesson for the children is that whenever we gather together, God will be there in the midst of us. When we have conflicts is a good time to pray together.

The Sacred Circle Time Focus: We will continue to emphasize Lent as an important holy time for prayer by teaching the children this story and encouraging them to pray together when they have arguments.

Sacred Circle Time Basic Format

Sacred Circle basket and contents:

- Sacred space cloth

174

- Symbols for Creator (globe), Christ (cross), and Holy Spirit (bell or chimes)
- Small, unbreakable bottle to hold water or oil for the blessing
- A journal page (one per child)
- Crayons and/or markers
- A Bible bookmarked to Matthew 18:19-20
- Focused objects from the Bible story: A heart cut out of paper. Leave one side blank and make a broken heart line on the other side.

The Lesson

Gathering

Begin by sitting down and placing the sacred basket in front of you. Pause so that the children notice it and begin to come closer.

Invite them to form a circle. Sit quietly until they settle in and are quiet.

Say: "It is time for Sacred Circle Time. I am so glad that you are here today. I love learning our stories and experiencing God with you."

Observing Lent as Forty-Six Holy Days

Say: "Lent is made up of forty-six holy days between Ash Wednesday and Easter. It is forty days and six Sundays. Let's count the days by clapping forty-six times."

Have the children stand. Let them count loudly while they clap. As the numbers get higher, lower your voice, and the children will follow. By the time you get to forty, be whispering; then sit down during 40 through 46. After you sit, be silent for a few seconds.

Say: "Lent is a holy time of forty-six days."

Creating the Sacred Space

Say: "First, we create our sacred space."

Slowly lay out the sacred cloth.

Slowly lift the globe (symbol of God, the Creator) and hold it at the eye level of the children. Say: "This is our symbol for God, the Creator." Carefully lay it on the sacred cloth. (*Pause.*)

Slowly lift the cross (symbol of God, the Son). Say: "This is our symbol for God, the Son." Carefully lay it on the sacred cloth. (*Pause.*)

Slowly lift the bell (symbol of God, the Holy Spirit). Say: "This is our symbol of God, the Holy Spirit." (*Pause.*)

Point to each symbol and say: "So we have God, the Creator; God, the Son; and God, the Holy Spirit. (*Pause.*) Our sacred space is ready. We are ready to begin our Sacred Circle Time together."

God, the Creator (A Time to Wonder)

Ask: "Do you like to play hide and seek? Would you like to play? I have hidden a heart somewhere in our room. I want you to try to find it."

Let them play this game two or three times, depending on how fast they find the heart the first time.

God, the Son (Telling the Story)

Say: "Today I want to tell you a story found in (*open the Bible*) Matthew, chapter eighteen, verses 19-20. In our story, Jesus is talking to the disciples. Did you know that even the friends of Jesus sometimes got mad at one another? They did. They got mad just like you sometimes get angry with one another, or maybe you get angry with your brother or sister or your mom or dad. Do you ever get angry?"

Invite the children to tell you about the things they get angry about. Do not correct them or judge what they say. Let them share freely.

Say: "And you know when we are angry, someone usually feels like this!"

Show them the broken side of the heart and ask, "Have you ever felt brokenhearted when someone was angry with you?" (*Let them share.*)

Say: "In our story today, Jesus tells us that when we are angry, one of the best things we can do is gather together and pray. And when we do that, God's love will be there."

Ask the children to stand up.

Say: "Let's pretend we are all angry with one another. Let me see your angriest faces!" (*Let them make angry faces. You should make one as well. Then place the broken heart in the center of the circle.*)

Say: "When we are angry, we hurt one another and make one another sad. Jesus told us that when we are angry, we should pray together, and look what happens . . ."

(*Turn the heart over.*)

Say: "When we pray together, God's love is with us; and we can forgive one another, be nice to one another, and no one will be hurt or upset. Jesus told his disciples that when they got angry with one another and broke one another's hearts and made one another sad, they should gather together and pray. And then God's love would be there to help them get along better."

God, the Holy Spirit (Quiet and Prayer Time)

Say: "It is now time to pray. For our prayer time, I want us to hold hands all together and just be together, praying silently. Let's see if any of us can feel God's love when we pray together." (*Pray silently for about 45 seconds.*)

Ask: "Did any of you feel God's love? What did it feel like?" Encourage the children to share.

(If using the extended Sacred Circle Time, stop here.)

A Time of Blessing

Explain: "The symbol for the story today is a cross because it is a symbol for Jesus."

Ask: "Where would you like your blessing today?" (*Let them tell you.*)

As you look into each child's eyes, make the symbol.

Say: "Thank you for being here today and spending time experiencing God with me. You are a blessing!"

Closing Time

Slowly put each Trinity symbol away.

Say: "And now we are finished with our Sacred Circle Time. We put away our symbol for God, the Creator. We put away our symbol for God, the Son. And we put away our symbol for God, the Holy Spirit."

Then quietly and gently put the sacred cloth away.

Conclude: "And we are all done with our Sacred Circle time. You did a great job. Yay!" Clap and celebrate a job well done.

Extended Format

(*10 minutes*) Begin with free-play time. Greet the children warmly and let them get used to the space. Have something in the free-play space for them to play with. Rotate each week:

Week One: Paper and crayons, markers, or paint.

Week Two: Clay, wire, pipe cleaners and beads, and tools to work the clay.

Week Three: Things to build with: blocks, Legos®, cans, boxes, or flat stones.

Week Four: Things that make noise.

(*3 minutes*) Transition Time. Let the children know that it is almost Sacred Circle Time. Say: "It is almost our Sacred Circle Time. I cannot wait to have sacred time with you today. Will you start to finish up? Then come join me for our special, holy time together."

Sit down in the Sacred Circle Time space and place your sacred basket in front of you.

(*10 minutes*) **Sacred Circle Time** (*Basic format*)—Use the Sacred Circle Basic Format, but do not include the blessing or closing.

(*10 minutes*) **Trinity Stations**

Explain the Trinity Stations procedure for new children and for those who might forget from time to time.

Walk with the children to the Trinity Stations and show them what they can do in the stations, but do not let them start until they have seen all three stations.

Tell the children that after the Trinity Stations, they will spend five minutes in quiet time thinking about the story and the activities they have completed. They will then return to the Sacred Circle Time space to draw pictures and talk about their activities.

Station One: God, the Creator (Wonder) Station

Walk with the children to this station and show them what they can do here.

In addition to the suggested supplies (page 469), you might want to add clay and heart-shaped cookie cutters of different sizes.

Station Two: God, the Son (Story) Station

Walk with the children to this station and show them what they can do here. In addition to the suggested supplies (page 469), you might want to include some dolls so the children can act out arguing and then praying together.

Station Three: God, the Holy Spirit (Prayer) Station

Walk with the children to this station and show them what they can do here. In addition to the suggested supplies (page 469), you might want to have paper and paint and encourage the children to create hearts of love.

Begin Quiet Time

Say: "Let's begin five minutes of thinking about how Jesus told us to pray together whenever we have an argument or are mad at someone. He promised us that when we pray together, God's love will be there. After five minutes, I will invite you, one at a time, to come to the Sacred Circle Time space and draw what you did or thought about so we can all share together."

(*2-minute transition time*) Start laying paper in the circle and laying out the crayons and other materials. Invite the children, one at a time, to come and draw what they did, thought about, or experienced.

(*10 minutes*) **Journal and Share Time**

Let them draw and journal as they gather and, as most of the children have finished, begin to share. Point out that listening to one another is important.

Say: "Thank you for spending time with me in the Trinity Stations. I cannot wait to find out what you experienced today. Who would like to share?" (Give each child time to talk, and you should talk as well.)

Place their activities in individual folders; or if they are to take the folders home, place them behind them so they will not be distracted. This will keep you from having to correct the children's behavior.

10 minutes (snack or toy time)

A Time of Blessing

Explain: "The symbol for the story today is a cross because it is a symbol for Jesus."

Ask: "Where would you like your blessing today?" (*Let them tell you.*)

As you look into each child's eyes, make the symbol.

Say: "Thank you for being here today and spending time experiencing God with me. You are a blessing!"

Closing Time

Slowly put each Trinity symbol away.

Say: "And now we are finished with our Sacred Circle Time. We put away our symbol for God, the Creator. We put away our symbol for God, the Son. And we put away our symbol for God, the Holy Spirit."

Then quietly and gently put the sacred cloth away.

Conclude: "And we are all done with our Sacred Circle time. You did a great job. Yay!" Clap and celebrate a job well done.

The Fifth Sunday of Lent

Story: Jesus Prayed for and Blessed the Children

Text: Matthew 19:13-14, NRSV

> Then little children were being brought to him in order that he might lay his hands on them and pray. The disciples spoke sternly to those who brought them; but Jesus said, "Let the little children come to me, and do not stop them; for it is to such as these that the kingdom of heaven belongs."

About the text: This story is so important to teach to children! Because so much of what happens at church, and especially in worship, is aimed at adults, children might get the impression that their journey with Jesus will begin when they grow up. This could not be further from the truth, as this text so beautifully illustrates. Jesus loves children, and he proved it to the adults, who thought his love and care was for adults only, by taking the time to lay his hands on each child as a prayer and a blessing.

The Sacred Circle Time Focus: We will continue to emphasize Lent as an important holy time for prayer by teaching the children this story and reminding them that Jesus prayed for children and still loves children today!

Sacred Circle Time Basic Format

Sacred Circle basket and contents:

- Sacred space cloth
- Symbols for Creator (globe), Christ (cross), and Holy Spirit (bell or chimes)
- Small, unbreakable bottle to hold water or oil for the blessing
- A journal page (one per child)
- Crayons and/or markers
- A Bible bookmarked to Matthew 19:13-14
- Focused objects from the Bible story: One paper heart for each child. Place the hearts in a clear container.

The Lesson

Gathering

Begin by sitting down and placing the sacred basket in front of you. Pause so that the children notice it and begin to come closer.

Invite them to form a circle. Sit quietly until they settle in and are quiet.

Say: "It is time for Sacred Circle Time. I am so glad that you are here today. I love learning our stories and experiencing God with you."

Observing Lent as Forty-Six Holy Days

Say: "Lent is made up of forty-six holy days between Ash Wednesday and Easter. It is forty days and six Sundays. Let's count the days by clapping forty-six times."

Have the children stand and begin counting loudly while they clap. As the numbers get higher, lower your voice, and the children will follow. By the time you get to forty, be whispering; and then sit down during 40 through 46. After you sit, be silent for a few seconds.

Say: "Lent is a holy time of forty-six days."

Creating the Sacred Space

Say: "First, we create our sacred space."

Slowly lay out the sacred cloth.

Slowly lift the globe (symbol of God, the Creator) and hold it at the eye level of the children. Say: "This is our symbol for God, the Creator." Carefully lay it on the sacred cloth. (*Pause.*)

Slowly lift the cross (symbol of God, the Son). Say: "This is our symbol for God, the Son." Carefully lay it on the sacred cloth. (*Pause.*)

Slowly lift the bell (symbol of God, the Holy Spirit). Say: "This is our symbol of God, the Holy Spirit." (*Pause.*)

Point to each symbol and say: "So we have God, the Creator; God, the Son; and God, the Holy Spirit. (*Pause.*) Our sacred space is ready. We are ready to begin our Sacred Circle Time together."

God, the Creator (A Time to Wonder)

Place the container of hearts in front of you. Ask the children, "How many hearts do you think I have in my container?"

Let them guess. After each child guesses, say, "Good guess!" Do not tell them if they are right or wrong. They are exploring and wondering. It does not matter if they are right or wrong. This is playtime.

Say: "Let's count the hearts and see how many there are." (*Count them.*)

Say: "Hummmm . . . How many people are in our Sacred Circle?" (*Count them.*)

Say: "Wow! We have enough hearts for everyone to have one." (*Do not pass the hearts out yet.*)

God, the Son (Telling the Story)

Say: "Today I want to tell you a story found in (*open the Bible*) Matthew, chapter nineteen, verses 13-14. In our story, some mommies and daddies brought their children to

184

see Jesus. They knew that Jesus loved them very much. So they wanted Jesus to give each child a little bit of his love." (*Start laying out the hearts. The kids will get excited knowing that each of them will get one.*)

"Jesus had enough love for all the children who came! But something happened. Some of his friends, the disciples, said to those parents, 'Go away. Jesus does not want your kids here.'" (*Pick up all the hearts.*)

Say: "They thought Jesus loved only the grown-ups." (*Pause and let this thought sink in. The children will not be happy!*)

Say: "But Jesus said to those people, 'No! I want these children here! I love them. They are wonderful!' And then Jesus touched each child, one at a time, and prayed for the children and blessed them." (*Slowly give a heart to each child.*)

Say: "Jesus loved each child who was brought to visit him, and he loves you."

God, the Holy Spirit (Quiet and Prayer Time)

Say: "It is now time to pray. For our prayer time, I am going to pray for each of you like Jesus did. The Bible tells us that Jesus laid his hands on each child as a prayer. I will lay my hands on top of your head or on your shoulders. You can tell me which one you want."

Ask the children whether they prefer that you lay hands on their head or shoulders. Then, lay your hands on them with great care and love.

(If using the extended Sacred Circle Time, stop here.)

A Time of Blessing

Explain: "The symbol for the story today is a cross because it is a symbol for Jesus."

Ask: "Where would you like your blessing today?" (*Let them tell you.*)

Make the symbol as you look into each child's eyes.

Say: "Thank you for being here today and spending time experiencing God with me. You are a blessing!"

Closing Time

Slowly put each Trinity symbol away.

Say: "And now we are finished with our Sacred Circle Time. We put away our symbol for God, the Creator. We put away our symbol for God, the Son. And we put away our symbol for God, the Holy Spirit."

Then quietly and gently put the sacred cloth away.

Conclude: "And we are all done with our Sacred Circle time. You did a great job. Yay!" Clap and celebrate a job well done.

Extended Format

(*10 minutes*) Begin with free-play time. Greet the children warmly and let them get used to the space. Have something in the free-play space for them to play with. Rotate each week:

Week One: Paper and crayons, markers, or paint.

Week Two: Clay, wire, pipe cleaners and beads, and tools to work the clay.

Week Three: Things to build with: blocks, Legos®, cans, boxes, or flat stones.

Week Four: Things that make noise.

(*3 minutes*) Transition Time. Let the children know that it is almost Sacred Circle Time. Say: "It is almost our Sacred Circle Time. I cannot wait to have sacred time with you today. Will you start to finish up? Then come join me for our special, holy time together."

Sit down in the Sacred Circle Time space and place your sacred basket in front of you.

(*10 minutes*) **Sacred Circle Time** (*Basic format*)—Use the Sacred Circle Basic Format, but do not include the blessing or closing.

(*10 minutes*) **Trinity Stations**

Explain the Trinity Stations procedure for new children and for those who might forget from time to time.

Walk with the children to the Trinity Stations and show them what they can do in the stations, but do not let them start until they have seen all three stations.

Tell the children that after the Trinity Stations, they will spend five minutes in quiet time thinking about the story and the activities they have completed. They will then return to the Sacred Circle Time space to draw pictures and talk about their activities.

Station One: God, the Creator (Wonder) Station

Walk with the children to this station and show them what they can do here. In addition to the suggested supplies (page 469), you might want to add pictures of children from around the world and children from different ethnic origins.

Station Two: God, the Son (Story) Station

Walk with the children to this station and show them what they can do here. In addition to the suggested supplies (page 469), you might want to have some dollhouse characters or babies to enable the children to act out the Bible story.

Station Three: God, the Holy Spirit (Prayer) Station

Walk with the children to this station and show them what they can do here. In addition to the suggested supplies (page 469), you might want to include blessing balm for the children to bless themselves or one another as Jesus blessed the children.

Begin Quiet Time

Instruct the children to begin five minutes of quiet time to think about the Bible story. Explain that after the time has elapsed, you will invite them, one at a time, to the Sacred Circle Time space to draw what they did or thought about.

(*2-minute transition time*) Place paper, crayons, and other material in the circle. Invite the children, one at a time, to come and draw what they did, thought about, or experienced.

(*10 minutes*) **Journal and Share Time**

Let them draw and journal as they gather. When most of the children have finished, let them begin to share. Tell them that listening to one another is important.

Say: "Thank you for spending time with me in the Trinity Stations. I cannot wait to find out what you experienced today. Who would like to share?" (Give each child a time to talk, and you should talk as well.)

Place their activities in individual folders; or if they are to take the folders home, place them behind them so they will not be distracted. This will keep you from having to correct the children's behavior.

10 minutes (snack or toy time)

A Time of Blessing

Explain: "The symbol for the story today is a cross because it is a symbol for Jesus."

Ask: "Where would you like your blessing today?" (*Let them tell you.*)

Make the symbol as you look into each child's eyes.

Say: "Thank you for being here today and spending time experiencing God with me. You are a blessing!"

Closing Time

Slowly put each Trinity symbol away.

Say: "And now we are finished with our Sacred Circle Time. We put away our symbol for God, the Creator. We put away our symbol for God, the Son. And we put away our symbol for God, the Holy Spirit."

Then quietly and gently put the sacred cloth away.

Conclude: "And we are all done with our Sacred Circle time. You did a great job. Yay!" Clap and celebrate a job well done.

The Sixth Sunday of Lent

Story: Palm Sunday and Jesus Prays When He is Sad

Text: Luke 22:39-46, NRSV

He came out and went, as was his custom, to the Mount of Olives; and the disciples followed him. When he reached the place, he said to them, "Pray that you may not come into the time of trial." Then he withdrew from them about a stone's throw, knelt down, and prayed, "Father, if you are willing, remove this cup from me; yet, not my will but yours be done." Then an angel from heaven appeared to him and gave him strength. In his anguish he prayed more earnestly, and his sweat became like great drops of blood falling down on the ground. When he got up from prayer, he came to the disciples and found them sleeping because of grief, and he said to them, "Why are you sleeping? Get up and pray that you may not come into the time of trial."

About the text: The last week of Lent is called Holy Week, because it is the last week of Jesus' life. It begins with Jesus' entry into Jerusalem on what came to be called "Palm Sunday," and ends with his death. The story moves from great joy to great sorrow. Young children do not have to hear all the details of this story to understand that Jesus was sad and scared. They cannot understand what "dying on the cross for our redemption" means, but they can understand his emotions.

The Sacred Circle Time Focus: We will continue to emphasize Lent as an important holy time for prayer and remind the children that we can pray to God any time. We do not need to feel embarrassed if we are sad or upset. God understands and cares.

Sacred Circle Time Basic Format

Sacred Circle basket and contents:

- Sacred space cloth
- Symbols for Creator (globe), Christ (cross), and Holy Spirit (bell or chimes)
- Small, unbreakable bottle to hold water or oil for the blessing
- A journal page (one per child)
- Crayons and/or markers
- A Bible bookmarked to Luke 22:39-46
- Focused objects from the Bible story: A palm or tree branch with leaves and branches that point up

The Lesson

Gathering

Begin by sitting down and placing the sacred basket in front of you. Pause so that the children notice it and begin to come closer.

Invite them to form a circle. Sit quietly until they settle in and are quiet.

Say: "It is time for Sacred Circle Time. I am so glad that you are here today. I love learning our stories and experiencing God with you."

Observing Lent as Forty-Six Holy Days

Say: "Lent is made up of forty-six holy days between Ash Wednesday and Easter. It is forty days and six Sundays. Let's count the days by clapping forty-six times."

Have the children stand and let them count loudly while they clap. As the numbers get higher, lower your voice, and the children will follow. By the time you get to forty, be whispering; then sit down during 40 through 46. After you sit, be silent for a few seconds.

Say: "Lent is a holy time of forty-six days. This is our last time to celebrate Lent because our 46 days are almost over. It has been a long time, and Easter is almost here."

Creating the Sacred Space

Say: "Let's create our sacred space."

Slowly lay out the sacred cloth.

Slowly lift the globe (symbol of God, the Creator) and hold it at the eye level of the children. Say: "This is our symbol for God, the Creator." Carefully lay it on the sacred cloth. (Pause.)

Slowly lift the cross (symbol of God, the Son). Say: "This is our symbol for God, the Son." Carefully lay it on the sacred cloth. (Pause.)

Slowly lift the bell (symbol of God, the Holy Spirit). Say: "This is our symbol of God, the Holy Spirit." (Pause.)

Point to each symbol and say: "So we have God, the Creator; God, the Son; and God, the Holy Spirit. (Pause.) Our sacred space is ready. We are ready to begin our Sacred Circle Time together."

God, the Creator (A Time to Wonder)

Show the children the palm branch or other tree branch. Shake it hard, so they can hear and see it. Shake it slowly, and let them see how it sounds and looks. Pass it around, and let them shake it either fast or slowly.

God, the Son (Telling the Story)

Say: "Today I want to tell you a story found in (*open the Bible*) Luke, chapter 22, verses 39-46. Our story for today begins with a very happy story. Jesus and his disciples are going to Jerusalem, and the people are so excited they start to break palms and branches off trees and shake them for joy! Do you think they shook the branches fast or slowly?" (*The children will say fast.*)

Ask: "This fast?" (*Shake the branch slowly, and let the children say, "Faster."*)

Ask: "This hard?" (*Shake the branch a bit harder, and let the children say, "Harder."*)

Ask: "This hard and fast?" (*Shake the branch as hard and fast as you can and while you are still shaking it.*)

Say: "Jesus rode into Jerusalem and people shook branches and waved and yelled, and it was a fun day! The people loved Jesus so much!" (*Stop shaking the branch and sit very still.*)

Say: "That day was called Palm Sunday. It was a happy day. That is the happy part of our story for today. The other part is a sad part." (*Lay the branch down and look sad.*)

Say: "Jesus never did anything wrong, but those people decided to be mean to him. Those same people who were so excited and waved their palms began to be mean to Jesus. And that made him very sad! In fact, they got so mad at Jesus (*pause*), they wanted him to be killed. And that made Jesus very, very sad. So he went to a garden to pray, and he prayed a very sad prayer."

Say: "Those mean people made Jesus sad. What makes you sad?"

Encourage the children to talk.

Say: "When Jesus was sad, he prayed to God and told God all about it."

God, the Holy Spirit (Quiet and Prayer Time)

Say: "It is now time to pray. I am going to pass our branch around two times. The first time, I want you to share something that makes you sad. The second time, share something that makes you happy; and you can shake the branch then."

Pass the branch around and have the children share something that makes them sad. Just listen and do not comment. You may nod your head in empathy, but try not to say anything.

Say: "Thank you for sharing your sadness in our prayer time. Jesus prayed when he was sad too. Now I am going to pass the branch around again. This time, I want you to share something that makes you happy and then shake the branch!"

(*Pass the branch around again.*)

Say: "Thank you for sharing what makes you sad and what makes you happy. You can always pray to God . . . when you are happy and when you are sad. God always listens to our prayers!"

(If using the extended Sacred Circle Time, stop here.)

A Time of Blessing

Explain: "The symbol for the story today is a cross because it is a symbol for Jesus."

Ask: "Where would you like your blessing today?" (*Let them tell you.*)

Make the symbol as you look into each child's eyes.

Say: "Thank you for being here today and spending time experiencing God with me. You are a blessing!"

Closing Time

Slowly put each Trinity symbol away.

Say: "And now we are finished with our Sacred Circle Time. We put away our symbol for God, the Creator. We put away our symbol for God, the Son. And we put away our symbol for God, the Holy Spirit."

Then quietly and gently put the sacred cloth away.

Conclude: "And we are all done with our Sacred Circle time. You did a great job. Yay!" Clap and celebrate a job well done.

Extended Format

(*10 minutes*) Begin with free-play time. Greet the children warmly and let them get used to the space. Have something in the free-play space for them to play with. Rotate each week:

Week One: Paper and crayons, markers, or paint.
Week Two: Clay, wire, pipe cleaners and beads, and tools to work the clay.
Week Three: Things to build with: blocks, Legos®, cans, boxes, or flat stones.
Week Four: Things that make noise.

(*3 minutes*) Transition Time. Let the children know that it is almost Sacred Circle Time. Say: "It is almost our Sacred Circle Time. I cannot wait to have sacred time with you today. Will you start to finish up? Then come join me for our special, holy time together."

Sit down in the Sacred Circle Time space and place your sacred basket in front of you.

(*10 minutes*) **Sacred Circle Time** (*Basic format*)—Use the Sacred Circle Basic Format, but do not include the blessing or closing.

(*10 minutes*) **Trinity Stations**

Explain the Trinity Stations procedure for new children and for those who might forget from time to time.

Walk with the children to the Trinity Stations and show them what they can do in the stations, but do not let them start until they have seen all three stations.

Tell the children that after the Trinity Stations, they will spend five minutes in quiet time thinking about the story and the activities they have completed. They will then return to the Sacred Circle Time space to draw pictures and talk about their activities.

Station One: God, the Creator (Wonder) Station

Walk with the children to this station and show them what they can do here. In addition to the suggested supplies (page 469), you might want to add different species of tree branches for the children to compare.

Station Two: God, the Son (Story) Station

Walk with the children to this station and show them what they can do here. In addition to the suggested supplies (page 469), you might want to include some palm branches to enable the children to act out the Bible story.

Station Three: God, the Holy Spirit (Prayer) Station

Walk with the children to this station and show them what they can do here. In addition to the suggested supplies (page 469), you might want to have a water bowl with cups and let the children play in it and think about sad prayers they might have. Also include a bowl with small balls or marbles or pretty stones to let them play in and think about happy prayers.

Begin Quiet Time

"Say: Let's begin five minutes of thinking about the story of Palm Sunday when Jesus entered Jerusalem and the people were so happy. And then think about how those people were mean to him, and he was sad and prayed to God about it. After five minutes, I will invite you, one at a time, to come to the Sacred Circle Time space and draw what you did or thought about, so we can all share together."

(2-minute transition time) Place paper, crayons, and other material in the circle. Invite the children, one at a time, to come and draw what they did, thought about, or experienced.

(*10 minutes*) **Journal and Share Time**

Let them draw and journal as they gather. When most of the children have finished, let them begin to share. Tell them that listening to one another is important.

Say: "Thank you for spending time with me in the Trinity Stations. I cannot wait to find out what you experienced today. Who would like to share?" (Give each child time to talk, and you should talk as well.)

Place their activities in individual folders; or if they are to take the folders home, place them behind them so they will not be distracted. This will keep you from having to correct the children's behavior.

10 minutes (snack or toy time)

A Time of Blessing

Explain: "The symbol for the story today is a cross because it is a symbol for Jesus."

Ask the children where they would like their blessing, and then make the symbol as you look into each child's eyes.

Say: "Thank you for being here today and spending time experiencing God with me. You are a blessing!"

Closing Time

Slowly put each Trinity symbol away.

Say: "And now we are finished with our Sacred Circle Time. We put away our symbol for God, the Creator. We put away our symbol for God, the Son. And we put away our symbol for God, the Holy Spirit."

Then quietly and gently put the sacred cloth away.

Conclude: "And we are all done with our Sacred Circle time. You did a great job. Yay!" Clap and celebrate a job well done.

About Easter and the
Fifty Days of Easter

While children, and most of society, like Christmas best, Easter is the most important day of the liturgical calendar. Why? Because the resurrection of Christ is the most important miracle God did for us. Jesus had promised that the light of God would never go out, that he would always be with us, that evil would never conquer good. Then he was killed on the cross. With his death, all hope was lost. All of the promises meant nothing until . . . he was resurrected by God on Easter!

The resurrection of Christ proved that he was the Son of God and that everything he had said was true. And because of the Resurrection, the church lives on, and we are promised life eternal. Easter proves that God is all-powerful, all-loving, and all-forgiving. It proves that we will be loved and cared for in this life and will live forever with God, Christ, and the Holy Spirit after we die.

Easter is so important that the early church decided it should be celebrated for fifty days!

After Easter Sunday, we celebrate Easter for fifty days. And at the end of the fifty days, we celebrate the day of Pentecost, where another promise of Jesus came true.

Jesus had promised to send the Holy Spirit to be with us always. On the day of Pentecost, the Holy Spirit descended, and the "church" officially began.

Easter should be a festive time for young children. It helps us that it lasts for fifty days because Easter Sunday can sometimes get overshadowed by Easter baskets and candy. Having fifty days to celebrate will help children learn that Easter is very special, even if they are too young to understand or grasp the theological significance.

Because the Resurrection and assumption of Jesus are difficult concepts for young children to grasp, these lessons will simply mention them so that the children begin to become familiar with them as important events. However, the fifty days of Easter will concentrate mainly on the love of Jesus. After all, the core of the Easter message is love! While young children cannot yet understand Resurrection and assumption, they can and do understand love.

(*Note: We will intentionally use a heart as the blessing symbol throughout the fifty days of Easter to associate Easter with great love!*)

The fifty days of Easter end with Pentecost Sunday. Pentecost Sunday is often referred to as the "birthday of the church" because it is the day when the Holy Spirit arrived and empowered the disciples to boldly proclaim the good news. Jesus had promised that after he died, the Holy Spirit would come and be God's presence. Jesus promised that he would not abandon them. So, while Pentecost is the birthday of the Christian church, it is also the completion of Easter. Jesus promised to send the spirit, and Jesus kept his promise.

Easter Sunday

Story: The Joy of the Resurrection

Text: Luke 24:1-12, NRSV

But on the first day of the week, at early dawn, they came to the tomb, taking the spices that they had prepared. They found the stone rolled away from the tomb, but when they went in, they did not find the body. While they were perplexed about this, suddenly two men in dazzling clothes stood beside them. The women were terrified and bowed their faces to the ground, but the men said to them, "Why do you look for the living among the dead? He is not here, but has risen. Remember how he told you, while he was still in Galilee, that the Son of Man must be handed over to sinners, and be crucified, and on the third day rise again." Then they remembered his words, and returning from the tomb, they told all this to the eleven and to all the rest. Now it was Mary Magdalene, Joanna, Mary the mother of James, and the other women with them who told this to the apostles. But these words seemed to them an idle tale, and they did not believe them. But Peter got up and ran to the tomb; stooping and looking in, he saw the linen cloths by themselves; then he went home, amazed at what had happened.

About the text: The story of the Resurrection is difficult even for adults to grasp. Young children cannot understand the notion of death, let alone that someone came back to life after death. The Resurrection is the miracle of miracles!! And as such, the day is a celebration of ALL that God is, does, and always will do. Let today be a day of joy, happiness, and celebration. For young children, that is enough.

The Sacred Circle Time Focus: We will focus on the happiness of Easter!

Sacred Circle Time Basic Format

Sacred Circle basket and contents:

- Sacred space cloth
- Symbols for Creator (globe), Christ (cross), and Holy Spirit (bell or chimes)
- Small, unbreakable bottle to hold water or oil for the blessing
- A journal page (one per child)
- Crayons and/or markers
- A Bible bookmarked at Luke 24:1-12
- Focused Objects from the Bible Story: Three regular eggs, a glass bowl to break the eggs into, a blown-out Easter egg with a pin hole in the top and bottom (Although the egg is empty, the shell should still be intact.)

The Lesson

Gathering

Sit down and place the sacred basket in front of you.

Pause so that the children notice it and begin to come closer.

Invite them to form a circle.

Sit quietly until they settle in and are quiet.

Say: "It is time for Sacred Circle Time. I am so glad that you are here today. I love learning our stories and experiencing God with you."

Creating the Sacred Space

Say: "First, we create our sacred space." Slowly lay out the sacred cloth.

Slowly lift the globe (symbol of God, the Creator) and hold it at the eye level of the children. Say: "This is our symbol for God, the Creator." Carefully lay it on the sacred cloth. (*Pause.*)

Slowly lift the cross (symbol of God, the Son). Say: "This is our symbol for God, the Son." Carefully lay it on the sacred cloth. (*Pause.*)

Slowly lift the bell (symbol of God, the Holy Spirit). Say: "This is our symbol of God, the Holy Spirit." (*Pause.*)

Point to each symbol and say: "So we have God, the Creator; God, the Son; and God, the Holy Spirit. (*Pause.*) Our sacred space is ready. We are ready to begin our Sacred Circle Time together."

God, the Creator (A Time to Wonder)

Ask: "Have you ever seen someone break eggs? What is inside an egg?" Encourage the children to respond.

Say: "Well, I have four eggs with me today to use later in my baking. I am going to crack them for you."

Crack the eggs one at a time. Young children will find this terribly entertaining!

Say: "Now I have one last egg. Ready for me to crack it?"

Let the children respond. They will be very excited!

Say: "Oh, no . . . what happened?" Let them see that the egg is empty.

Say: "This empty egg will help me tell my story."

God, the Son (Telling the Story)

Say: "Today I want to tell you the Easter story! It is found in (*open the Bible*) Luke, chapter 24, verses 1-12. Jesus was such a good person. He loved everyone, but not everyone loved him. In fact, some people hated Jesus so much that they killed him. And when he died, they put him in a tomb and put a big rock in front of it! The rock was so big! It was bigger than the ceiling of our room! Do you think that rock was heavy?"

Let the children respond.

Say: "You are so smart! It was heavy. Soooooo heavy! And on Easter morning, some of the women missed Jesus and were very sad because he had died. They wanted to put some good smelling perfume on his body and see his body one more time. They knew that his body had been laid in a cave and that a big rock had been placed in front of the cave. So they wanted to see Jesus' body, but they did not know how they would move the big heavy rock. And when they got to the tomb, guess what?"

Let the children guess.

Say (*with total amazement*): "The rock had been moved; two angels were sitting in the tomb; and Jesus was gone! He had risen! Happy Easter! Easter is the day when we are so happy because Jesus, who had been killed, rose from the tomb and now lives with God forever in heaven! HAPPY EASTER!!!"

Let them clap and say "Happy Easter!"

God, the Holy Spirit (Quiet and Prayer Time)

Say: "It is now time to pray. Usually our prayer time is quiet, but on Easter, this happy day, we just can't be quiet, even when we pray! So we are going to show God how happy we are, and that will be our Easter prayer for today. Let's show God how happy we are for Easter by clapping our hands!"

Let them clap!

Say: "Let's show God how happy we are by stomping our feet!"

Let them stomp their feet!

Say: "Let's show God how happy we are by clapping our hands and stomping our feet at the same time!"

Let them clap and stomp!

Say: "Let's show God how happy we are by holding our bodies very still."

Let them quiet down and be still.

Say: "Thank you, God, for this happy Easter day! Let's show God how happy we are by smiling!"

They will all smile!

(If using the extended Sacred Circle Time, stop here.)

A Time of Blessing

Explain, "The symbol for the story today is a smile because today is our happy Easter celebration!"

Ask the children where they would like their blessing; then make the symbol as you look into each child's eyes.

Say: "Thank you for being here today and spending time experiencing God with me. You are a blessing!"

Closing Time

Slowly put each Trinity symbol away.

Say: "And now we are finished with our Sacred Circle Time. We put away our symbol for God, the Creator. We put away our symbol for God, the Son. And we put away our symbol for God, the Holy Spirit."

Then quietly and gently put the sacred cloth away.

Conclude: "And we are all done with our Sacred Circle time. You did a great job. Yay!" Clap and celebrate a job well done.

Extended Format

(10 minutes) Begin with free-play time. Greet the children warmly and let them get used to the space. Have something in the free-play space for them to play with. Rotate each week:

Week One: Paper and crayons, markers, or paint.

Week Two: Clay, wire, pipe cleaners and beads, and tools to work the clay.

Week Three: Things to build with: blocks, Legos®, cans, boxes, or flat stones.

Week Four: Things that make noise.

(*3 minutes*) Transition Time. Let the children know that it is almost Sacred Circle Time. Say: "It is almost our Sacred Circle Time. I cannot wait to have sacred time with you today. Will you start to finish up? Then come join me for our special, holy time together."

Sit down in the Sacred Circle Time space and place your sacred basket in front of you.

(*10 minutes*) **Sacred Circle Time** (*Basic format*)—Use the Sacred Circle Basic Format, but do not include the blessing or closing.

(*10 minutes*) **Trinity Stations**

Explain the Trinity Stations procedure for new children and for those who might forget from time to time.

Walk with the children to the Trinity Stations and show them what they can do in the stations, but do not let them start until they have seen all three stations.

Tell the children that after the Trinity Stations, they will spend five minutes in quiet time thinking about the story and the activities they have completed. They will then return to the Sacred Circle Time space to draw pictures and talk about their activities.

Station One: God, the Creator (Wonder) Station

Walk with the children to this station and show them what they can do here. In addition to the suggested supplies (page 469), you might want to add noisemakers of all kinds for the children to shake, rattle, and drum to express happiness. Or, if you want a *fun mess*, let them try to break eggs.

Station Two: God, the Son (Story) Station

Walk with the children to this station and show them what they can do here.

In addition to the suggested supplies (page 469), you might want to have some clay and stones so the children can create the empty tomb and the angels.

Station Three: God, the Holy Spirit (Prayer) Station

Walk with the children to this station and show them what they can do here. In addition to the suggested supplies (page 469), you might want to have some glitter and glue so the children can create a special Easter prayer picture.

Begin Quiet Time

Say: "Let's begin five minutes of thinking about the happy story of Easter and about how the women went to the tomb and found that Jesus has been resurrected and was not there! After five minutes, I will invite you, one at a time, to come to the Sacred Circle Time space and draw what you did or thought about, so we can all share together."

(*2-minute transition time*) Lay paper in the circle and lay out the crayons and other materials. Invite the children, one at a time, to come and draw what they did, thought about, or experienced.

(*10 minutes*) Journal and Share Time

Let them draw and journal as they gather. When most of the children have finished, ask the children to begin to share. Remind the children that listening to one another is important.

Say: "Thank you for spending time with me in the Trinity Stations. I cannot wait to discover what you experienced today. Who would like to share?" (Give each child time to talk, and you should talk as well.)

Place their activities in individual folders; or if they are to take the folders home, place them behind them so they will not be distracted. This will keep you from having to correct the children's behavior.

10 minutes (snack or toy time)

A Time of Blessing

Explain: "The symbol for the story today is a smile, because today is our happy Easter celebration!"

Ask: "Where would you like your blessing today?" (*Let them tell you.*)

Make the symbol as you look into each child's eyes.

Say: "Thank you for being here today and spending time experiencing God with me. You are a blessing!"

Slowly put each Trinity symbol away.

Say: "And now we are finished with our Sacred Circle Time. We put away our symbol for God, the Creator. We put away our symbol for God, the Son. And we put away our symbol for God, the Holy Spirit."

Then quietly and gently put the sacred cloth away.

Conclude: "And we are all done with our Sacred Circle time. You did a great job. Yay!" Clap and celebrate a job well done.

Say: "HAPPY EASTER!!!"

Fifty Days of Easter 1

Story: Jesus Loved His Friends

Text: Luke 10:38-42, NRSV

> Now as they went on their way, he entered a certain village, where a woman named Martha welcomed him into her home. She had a sister named Mary, who sat at the Lord's feet and listened to what he was saying. But Martha was distracted by her many tasks; so she came to him and asked, "Lord, do you not care that my sister has left me to do all the work by myself? Tell her then to help me." But the Lord answered her, "Martha, Martha, you are worried and distracted by many things; there is need of only one thing. Mary has chosen the better part, which will not be taken away from her."

About the text: It is interesting to me that, while the twelve disciples were chosen by Jesus to be his followers, they were not his closest friends. His closest friends seem to be Mary, Martha, and Lazarus. It was at their home he often retreated when he wanted to get away, have a good dinner, and relax. Friends were important to Jesus, just as our friends are important to us. The gospels tell us much about Jesus' public ministry, but we have very few glimpses of Jesus' personal life. The stories that take place at the home of Mary, Martha, and Lazarus are rare and important. Friends are a gift . . . even Jesus had them!

The Sacred Circle Time Focus: We will focus on telling this story about the way Jesus loved his friends and also on the gift of friendship.

Sacred Circle Time Basic Format

Sacred Circle basket and contents:

- Sacred space cloth
- Symbols for Creator (globe), Christ (cross), and Holy Spirit (bell or chimes)
- Small, unbreakable bottle to hold water or oil for the blessing
- A journal page (one per child)
- Crayons and/or markers
- A Bible bookmarked to Luke 10:38-42
- Focused objects from the Bible story: Three different pictures, including one of a relative, one of someone you have worked or volunteered with, and one of a friend. (These may be photographs or drawings.)

The Lesson

Gathering

Begin by sitting down and placing the sacred basket in front of you. Pause so that the children notice it and begin to come closer.

Invite them to form a circle. Sit quietly until they settle in and are quiet.

Say: "It is time for Sacred Circle Time. I am so glad that you are here today. I love learning our stories and experiencing God with you."

Celebrating the Fifty Days of Easter

Say: "Before we create our Sacred Circle, I want to tell you that Easter is such an important holiday that we celebrate it at our church for fifty days! We are happy because

Jesus was resurrected for fifty days! So let's count and clap with happy hands fifty times to celebrate Easter!"

Clap and count to fifty.

Say: "Easter lasts for fifty days! Let's all say 'Happy Easter!' 1-2-3 . . ."

Everyone shouts "Happy Easter!"

Say: "And during our fifty days of Easter, we are going to learn all about love!"

Creating the Sacred Space

Say: "Let's create our sacred space."

Slowly lay out the sacred cloth.

Slowly lift the globe (symbol of God, the Creator) and hold it at the eye level of the children. Say: "This is our symbol for God, the Creator." Carefully lay it on the sacred cloth. (Pause.)

Slowly lift the cross (symbol of God, the Son). Say: "This is our symbol for God, the Son." Carefully lay it on the sacred cloth. (Pause.)

Slowly lift the bell (symbol of God, the Holy Spirit). Say: "This is our symbol of God, the Holy Spirit." Carefully lay it on the sacred cloth. (Pause.)

Point to each symbol and say: "So we have God, the Creator; God, the Son; and God, the Holy Spirit. (Pause.) Our sacred space is ready. We are ready to begin our Sacred Circle Time together."

God, the Creator (A Time to Wonder)

Show the children the photographs or drawings, but do not tell them who the people in the pictures are.

Say: "I have brought these pictures today, and all of these people are important to me. Who do you think they are?"

Let them guess who they think the people in the pictures are. They may make such guesses as, "Your mommy or daddy," or "your daughter or son." They may guess "friend." Give them all time to guess, and do not tell them if they are correct or not.

Next, take a few minutes to talk about the people in the photographs and why they are important to you. The children will like hearing about them.

Say: "Tell me about your friends." (*Let them tell you about their friends.*)

God, the Son (Telling the Story)

Say: "In our story today, which is found in (*open the Bible*) Luke, chapter ten, verses 38-42, we learn about some people who were very special friends to Jesus: Mary, Martha, and Lazarus. And they were brothers and sisters. Jesus went to their house to eat dinner. Martha was busy cooking dinner, and she got grumpy because her sister, Mary, was not helping her. Do you ever get grumpy with your brother or sister?" (*Let them share.*)

"Well, Mary and Martha were sisters, and Martha got angry with Mary; but they still loved each other. They both wanted to spend time with their friend Jesus, because he was their very special friend; and they were his very special friends. Friends are very special people! Jesus had friends, I have friends, and you have friends. Friends are very special people!"

God, the Holy Spirit (Quiet and Prayer Time)

Say: "Friends were very special to Jesus, and they are very special to each of us. I am going to invite each of you to pray for a friend today. When it is your turn, you can say the name of a special friend; and we will all say, 'God, please bless (*name of friend.*)'"

Let each child name a friend and hear the response.

Pray: "God, thank you for the friends we love! Mary, Martha, and Lazarus were some friends that Jesus loved. Help us to always remember that Jesus loves us very much as well. In the name of Jesus, we pray. Amen."

(If using the extended Sacred Circle Time, stop here.)

A Time of Blessing

Say: "The symbol for the story today is a heart because Easter is all about Jesus and his love! Where would you like your blessing today?"

Let them tell you. Make the symbol as you look into each child's eyes.

Say: "Thank you for being here today and spending time experiencing God with me. You are a blessing!"

Closing Time

Slowly put each Trinity symbol away.

Say: "And now we are finished with our Sacred Circle Time. We put away our symbol for God, the Creator. We put away our symbol for God, the Son. And we put away our symbol for God, the Holy Spirit."

Then quietly and gently put the sacred cloth away.

Conclude: "And we are all done with our Sacred Circle time. You did a great job. Yay!" Clap and celebrate a job well done.

Extended Format

(*10 minutes*) Begin with free-play time. Greet the children warmly and let them get used to the space. Have something in the free-play space for them to play with. Rotate each week:

Week One: Paper and crayons, markers, or paint.

Week Two: Clay, wire, pipe cleaners and beads, and tools to work the clay.

Week Three: Things to build with: blocks, Legos®, cans, boxes, or flat stones.

Week Four: Things that make noise.

(*3 minutes*) Transition Time. Let the children know that it is almost Sacred Circle Time. Say: "It is almost our Sacred Circle Time. I cannot wait to have sacred time with you today. Will you start to finish up? Then come join me for our special, holy time together."

Sit down in the Sacred Circle Time space and place your sacred basket in front of you.

(*10 minutes*) **Sacred Circle Time** (*Basic format*)—Use the Sacred Circle Basic Format, but do not include the blessing or closing.

(*10 minutes*) **Trinity Stations**

Explain the Trinity Stations procedure for new children and for those who might forget from time to time.

Walk with the children to the Trinity Stations and show them what they can do at the stations, but do not let them start until they have seen all three stations.

Tell the children that after the Trinity Stations, they will spend five minutes in quiet time thinking about the story and the activities they have completed. They will then return to the Sacred Circle Time space to draw pictures and talk about their activities.

Station One: God, the Creator (Wonder) Station

Walk with the children to this station and show them what they can do here. In addition to the suggested supplies (page 469), you might want to have some bags of fifty items each, such as small stones, marbles, coins, and shells for the children to explore and think about the fifty days of Easter.

Station Two: God, the Son (Story) Station

Walk with the children to this station and show them what they can do here. In addition to the suggested supplies (page 469), you might want to include dishes and play food, so the children can pretend to make dinner for Jesus or a friend.

Station Three: God, the Holy Spirit (Prayer) Station

Walk with the children to this station and show them what they can do here. In addition to the suggested supplies (page 469), you might want to have some paper for children to draw pictures of their friends so that they can pray for them.

Begin Quiet Time

Say: "Let's begin five minutes of thinking about the story and how Jesus had dinner with his friends Mary, Martha, and Lazarus. After five minutes, I will invite you, one at a time, to come to the Sacred Circle Time space and draw what you did or thought about, so we can all share together."

(*2-minute transition time*) Place paper, crayons, and other materials in the circle. Invite the children to come and draw what they did, thought about, or experienced.

(*10 minutes*) **Journal and Share Time**

Let the children draw and journal as they gather. As most of the children finish, have them begin to share. Tell them that listening to one another is important.

Say: "Thank you for spending time with me in the Trinity Stations. I cannot wait to hear what you experienced today. Who would like to share?" (Give each child time to talk, and you should talk as well.)

Place their activities in individual folders; or if they are to take the folders home, place them behind them so they will not be distracted. This will keep you from having to correct the children's behavior.

10 minutes (snack or toy time)

A Time of Blessing

Explain: "The symbol for the story today is a heart because Easter is all about Jesus and his love! Where would you like your blessing today?"

Let them tell you. Make the symbol as you look into each child's eyes.

Say: "Thank you for being here today and spending time experiencing God with me. You are a blessing!"

Closing Time

Slowly put each Trinity symbol away.

Say: "And now we are finished with our Sacred Circle Time. We put away our symbol for God, the Creator. We put away our symbol for God, the Son. And we put away our symbol for God, the Holy Spirit."

Then quietly and gently put the sacred cloth away.

Conclude: "And we are all done with our Sacred Circle time. You did a great job. Yay!" Clap and celebrate a job well done.

Fifty Days of Easter 2

Story: Jesus Loved the Crowds

Text: Matthew 14:13-21, NRSV

Now when Jesus heard this, he withdrew from there in a boat to a deserted place by himself. But when the crowds heard it, they followed him on foot from the towns. When he went ashore, he saw a great crowd; and he had compassion for them and cured their sick. When it was evening, the disciples came to him and said, "This is a deserted place, and the hour is now late; send the crowds away so that they may go into the villages and buy food for themselves." Jesus said to them, "They need not go away; you give them something to eat." They replied, "We have nothing here but five loaves and two fish." And he said, "Bring them here to me." Then he ordered the crowds to sit down on the grass. Taking the five loaves and the two fish, he looked up to heaven, and blessed and broke the loaves, and gave them to the disciples, and the disciples gave them to the crowds. And all ate and were filled; and they took up what was left over of the broken pieces, twelve baskets full. And those who ate were about five thousand men, besides women and children.

About the text: This text is a beautiful story of the deep care that Jesus had for the crowds of people who came to hear him speak. The disciples were ready to send the people away hungry. But Jesus had deep compassion and wanted them fed. So "the

Bread of the World" fed the people by multiplying bread with two loaves of bread and two fish. The theological question is, "What did Jesus feed the people with? Bread and fish or love?"

The Sacred Circle Time Focus: We will focus on telling this story about the way Jesus loved the crowd and compassionately fed them.

Sacred Circle Time Basic Format

Sacred Circle basket and contents:

- Sacred space cloth
- Symbols for Creator (globe), Christ (cross), and Holy Spirit (bell or chimes)
- Small, unbreakable bottle to hold water or oil for the blessing
- A journal page (one per child)
- Crayons and/or markers
- A Bible bookmarked to Matthew 14:13-21
- Focused objects from the Bible story: Pots and pans of all different sizes from very small to very large and everything in between

The Lesson

Gathering

Begin by sitting down and placing the sacred basket in front of you. Pause so that the children notice it and begin to come closer.

Invite them to form a circle. Sit quietly until they settle in and are quiet.

Say: "It is time for Sacred Circle Time. I am so glad that you are here today. I love learning our stories and experiencing God with you."

Celebrating the Fifty Days of Easter

Say: "Before we create our Sacred Circle, I want to tell you that Easter is such an important holiday that we celebrate it at our church for fifty days! We are happy because Jesus was resurrected for fifty days! So let's count and clap with happy hands fifty times to celebrate Easter!"

(*Clap and count to fifty.*)

Say: "Easter lasts for fifty days! Let's all say 'Happy Easter!' 1-2-3 . . ."

Everyone shouts "Happy Easter!"

Say: "And during our fifty days of Easter we are going to learn all about love!"

Creating the Sacred Space

Say: "Let's create our sacred space."

Slowly lay out the sacred cloth.

Slowly lift the globe (symbol of God, the Creator) and hold it at the eye level of the children. Say: "This is our symbol for God, the Creator." Carefully lay it on the sacred cloth. (*Pause.*)

Slowly lift the cross (symbol of God, the Son). Say: "This is our symbol for God, the Son." Carefully lay it on the sacred cloth. (*Pause.*)

Slowly lift the bell (symbol of God, the Holy Spirit). Say: "This is our symbol of God, the Holy Spirit." Carefully lay it on the sacred cloth. (*Pause.*)

Point to each symbol and say: "So we have God, the Creator; God, the Son; and God, the Holy Spirit. (*Pause.*) Our sacred space is ready. We are ready to begin our Sacred Circle Time together."

God, the Creator (A Time to Wonder)

Start by showing the children the smallest pan.

Ask: "If I filled this pan with food, how many people do you think might be able to eat?"

Let them guess. Then show them the next largest pan.

Say: "This would serve one person and maybe two people. How many people do you think this pan would feed?"

Keep doing this pattern until you have shown the children all of the pans you have. The numbers should get higher and higher, and maybe even outrageous. Have fun, and let them imagine a hundred or more people eating from the largest pan!

God, the Son (Telling the Story)

Say: "Well, in our story today, which is found in (*open the Bible*) Matthew, chapter fourteen, verses 13-21, we learn about a day when five thousand people came to hear Jesus tell them about God! Five thousand people is so many people! If we filled this entire room with people, it would not be 5000. Five thousand people is sooooo many people! And they spent the whole day listening to Jesus talk. Breakfast time came, but they did not have any food. Lunch time came, and they did not have any food. Dinner time came, and they did not have any food; and those people were soooooo hungry. And there were sooooo many of them! So Jesus' disciples told the people to go away and find their own food someplace else. But Jesus loved those people, and he wanted to feed them. Which size pan do you think Jesus might need to fill with food to feed 5000 people?"

They will say, "The big one!"

Say: "Yes, Jesus would need that much food."

Take the big pan away.

Say: "And Jesus did not have this much food."

Take away the next largest pan.

Say: "Or this much food."

Take away the next largest pan and do this until you have only the smallest pan left.

Say: "And Jesus did not even have this much food. Jesus only had this much food." (*Cup your hands into a tiny cup*).

Say: "And everyone knew it wasn't enough food. I mean, could this much food possibly feed 5000 people?"

The children will say, "No!"

Say: "But Jesus loved those people and wanted to feed them, so he started passing out this tiny bit of food, and a miracle of love happened. The people starting eating the food, and there was enough. In fact, there was so much food that they had this much left over (*get the smallest pan out*), and this much left over (*get the next largest pan*) and this much left over (*get out the largest pan*). The love of Jesus made a miracle, and this much food (*cup your hands*) fed 5000 people! Jesus loved all of the people who came to hear him teach!"

God, the Holy Spirit (Quiet and Prayer Time)

Say: "It is now time to pray. For our prayer today, I want you to think about how much Jesus loved those people and how much he loves us today! Jesus' love made that little bit of food (*hold hands close together palms facing each other*) feed all those 5000 people!" (*Stretch your hands out as wide as you can.*)

Say: "For our prayer, I want you to begin with a little love." (*Have them put their palms nearly touching*).

Say: "This is not how much Jesus loves you." (*Have them put their hands a little farther apart.*)

Say: "This is not how much Jesus loves you." (*Have them stretch their hands out as wide as possible.*)

Say: "This is how much Jesus loves you! Now sit here and see if you can feel how BIG the love of Jesus is!" (*Be silent for about 30 seconds.*)

Pray: "Dear God, thank you for the love that helped Jesus feed all those people long ago and thank you that he loves us so much! In his name, we pray. Amen."

(If using the extended Sacred Circle Time, stop here.)

A Time of Blessing

Explain that the symbol for the story today is a heart because Easter is all about Jesus and his love! Ask the children where they would like their blessing, then make the symbol as you look into each child's eyes.

Say: "Thank you for being here today and spending time experiencing God with me. You are a blessing!"

Closing Time

Slowly put each Trinity symbol away.

Say: "And now we are finished with our Sacred Circle Time. We put away our symbol for God, the Creator. We put away our symbol for God, the Son. And we put away our symbol for God, the Holy Spirit."

Then quietly and gently put the sacred cloth away.

Conclude: "And we are all done with our Sacred Circle time. You did a great job. Yay!" Clap and celebrate a job well done.

Extended Format

(*10 minutes*) Begin with free-play time. Greet the children warmly and let them get used to the space. Have something in the free-play space for them to play with. Rotate each week:

Week One: Paper and crayons, markers, or paint.

Week Two: Clay, wire, pipe cleaners and beads, and tools to work the clay.

Week Three: Things to build with: blocks, Legos®, cans, boxes, or flat stones.

Week Four: Things that make noise.

(*3 minutes*) Transition Time. Let the children know that it is almost Sacred Circle Time. Say: "It is almost our Sacred Circle Time. I cannot wait to have sacred time with you today. Will you start to finish up? Then come join me for our special, holy time together."

Sit down in the Sacred Circle Time space and place your sacred basket in front of you.

(*10 minutes*) **Sacred Circle Time** (*Basic format*)—Use the Sacred Circle Basic Format, but do not include the blessing or closing.

(*10 minutes*) **Trinity Stations**

Explain the Trinity Stations procedure for new children and for those who might forget from time to time.

Walk with the children to the Trinity Stations and show them what they can do in the stations, but do not let them start until they have seen all three stations.

Tell the children that after the Trinity Stations, they will spend five minutes in quiet time thinking about the story and the activities they have completed. They will then return to the Sacred Circle Time space to draw pictures and talk about their activities.

Station One: God, the Creator (Wonder) Station

Walk with the children to this station and show them what they can do here. In addition to the suggested supplies (page 469), you might want to have the pans used in the Sacred Circle Time and things to fill them with (blocks or Legos® to help the children explore differences in size).

Station Two: God, the Son (Story) Station

Walk with the children to this station and show them what they can do here. In addition to the suggested supplies (page 469), you might want to include dishes and play food so the children can pretend to serve others.

Station Three: God, the Holy Spirit (Prayer) Station

Walk with the children to this station and show them what they can do here. In addition to the suggested supplies (page 469), you might want to include items that can demonstrate growing larger or smaller, such as a wire coil or a paper plate cut circularly so when one end is lifted it grows like a snake.

Begin Quiet Time

Say: "Let's begin five minutes of thinking about how Jesus fed all those people with a loving miracle and how much Jesus loves you!"

And then, after five minutes, I will invite you, one at a time, to come to the Sacred Circle Time space and draw what you did or thought about, so we can all share together.

(*2-minute transition time*) Place paper, crayons, and other materials in the circle. Invite the children to come and draw what they did, thought about, or experienced.

(*10 minutes*) **Journal and Share Time**

Let them draw and journal as they gather. When most of the children have finished, let them begin to share. Remind them that listening to one another is important.

Say: "Thank you for spending time with me in the Trinity Stations. I cannot wait to see what you experienced today. Who would like to share?" (Give each child time to talk, and you should talk as well.)

Place their activities in individual folders; or if they are to take the folders home, place them behind them so they will not be distracted. This will keep you from having to correct the children's behavior.

10 minutes (snack or toy time)

A Time of Blessing

Explain: "The symbol for the story today is a heart because Easter is all about Jesus and his love! Where would you like your blessing today?"

Let them tell you. Make the symbol as you look into each child's eyes.

Say: "Thank you for being here today and spending time experiencing God with me. You are a blessing!"

Closing Time

Slowly put each Trinity symbol away.

Say: "And now we are finished with our Sacred Circle Time. We put away our symbol for God, the Creator. We put away our symbol for God, the Son. And we put away our symbol for God, the Holy Spirit."

Then quietly and gently put the sacred cloth away.

Conclude: "And we are all done with our Sacred Circle time. You did a great job. Yay!" Clap and celebrate a job well done.

Fifty Days of Easter 3

Story: Jesus Loved the Sick Woman

Text: Mark 5:25-34, NRSV

Now there was a woman who had been suffering from hemorrhages for twelve years. She had endured much under many physicians, and had spent all that she had; and she was no better, but rather grew worse. She had heard about Jesus, and came up behind him in the crowd and touched his cloak, for she said, "If I but touch his clothes, I will be made well." Immediately her hemorrhage stopped; and she felt in her body that she was healed of her disease. Immediately aware that power had gone forth from him, Jesus turned about in the crowd and said, "Who touched my clothes?" And his disciples said to him, "You see the crowd pressing in on you; how can you say, 'Who touched me?'" He looked all around to see who had done it. But the woman, knowing what had happened to her, came in fear and trembling, fell down before him, and told him the whole truth. He said to her, "Daughter, your faith has made you well; go in peace, and be healed of your disease."

About the text: This text is a beautiful story of a desperate woman who has been ill for many years. We know that she is desperate because being ill for such a lengthy time would make any of us desperate. But we also know that she is desperate because she breaks a huge Jewish law. This woman was unclean in the eyes of her religious community, and she certainly was not supposed to touch a man while she was considered unclean. However, she was desperate, so she tried to touch Jesus quickly from behind, hoping that he would never notice. She was a desperate woman, but she had great faith in Jesus and what he could do for her. After she touched Jesus, he stopped and asked who had touched him. The woman was terrified. Why? Because Jesus had been religiously violated by her touch, and he had the right to have her punished. When she fell down before him, he had love and compassion for her. Instead of condemning her, he admired her faith and sent her away in peace. The respect and love Jesus showed to this woman is especially powerful when told in context.

The Sacred Circle Time Focus: We will focus on telling this story about this woman who was so brave and Jesus who was so respectful and loving toward her in return.

Sacred Circle Time Basic Format

Sacred Circle basket and contents:

- Sacred space cloth
- Symbols for Creator (globe), Christ (cross), and Holy Spirit (bell or chimes)
- Small, unbreakable bottle to hold water or oil for the blessing
- A journal page (one per child)
- Crayons and/or markers
- A Bible bookmarked to Mark 5:25-34
- Focused objects from the Bible story: A first-aid kit. (You may use a toy one, a real one, or one you make out of shoebox. It should have things inside that make people feel better after they are hurt or sick.)

The Lesson

Gathering

Begin by sitting down and placing the sacred basket in front of you. Pause so that the children notice it and begin to come closer.

Invite them to form a circle. Sit quietly until they settle in and are quiet.

Say: "It is time for Sacred Circle Time. I am so glad that you are here today. I love learning our stories and experiencing God with you."

Celebrating the Fifty Days of Easter

Say: "Before we create our Sacred Circle, I want to tell you that Easter is such an important holiday that we celebrate it at our church for fifty days! We are happy because Jesus was resurrected for fifty days! So let's count and clap with happy hands fifty times to celebrate Easter!

(*Clap and count to fifty.*)

Say: "Easter lasts for fifty days! Let's all say 'Happy Easter!' 1-2-3 . . .'"

Everyone shouts "Happy Easter!"

Say: "And during our fifty days of Easter, we are going to learn all about love!"

Creating the Sacred Space

Say: "Let's create our sacred space."

Slowly lay out the sacred cloth.

Slowly lift the globe (symbol of God, the Creator) and hold it at the eye level of the children. Say: "This is our symbol for God, the Creator." Carefully lay it on the sacred cloth. (*Pause.*)

Slowly lift the cross (symbol of God, the Son). Say: "This is our symbol for God, the Son." Carefully lay it on the sacred cloth. (*Pause.*)

Slowly lift the bell (symbol of God, the Holy Spirit). Say: "This is our symbol of God, the Holy Spirit." Carefully lay it on the sacred cloth. (*Pause.*)

Point to each symbol and say: "So we have God, the Creator; God, the Son; and God, the Holy Spirit. (*Pause.*) Our sacred space is ready. We are ready to begin our Sacred Circle Time together."

God, the Creator (A Time to Wonder)

Show the children the first-aid kit. Ask them what they think is inside. (They might know and they might not.)

Say: "This is a first-aid kit. When people are hurt or sick, this box has many things that might make them better. Shall we take a look inside?" (*Pause for dramatic effect*).

Say: "Let's see what we can find." (Pull various items out of the kit and let them guess how it might be used—aspirin, a Band-aid®, a bandage, gauze, ointment.)

Explain: "When we get hurt or sick, we can use a first-aid kit. What else could we do?" (*Let them guess that they might go to a doctor or nurse or to their mom or dad.*)

Say: "You are so smart! In today's story, I want to tell you about a woman who was very sick and how she got better."

God, the Son (Telling the Story)

Say: "Our story today, which is found in (*open the Bible*) Mark, chapter five, verses 25-34, tells about a day when Jesus and his followers were walking down the street, and a very sick woman saw Jesus. She had been sick for a very long time, and none of the doctors or nurses could help her get better. She was so tired of being sick, and she wanted to be better. So she decided to touch Jesus because she believed that touching Jesus would make her better. But the weird part of this story is that Jesus was not a doctor. Jesus was not a nurse. Jesus did not have any of the things we just looked at in this first-aid kit. He didn't have a Band-aid®, he didn't have a bandage; he didn't even have any medicine." (*Pause so this can all soak in.*)

Say: "So the woman thought Jesus would make her better if only she could touch him. So she reached out and touched a very tiny part of his coat. And guess what? She was healed! What do you think Jesus used to heal this woman? I mean, he didn't have a Band-aid® or anything! What could have healed her?" (*Let them guess.*)

Say: "Jesus was not a doctor or nurse. He didn't have a Band-aid® or bandage or anything. Do you know what healed that woman? Love! Jesus had so much love in his heart that when the woman touched him and believed she would be healed, she was.

Jesus loved people who were sick, and often used his love to make them better. He healed this woman; and he also healed a blind man, a little girl, a soldier's son, and many, many others. Love is very powerful, and Jesus has lots of it!"

God, the Holy Spirit (Quiet and Prayer Time)

Say: "It is now time to pray. I want to pray for sick people today; and after I name a sickness, you can make a heart with your finger in the air as a way of asking God to heal the person."

Have the children practice making the heart movement with their fingers.

Pray: "God, we ask you to heal anyone in our homes who is sick today."

Instruct the children to make the heart sign.

Pray: "God, we ask you to heal anyone in our church who is sick today." (The children make the heart sign.)

Pray: "God, we ask you to heal anyone in our community who is sick today." (The children make the heart sign.)

Pray: "God, we ask you to heal anyone in our world who is sick today." (The children make the heart sign.)

Pray: "God, remind us that your healing love is very powerful and that you love us when we are well and when we are sick. Your love is always with us. In Christ's name, we pray. Amen."

(If using the extended Sacred Circle Time, stop here.)

A Time of Blessing

Tell the children that the symbol for today is a heart because Easter is all about Jesus and his love! Ask the children where they would like their blessing, then make the symbol as you look into each child's eyes.

Say: "Thank you for being here today and spending time experiencing God with me. You are a blessing!"

Closing Time

Slowly put each Trinity symbol away.

Say: "And now we are finished with our Sacred Circle Time. We put away our symbol for God, the Creator. We put away our symbol for God, the Son. And we put away our symbol for God, the Holy Spirit."

Then quietly and gently put the sacred cloth away.

Conclude: "And we are all done with our Sacred Circle time. You did a great job. Yay!" Clap and celebrate a job well done.

Extended Format

(*10 minutes*) Begin with free-play time. Greet the children warmly and let them get used to the space. Have something in the free-play space for them to play with. Rotate each week:

Week One: Paper and crayons, markers, or paint.

Week Two: Clay, wire, pipe cleaners and beads, and tools to work the clay.

Week Three: Things to build with: blocks, Legos®, cans, boxes, or flat stones.

Week Four: Things that make noise.

(*3 minutes*) Transition Time. Let the children know that it is almost Sacred Circle Time. Say: "It is almost our Sacred Circle Time. I cannot wait to have sacred time with you today. Will you start to finish up? Then come join me for our special, holy time together."

Sit down in the Sacred Circle Time space and place your sacred basket in front of you.

(*10 minutes*) **Sacred Circle Time** (*Basic format*)—Use the Sacred Circle Basic Format, but do not include the blessing or closing.

(*10 minutes*) **Trinity Stations**

Explain the Trinity Stations procedure for new children and for those who might forget from time to time.

Walk with the children to the Trinity Stations and show them what they can do at the stations, but do not let them start until they have seen all three stations.

Tell the children that after the Trinity Stations, they will spend five minutes in quiet time thinking about the story and the activities they have completed. They will then return to the Sacred Circle Time space to draw pictures and talk about their activities.

Station One: God, the Creator (Wonder Station)

Walk with the children to this station and show them what they can do here. In addition to the suggested supplies (page 469), you might want to add some medical items such as a stethoscope to allow children to hear their heartbeats.

Station Two: God, the Son (Story) Station

Walk with the children to this station and show them what they can do here. In addition to the suggested supplies (page 469), you might want to include a play doctor kit and some white coats so the children can play doctors and nurses and pretend to make a doll baby better.

Station Three: God, the Holy Spirit (Prayer) Station

Walk with the children to this station and show them what they can do here. In addition to the suggested supplies (page 469), you might want to add some photos of people who need healing: a person with a broken leg, someone in a wheelchair, a blind person. Encourage the children to pray for healing.

Begin Quiet Time

Say: "Let's begin five minutes of thinking about the story and how powerful the love of Jesus is. Let's also think of how deep the faith of the woman who was so sick for such a long time was. Let's think about the love of Jesus that healed her. After five minutes, I will invite you, one at a time, to come to the Sacred Circle Time space and draw what you did or thought about so we can all share together."

(*2-minute transition time*) Place paper, crayons, and other materials in the circle. Invite the children, one at a time, to come and draw what they did, thought about, or experienced.

(*10 minutes*) Journal and Share Time

Let them draw and journal as they gather. When most of the children have finished, let them begin to share. Remind the children that listening to one another is important.

Say: "Thank you for spending time with me in the Trinity Stations. I cannot wait to discover what you experienced today. Who would like to share?" (Give each child time to talk, and you should talk as well.)

Place their activities in individual folders; or if they are to take the folders home, place them behind them so they will not be distracted. This will keep you from having to correct the children's behavior.

10 minutes (snack or toy time)

A Time of Blessing

Explain: "The symbol for the story today is a heart because Easter is all about Jesus and his love! Where would you like your blessing today?" (*Let them tell you.*)

Make the symbol as you look into each child's eyes.

Say: "Thank you for being here today and spending time experiencing God with me. You are a blessing!"

Closing Time

Slowly put each Trinity symbol away.

Say: "And now we are finished with our Sacred Circle Time. We put away our symbol for God, the Creator. We put away our symbol for God, the Son. And we put away our symbol for God, the Holy Spirit."

Then quietly and gently put the sacred cloth away.

Conclude: "And we are all done with our Sacred Circle time. You did a great job. Yay!" Clap and celebrate a job well done.

Fifty Days of Easter 4

Story: Jesus Loved Zacchaeus

Text: Luke 19:1-10, NRSV

He entered Jericho and was passing through it. A man was there named Zacchaeus; he was a chief tax collector and was rich. He was trying to see who Jesus was, but on account of the crowd he could not, because he was short in stature. So he ran ahead and climbed a sycamore tree to see him, because he was going to pass that way. When Jesus came to the place, he looked up and said to him, "Zacchaeus, hurry and come down; for I must stay at your house today." So he hurried down and was happy to welcome him. All who saw it began to grumble and said, "He has gone to be the guest of one who is a sinner." Zacchaeus stood there and said to the Lord, "Look, half of my possessions, Lord, I will give to the poor; and if I have defrauded anyone of anything, I will pay back four times as much." Then Jesus said to him, "Today salvation has come to this house, because he too is a son of Abraham. For the Son of Man came to seek out and to save the lost."

About the text: This text is a beautiful story of the sensitivity, love, and compassion Jesus gave to people others despised. Zacchaeus was a tax collector. He worked for the Romans, who took nearly everything that the common Jewish people had. And Zacchaeus was seen as particularly bad because he was a Jew. One of their own had "sold out" and was supporting the enemy. And this bad person had come to see Jesus.

No wonder he had to climb a tree. No one wanted him around! He was short, and people would have had to let him get in front of them to see, but he was pushed to the back. Jesus, however, noticed Zacchaeus alone in a tree and chose to have dinner with him. Jesus is always stepping out to love others . . . the good and the bad. And the message is clear: loving others is the way God changes hearts.

The Sacred Circle Time Focus: We will focus on telling this story about being kind to people, ALL people, even those we don't like.

Sacred Circle Time Basic Format

Sacred Circle basket and contents:

- Sacred space cloth
- Symbols for Creator (globe), Christ (cross), and Holy Spirit (bell or chimes)
- Small, unbreakable bottle to hold water or oil for the blessing
- A journal page (one per child)
- Crayons and/or markers
- A Bible bookmarked to Luke 19:1-10
- Focused objects from the Bible story:
    - Things for a parade: Noisemakers, streamers, drums—anything to make lots of fun noise!
    - A little cut-out of Zacchaeus hidden high on a shelf in the room, but visible.

The Lesson

Gathering

Begin by sitting down and placing the sacred basket in front of you. Pause so that the children notice it and begin to come closer.

Invite them to form a circle. Sit quietly until they settle in and are quiet.

Say: "It is time for Sacred Circle Time. I am so glad that you are here today. I love learning our stories and experiencing God with you."

Celebrating the Fifty Days of Easter

Explain again to the children that we celebrate Easter for fifty days.

Say: "We are happy because Jesus was resurrected for fifty days! So let's count and clap with happy hands fifty times to celebrate Easter!" (*Clap and count to fifty.*)

Say: "Easter lasts for fifty days! Let's all say 'Happy Easter!' 1-2-3 . . .'"

Everyone shouts "Happy Easter!"

Say: "And during our fifty days of Easter, we are going to learn all about love!"

Creating the Sacred Space

Say: "Let's create our sacred space."

Slowly lay out the sacred cloth.

Slowly lift the globe (symbol of God, the Creator) and hold it at the eye level of the children. Say: "This is our symbol for God, the Creator." Carefully lay it on the sacred cloth. (*Pause.*)

Slowly lift the cross (symbol of God, the Son). Say: "This is our symbol for God, the Son." Carefully lay it on the sacred cloth. (*Pause.*)

Slowly lift the bell (symbol of God, the Holy Spirit). Say: "This is our symbol of God, the Holy Spirit." Carefully lay it on the sacred cloth. (*Pause.*)

Point to each symbol and say: "So we have God, the Creator; God, the Son; and God, the Holy Spirit. (*Pause.*) Our sacred space is ready. We are ready to begin our Sacred Circle Time together."

God, the Creator (A Time to Wonder)

Ask: "Have you ever been to a parade? What was it like?"

Let the children share. Then show them the fun noisy things you brought to make a parade! Shake the noisemakers and get the kids excited!

Say: "As part of our Bible story today, we are going to have a parade! Are you excited?"

They will be very excited. Do not correct them or try to quiet them . . . It is okay!

God, the Son (Telling the Story)

Say: "Our story today, which is found in (*open the Bible*) Luke, chapter 19, verses 1-10, tells about a day when Jesus and his followers were walking through a town called Jericho. The people of Jericho had heard about how amazing Jesus was, and they were excited that he was coming to town. When Jesus arrived, it was like a parade! The people were clapping and waving things. It was an exciting day! Let's try to make a parade that was as exciting as the day Jesus and his followers arrived in Jericho. I am going to give each of you something to carry in the parade; and then I will be Jesus, and all of you follow me!"

Give them the noise makers, and have them line up after you. They will be super-excited, so just talk over them and march all over the room!

Say: "Oh those people loved Jesus! They wanted to see him and maybe be healed by him. They were so excited that they cheered, made noise, and yelled out to him to try and get his attention."

Keep marching and having fun; then point at Zacchaeus. Stop marching. Be still. The children will do the same, but you might have to gently help them settle.

Say: "Children, look at this little man sitting up here. Come back to the circle, I want to tell you about him!"

Go to the circle. If you are quiet, the children will be quiet.

Say: "This little man is named Zacchaeus. And on that day when Jesus and his followers went into Jericho and everyone was so excited at the big parade? Well poor Zacchaeus had to climb a tree because he was so short that he could not see. And, guess what?" (*Pause for dramatic affect.*)

"No one liked him! No one. He was a tax collector, and no one liked tax collectors. They (*pause*) hated tax collectors." (*Pause because the children will be shocked.*)

Continue: "So, in the middle of the big parade, do you know what Jesus did? He saw poor Zacchaeus sitting alone in a tree; and he stopped and said, "Zacchaeus, come down! I am coming to YOUR house to eat dinner!" Poor little Zacchaeus that no one loved . . . that everyone hated . . . Jesus loved!"

God, the Holy Spirit (Quiet and Prayer Time)

Say: "It is now time to pray. And for our prayer today, I want us to pray for all of the people in the world who feel unloved today. Isn't it sad that there are people in the world who do not have anyone who loves them? But you know who does love them? Jesus! He loves everyone everyday and all the time! Jesus' love is huge!

"So for the prayer, I want us to be still and pray for those people who are unloved . . . who do not have anyone in the world who loves them. (*Enter about 30 seconds of silent prayer.*)

"And now I want us to thank Jesus for loving everyone, all the time! Let's thank Jesus by making lots of noise like we did in the parade!" (*Let them wave, cheer, and enjoy! After all, Jesus' love is amazing and exciting!*)

Pray: "Jesus, your love is amazing! Thank you for loving Zacchaeus; and thank you for loving us, everyday, and all the time! Amen."

(If using the extended Sacred Circle Time, stop here.)

A Time of Blessing

Say: "The symbol for the story today is a heart because Easter is all about Jesus and his love! Where would you like your blessing today?" (*Let them tell you.*)

Make the symbol as you look in each child's eyes.

Say: "Thank you for being here today and spending time experiencing God with me. You are a blessing!"

Closing Time

Slowly put each Trinity symbol away.

Say: "And now we are finished with our Sacred Circle Time. We put away our symbol for God, the Creator. We put away our symbol for God, the Son. And we put away our symbol for God, the Holy Spirit."

Then quietly and gently put the sacred cloth away.

Conclude: "And we are all done with our Sacred Circle time. You did a great job. Yay!" Clap and celebrate a job well done.

Extended Format

(*10 minutes*) Begin with free-play time. Greet the children warmly and let them get used to the space. Have something in the free-play space for them to play with. Rotate each week:

Week One: Paper and crayons, markers, or paint.

Week Two: Clay, wire, pipe cleaners and beads, and tools to work the clay.

Week Three: Things to build with: blocks, Legos®, cans, boxes, or flat stones.

Week Four: Things that make noise.

(*3 minutes*) Transition Time. Let the children know that it is almost Sacred Circle Time. Say: "It is almost our Sacred Circle Time. I cannot wait to have sacred time with you today. Will you start to finish up? Then come join me for our special, holy time together."

Sit down in the Sacred Circle Time space and place your sacred basket in front of you.

(*10 minutes*) **Sacred Circle Time** (*Basic format*)—Use the Sacred Circle Basic Format, but do not include the blessing or closing.

(*10 minutes*) **Trinity Stations**

Explain the Trinity Stations procedure for new children and for those who might forget from time to time.

Walk with the children to the Trinity Stations and show them what they can do in the stations, but do not let them start until they have seen all three stations.

Tell the children that after the Trinity Stations, they will spend five minutes in quiet time thinking about the story and the activities they have completed. They will then return to the Sacred Circle Time space to draw pictures and talk about their activities.

Station One: God, the Creator (Wonder) Station

Walk with the children to this station and show them what they can do here. In addition to the suggested supplies (page 469), you might want to add some different tree leaves and magnifying glasses for them to explore.

Station Two: God, the Son (Story) Station

Walk with the children to this station and show them what they can do here. In addition to the suggested supplies (page 469), you might want to include a tree made out of pipe cleaners or wire and clay so that the children can make the characters and act out the story.

Station Three: God, the Holy Spirit (Prayer) Station

Walk with the children to this station and show them what they can do here. In addition to the suggested supplies (page 469), you might want to add some photos of people looking lonely and sad for the children to contemplate and pray about.

Begin Quiet Time

Say: "Let's begin five minutes of thinking about the story and how amazing the love of Jesus is. Let's also think of Zacchaeus and how happy he must have been when he discovered that Jesus loved him! After five minutes, I will invite you, one at a time, to come to the Sacred Circle Time space to draw what you did or thought about."

(*2-minute transition time*) Place paper, crayons, and other materials in the circle. Invite the children, one at a time, to come and draw what they did, thought about, or experienced.

(*10 minutes*) **Journal and Share Time**

Let them draw and journal as they gather. When most of the children have finished, let them begin to share. Remind the children that listening is important.

Say: "Thank you for spending time with me in the Trinity Stations. I cannot wait to discover what you experienced today. Who would like to share?" (Give each child time to talk, and you should talk as well.)

Place their activities in individual folders; or if they are to take the folders home, place them behind them so they will not be distracted. This will keep you from having to correct the children's behavior.

10 minutes (snack or toy time)

A Time of Blessing

Say: "The symbol for the story today is a heart because Easter is all about Jesus and his love! Where would you like your blessing today?" (*Let them tell you.*)

Make the symbol as you look into each child's eyes.

Say: "Thank you for being here today and spending time experiencing God with me. You are a blessing!"

Closing Time

Slowly put each Trinity symbol away.

Say: "And now we are finished with our Sacred Circle Time. We put away our symbol for God, the Creator. We put away our symbol for God, the Son. And we put away our symbol for God, the Holy Spirit."

Then quietly and gently put the sacred cloth away.

Conclude: "And we are all done with our Sacred Circle time. You did a great job. Yay!" Clap and celebrate a job well done.

Fifty Days of Easter 5

Story: Jesus Loved God

Text: Deuteronomy 6:4-9, NRSV

Hear, O Israel: The Lord is our God, the Lord alone. You shall love the Lord your God with all your heart, and with all your soul, and with all your might. Keep these words that I am commanding you today in your heart. Recite them to your children and talk about them when you are at home and when you are away, when you lie down and when you rise. Bind them as a sign on your hand, fix them as an emblem on your forehead, and write them on the doorposts of your house and on your gates.

And . . . Matthew 22:36-40, NRSV

"Teacher, which commandment in the law is the greatest?" He said to him, 'You shall love the Lord your God with all your heart, and with all your soul, and with all your mind.' This is the greatest and first commandment. And a second is like it: 'You shall love your neighbor as yourself.' On these two commandments hang all the law and the prophets."

About the texts: The text from Deuteronomy is known as the *Shema*, and it is a sacred and central prayer in Judaism. It was told to Moses, and he told the people of God that God had commanded them to recite it day and night, to bind it to their arms and foreheads and on the door posts of their homes. They took this command

243

seriously and still recite it, bind it, and post it on their doors today. It is likely that the *Shema* was the first prayer that Jesus learned as a child and he, like other Jews, would have had it posted on the door to his home and worn it as *teffillin* (small box) on his hand and forehead. When asked which commandment is the greatest, Jesus recited the *Shema* and then added that loving one another is the second greatest. In this passage in Matthew, Jesus makes clear that the love of God is the starting point of faith. And he did not mean just a casual love. Living as God calls us takes us loving God completely!

The Sacred Circle Time Focus: We will tell the story and emphasize how Jesus loved God with his whole being, and we should try to do so as well.

Sacred Circle Time Basic Format

Sacred Circle basket and contents:

- Sacred space cloth
- Symbols for Creator (globe), Christ (cross), and Holy Spirit (bell or chimes)
- Small, unbreakable bottle to hold water or oil for the blessing
- A journal page (one per child)
- Crayons and/or markers
- A Bible with these passages bookmarked: Deuteronomy 6:4-9 and Matthew 22:36-40
- Focused objects from the Bible story: None. We will use our hands and bodies today.

The Lesson

Gathering

Begin by sitting down and placing the sacred basket in front of you. Pause so that the children notice it and begin to come closer.

Invite them to form a circle. Sit quietly until they settle in and are quiet.

Say: "It is time for Sacred Circle Time. I am so glad that you are here today. I love learning our stories and experiencing God with you."

Celebrating the Fifty Days of Easter

Explain that Easter is such an important holiday that we celebrate it for fifty days!

Say: "We are happy because Jesus was resurrected for fifty days! So let's count and clap with happy hands fifty times to celebrate Easter!" (*Clap and count to fifty.*)

Say: "Easter lasts for fifty days! Let's all say 'Happy Easter!' 1-2-3 . . ."

Everyone shouts, "Happy Easter!"

Say: "And during our fifty days of Easter, we are going to learn all about love!"

Creating the Sacred Space

Say: "Let's create our sacred space."

Slowly lay out the sacred cloth.

Slowly lift the globe (symbol of God, the Creator) and hold it at the eye level of the children. Say: "This is our symbol for God, the Creator." Carefully lay it on the sacred cloth. (*Pause.*)

Slowly lift the cross (symbol of God, the Son). Say: "This is our symbol for God, the Son." Carefully lay it on the sacred cloth. (*Pause.*)

Slowly lift the bell (symbol of God, the Holy Spirit). Say: "This is our symbol of God, the Holy Spirit." Carefully lay it on the sacred cloth. (*Pause.*)

Point to each symbol and say: "So we have God, the Creator; God, the Son; and God, the Holy Spirit. (*Pause.*) Our sacred space is ready. We are ready to begin our Sacred Circle Time together."

God, the Creator (A Time to Wonder)

Stand up and bend over until your finger tips touch the floor. Slowly stand up as you say, "We can love people this much (*leave hands close to ground*), or this much (*stand up a bit more*), or this much (*hands at knees*), or this much (*hands at waist*), or this much (*hands by shoulders*), or this much (*hands over head*), or this much (*hands stretching clear up to sky*), or this much." (*Act as if you cannot stretch any further!*)

Say: "Now you stand up; and I will name something, and you show me how much you love it."

Name several things, such as broccoli, sunny days, swimming, playing with friends, bedtime, and end with parents. Let them use their bodies to show you if they like those things or not.

God, the Son (Telling the Story)

Say: "Today we have two Bible stories. The first one is found in (*open the Bible*), Deuteronomy, chapter six, verses 4-9. It is a special prayer that God told the people to pray every day. It was a very important prayer because it told the people to love God . . .

With all of their heart (*place hands over heart*)

With all of their soul (*move hands down in front of you from your head to the floor*)

And with all of their mind (*point to temples*)

"This prayer told the people to love God with their whole self. This (*stretch your arms way, way up*) much!

"And Jesus learned this prayer when he was a little boy. Let's learn the prayer."

Repeat the prayer (above) and let the children follow as they can. The motions are what they will remember, and that is the goal.

Say: "Jesus learned this prayer as a child. When he grew up, someone asked him how to love God. Guess what Jesus told them?" (*Let them guess the prayer.*)

Say: "Yes, he told them to love God with . . ." (*repeat the prayer and motions from above*).

God, the Holy Spirit (Quiet and Prayer Time)

Say: "It is now time to pray. And for our prayer today, I want us to pray the prayer God taught the people, the prayer that Jesus then learned as a child and taught us to pray. It is called a special word, *Shema*. Can you say that word?" (*Let them say it several times.*)

Say: "Let us pray the *Shema*, the special prayer.

> We should love God with:
> Our whole heart (*place hands over heart*),
> Our whole soul (*move hands down in front of you from your head to the floor*)
> And with our whole mind (*point to temples*)
> God told us to love God with our whole self. This (*stretch your arms way, way up*) much!"

(If using the extended Sacred Circle Time, stop here.)

A Time of Blessing

Explain that the symbol for today is a heart because Easter is all about Jesus and his love! Bless the children where they request, being sure to look them directly in their eyes. Thank them and say, "You are a blessing!"

Closing Time

Slowly put each Trinity symbol away.

Say: "And now we are finished with our Sacred Circle Time. We put away our symbol for God, the Creator. We put away our symbol for God, the Son. And we put away our symbol for God, the Holy Spirit."

Then quietly and gently put the sacred cloth away.

Conclude: "And we are all done with our Sacred Circle time. You did a great job. Yay!" Clap and celebrate a job well done.

Extended Format

(*10 minutes*) Begin with free-play time. Greet the children warmly and let them get used to the space. Have something in the free-play space for them to play with. Rotate each week:

Week One: Paper and crayons, markers, or paint.
Week Two: Clay, wire, pipe cleaners and beads, and tools to work the clay.
Week Three: Things to build with: blocks, Legos®, cans, boxes, or flat stones.
Week Four: Things that make noise.

(*3 minutes*) Transition Time. Let the children know that it is almost Sacred Circle Time. Say: "It is almost our Sacred Circle Time. I cannot wait to have sacred time with you today. Will you start to finish up? Then come join me for our special, holy time together."

Sit down in the Sacred Circle Time space and place your sacred basket in front of you.

(*10 minutes*) **Sacred Circle Time** (*Basic format*)—Use the Sacred Circle Basic Format, but do not include the blessing or closing.

(*10 minutes*) **Trinity Stations**

Explain the Trinity Stations procedure for new children and for those who might forget from time to time.

Walk with the children to the Trinity Stations and show them what they can do at the stations, but do not let them start until they have seen all three stations.

Tell the children that after the Trinity Stations, they will spend five minutes in quiet time thinking about the story and the activities they have completed. They will then return to the Sacred Circle Time space to draw pictures and talk about their activities.

Station One: God, the Creator (Wonder) Station

Walk with the children to this station and show them what they can do here.
See the supply list on page 469.

Station Two: God, the Son (Story) Station

Walk with the children to this station and show them what they can do here. See the
supply list on page 469.

Station Three: God, the Holy Spirit (Prayer) Station

Walk with the children to this station and show them what they can do here. In addition to the suggested supplies (page 469), you might want to add a "slinky" or other
toys that stretch big and then small.

Begin Quiet Time

Say: "Let's begin five minutes of thinking about the Shema prayer and how it asks us
to love God so much! After five minutes, I will invite you to the Sacred Circle Time
space to draw what you did or thought about."

(*2-minute transition time*) Place paper, crayons, and other supplies in the circle. Invite
the children, one at a time, to come and draw what they did, thought about, or
experienced.

(10 minutes) **Journal and Share Time**

Let them draw and journal as they gather. When most of the children have finished, let them begin to share. Remind the children that listening to one another is
important.

Say: "Thank you for spending time with me in the Trinity Stations. I cannot wait to hear what you experienced today. Who would like to share?" (Give each child time to talk, and you should talk as well.)

Place their activities in individual folders; or if they are to take the folders home, place them behind them so they will not be distracted. This will keep you from having to correct the children's behavior.

10 minutes (snack or toy time)

A Time of Blessing

Explain that the symbol for today is a heart because Easter is all about Jesus and his love! Bless the children where they request, being sure to look them directly in their eyes. Thank them and say, "You are a blessing!"

Closing Time

Slowly put each Trinity symbol away.

Say: "And now we are finished with our Sacred Circle Time. We put away our symbol for God, the Creator. We put away our symbol for God, the Son. And we put away our symbol for God, the Holy Spirit."

Then quietly and gently put the sacred cloth away.

Conclude: "And we are all done with our Sacred Circle time. You did a great job. Yay!" Clap and celebrate a job well done.

Fifty Days of Easter 6

Story: Jesus Asks Us to Love One Another

Text: Mark 12:31, NRSV

"The second is this, 'You shall love your neighbor as yourself.' There is no other commandment greater than these."

About the text: When questioned by religious authorities of the day about which commandment was the greatest, Jesus gave the "correct answer." He quoted the Shema that we learned in the last lesson. They must have been satisfied with his answer. As is typical for Jesus, he always pushed everyone into a deeper understanding of what love truly means. Because the Shema had become such a familiar and ritualized part of the Jewish faith, many people believed that posting it on their door and wearing it in the *tefillin* was all they needed to do. They had met the *requirement* of the Shema. Christ adds another sentence in his reply and says, "And you must love your neighbor as yourself." When he says this, he reminds them that loving God means loving others deeply. Jesus took what the people had come to believe was a familiar and easy Scripture to follow and reminded them that following God always calls them to deeper love of self and neighbors.

The Sacred Circle Time Focus: We will focus on Jesus asking us to love one another and that, the more we love, the more love grows.

Sacred Circle Time Basic Format

Sacred Circle basket and contents:

- Sacred space cloth
- Symbols for Creator (globe), Christ (cross), and Holy Spirit (bell or chimes)
- Small, unbreakable bottle to hold water or oil for the blessing
- A journal page (one per child)
- Crayons and/or markers
- A Bible bookmarked to Mark 12:31
- Focused objects from the Bible story: Red paper (About three sheets and scissors. If you don't have red paper, any color will do.)

The Lesson

Gathering

Begin by sitting down and placing the sacred basket in front of you. Pause so that the children notice it and begin to come closer.

Invite them to form a circle. Sit quietly until they settle in and are quiet.

Say: "It is time for Sacred Circle Time. I am so glad that you are here today. I love learning our stories and experiencing God with you."

Celebrating the Fifty Days of Easter

Explain that we celebrate for fifty days. We are happy because Jesus resurrected for fifty days. Say, "So let's count and clap with happy hands fifty times to celebrate Easter!" (*Clap and count to fifty.*)

Say: "Easter lasts for fifty days! Let's all say 'Happy Easter!' 1-2-3 . . ."

Everyone shouts "Happy Easter!"

Say: "And today is our last day to celebrate Easter until next year because the fifty days are almost over! As you know, we have been learning about love during Easter. Easter will end. Will God's love ever end?" (*Let them answer.*)

"No, love is always with us! Easter for this year will end, but love never ends, especially the love God and Jesus and the Holy Spirit have for us! That love goes on and on and never ends!"

Creating the Sacred Space

Say: "Let's create our sacred space."

Slowly lay out the sacred cloth.

Slowly lift the globe (symbol of God, the Creator) and hold it at the eye level of the children. Say: "This is our symbol for God, the Creator." Carefully lay it on the sacred cloth. (*Pause.*)

Slowly lift the cross (symbol of God, the Son). Say: "This is our symbol for God, the Son." Carefully lay it on the sacred cloth. (*Pause.*)

Slowly lift the bell (symbol of God, the Holy Spirit). Say: "This is our symbol of God, the Holy Spirit." Carefully lay it on the sacred cloth. (*Pause.*)

Point to each symbol and say: "So we have God, the Creator; God, the Son; and God, the Holy Spirit. (*Pause.*) Our sacred space is ready. We are ready to begin our Sacred Circle Time together."

God, the Creator (A Time to Wonder)

Say: "I have some paper, and I am going to use my scissors to cut out some hearts. I am going to cut different sizes." (*Cut several hearts of different sizes from very tiny to very large. The beautiful thing about young children is that they will marvel at the different sizes.*)

God, the Son (Telling the Story)

Say: "Our Scripture today is one sentence. It is found in Mark, chapter 12, verse 31. Let's see if we remember the special prayer called the *Shema* that is found in the Bible. Remember? Jesus tells us to love God with:

> Our whole heart (*place hands over heart*),
> Our whole soul (*move hands down in front of you from your head to the floor*)
> And with our whole mind (*point to temples*)
> God told us to love God with our whole self. This (*stretch your arms way, way up*) much!

"And then he tells us something else. He tells us to love one another as much as we love God. We are supposed to love one another with . . ." (*repeat the prayer and motions from above*).

"That is a lot of love. And do you know what happens with all that love? It grows bigger!

"We start with love and we give it to one another (*pass a little heart all the way around the circle*), and then (*pass the next large heart*) love grows; and we pass that love." (*Get the next largest heart out and pass it and continue until the children are amazed at how love that is shared grows bigger as we pass it to one another.*)

God, the Holy Spirit (Quiet and Prayer Time)

Say: "It is now time to pray. And for our prayer today I want us to show that we love one another. I am going to use one of the hearts we cut out and passed around. I am going to give it to one of you. When I give it to you, it is a way of saying, 'God loves you, and so do I.' But instead of using words to share God's love, we will just use the heart. I will give it to the first person, and then he (or she) will give it to someone else. We will do this until everyone has had the love of God shared with him or her."

You will need to be careful that no child is left out and make sure everyone gets the heart. The last child should give the heart back to you. After the heart has returned to you, say: "Thank you, God, that your love is given to everyone. Help us to share your love with everyone and to love others as you love us! Amen."

(If using the extended Sacred Circle Time, stop here.)

A Time of Blessing

Explain that the symbol for today is a heart because Easter is all about Jesus and his love! Bless the children where they request, being sure to look them directly in their eyes. Thank them and say, "You are a blessing!"

Closing Time

Slowly put each Trinity symbol away.

Say: "And now we are finished with our Sacred Circle Time. We put away our symbol for God, the Creator. We put away our symbol for God, the Son. And we put away our symbol for God, the Holy Spirit."

Then quietly and gently put the sacred cloth away.

Conclude: "And we are all done with our Sacred Circle time. You did a great job. Yay!" Clap and celebrate a job well done.

Extended Format

(10 minutes) Begin with free-play time. Greet the children warmly and let them get used to the space. Have something in the free-play space for them to play with. Rotate each week:

Week One: Paper and crayons, markers, or paint.

Week Two: Clay, wire, pipe cleaners and beads, and tools to work the clay.

Week Three: Things to build with: blocks, Legos®, cans, boxes, or flat stones.

Week Four: Things that make noise.

(*3 minutes*) Transition Time. Let the children know that it is almost Sacred Circle Time. Say: "It is almost our Sacred Circle Time. I cannot wait to have sacred time with you today. Will you start to finish up? Then come join me for our special, holy time together."

Sit down in the Sacred Circle Time space and place your sacred basket in front of you.

(*10 minutes*) **Sacred Circle Time** (*Basic format*)—Use the Sacred Circle Basic Format, but do not include the blessing or closing.

(*10 minutes*) **Trinity Stations**

Explain the Trinity Stations procedure for new children and for those who might forget from time to time.

Walk with the children to the Trinity Stations and show them what they can do in the stations, but do not let them start until they have seen all three stations.

Tell the children that after the Trinity Stations, they will spend five minutes in quiet time thinking about the story and the activities they have completed. They will then return to the Sacred Circle Time space to draw pictures and talk about their activities.

Station One: God, the Creator (Wonder) Station

Walk with the children to this station and show them what they can do here. In addition to the suggested supplies (page 469), you might want to have a Bible for the children to explore and touch.

Station Two: God, the Son (Story) Station

Walk with the children to this station and show them what they can do here. In addition to the suggested supplies (page 469), you might want to add some blessing water to let the children bless one another.

Station Three: God, the Holy Spirit (Prayer) Station

Walk with the children to this station and show them what they can do here. In addition to the suggested supplies (page 469), you might want to have the same photos from last week of people looking lonely and sad for the children to contemplate and pray about.

Begin Quiet Time

Say: "Let's begin five minutes of thinking about how much God loves us and how Jesus asks us to love one another. After five minutes, I will invite you to the Sacred Circle Time space to draw what you did or thought about."

(*2-minute transition time*) Place paper, crayons, and other materials in the circle. Invite the children, one at a time, to come and draw what they did, thought about, or experienced.

(*10 minutes*) **Journal and Share Time**

Let them draw and journal as they gather. When most of the children have finished, let them begin to share. Remind the children that listening to one another is important.

Say: "Thank you for spending time with me in the Trinity Stations. I cannot wait to hear what you experienced today. Who would like to share?" (Give each child time to talk, and you should talk as well.)

Place their activities in individual folders; or if they are to take the folders home, place them behind them so they will not be distracted. This will keep you from having to correct the children's behavior.

10 minutes (snack or toy time)

A Time of Blessing

Explain that the symbol for today is a heart because Easter is all about Jesus and his love! Bless the children where they request, being sure to look them directly in their eyes. Thank them and say, "You are a blessing!"

Closing Time

Slowly put each Trinity symbol away.

Say: "And now we are finished with our Sacred Circle Time. We put away our symbol for God, the Creator. We put away our symbol for God, the Son. And we put away our symbol for God, the Holy Spirit."

Then quietly and gently put the sacred cloth away.

Conclude: "And we are all done with our Sacred Circle time. You did a great job. Yay!" Clap and celebrate a job well done.

Pentecost Sunday

Story: Jesus Keeps His Promise to Send the Spirit

Text: Acts 2:1-4, NRSV

> When the day of Pentecost had come, they were all together in one place. And suddenly from heaven there came a sound like the rush of a violent wind, and it filled the entire house where they were sitting. Divided tongues, as of fire, appeared among them, and a tongue rested on each of them. All of them were filled with the Holy Spirit and began to speak in other languages, as the Spirit gave them ability.

About the text: Before Jesus died, he promised his disciples and followers that he would not leave them orphaned and alone. He died, was resurrected for fifty days, and then ascended into heaven. After he leaves, his followers do not know what to do next. This is clear because there is no record of activity. They do not teach, preach, or heal. And then on the Day of Pentecost (a Jewish agricultural celebration that happens each year fifty days after the Passover), the dramatic events of the Christian Pentecost happen. There is wind, fire, and speaking in different languages. It seems like a very confusing event and an event that was hard to describe with words. However, the result of these confusing events, is that the followers were transformed, and they were empowered to continue the ministry Jesus had begun. These same people had felt alone and scared, and now they were filled with courage, direction, and zeal. The Holy Spirit promised by Jesus had arrived. They were not alone.

The Sacred Circle Time Focus: Young children will not be able to understand the events of the Day of Pentecost. So rather than recreate the story, we will focus on the heart of the story: Jesus did not leave his followers alone. And the Holy Spirit is God with us.

Sacred Circle Time Basic Format

Sacred Circle basket and contents:

- Sacred space cloth
- Symbols for Creator (globe), Christ (cross), and Holy Spirit (bell or chimes)
- Small, unbreakable bottle to hold water or oil for the blessing
- A journal page (one per child)
- Crayons and/or markers
- A Bible bookmarked at Acts 2:1-4
- Focused object from the Bible story: A huggable stuffed animal

The Lesson

Gathering

Sit down and place the sacred basket in front of you.

Pause so that the children notice it and begin to come closer.

Invite them to form a circle.

Sit quietly until they settle in and are quiet.

Say: "It is almost time for our Sacred Circle. I am so glad that you are here today. I love learning our stories and experiencing God with you."

Celebrating that the Fifty Days of Easter Lead to Pentecost

Say: "Before we create our Sacred Circle, I want to remind you that Easter is such an important holiday that we celebrate at our church for fifty days! We are happy because

Jesus was resurrected for fifty days! And we have spent the last fifty days celebrating. Easter is now over. Today, after the fifty days of Easter, we have a new holiday. So let's count and clap with happy hands fifty times to celebrate Easter, and then let's see what happens at the end of Easter." (*Clap and count to fifty.*)

Say: "Easter lasts for fifty days; then we have a new holiday called the Day of Pentecost. Say that with me." (*Let them practice saying "Pentecost."*)

Say: "So for fifty days we celebrate Easter, and then today is Pentecost.

I am going to count to three and you can shout 'Happy Pentecost!' (*Count to three, and let them shout!*) And now, let's learn about what happened on Pentecost."

Creating the Sacred Space

Say: "First, we create our sacred space."

Slowly lay out the sacred cloth.

Slowly lift the globe (symbol of God, the Creator) and hold it at the eye level of the children. Say: "This is our symbol for God, the Creator." Carefully lay it on the sacred cloth. (*Pause.*)

Slowly lift the cross (symbol of God, the Son). Say: "This is our symbol for God, the Son." Carefully lay it on the sacred cloth. (*Pause.*)

Slowly lift the bell (symbol of God, the Holy Spirit). Say: "This is our symbol of God, the Holy Spirit." Carefully lay it on the sacred cloth. (*Pause.*)

Point to each symbol and say: "So we have God, the Creator; God, the Son; and God, the Holy Spirit. (*Pause.*) Our sacred space is ready. We are ready to begin our Sacred Circle Time together."

God, the Creator (A Time to Wonder)

Show the children the stuffed animal. Ask, "Do any of you have something you like to snuggle with?" (*Let them respond.*)

Ask: "How do you feel when you snuggle?"

Say: "We all need things to snuggle! They make us feel safe and warm and wonderful!"

God, the Son (Telling the Story)

"Say: Our story for today is found in the Book of Acts, chapter 2, verses 1-4. It is a happy story; but before I tell it, I have to tell you a sad story.

"Jesus and his followers and friends loved one another very much. Having Jesus with them felt like this stuffed animal feels when you snuggle with it. (*Hug the stuffed animal.*)

"All of Jesus' friends and followers loved having Jesus with them. (*Hug the stuffed animal again and demonstrate to the children how great it felt to have Jesus around by the enjoyment of the hug!*)

"But one day Jesus had to tell his friends and followers that he had to go away. They were very sacred and sad. Jesus told them, 'Do not be sad or scared. I promise that after I go away, I will send my spirit to be with you.' But they did not know what he meant, so they were sad. And then Jesus was hanged on the cross, and he died. (*Lay the stuffed animal on the ground and pause looking sadly at it.*)

"Everyone was so sad because Jesus had died, and they thought they would never feel his love again! But on the day of Pentecost, they were praying; and all of a sudden, a big wind came; and in that wind, Jesus sent his Holy Spirit to be with them.

"Jesus went to heaven to live with God. (*Move the stuffed animal behind you and pause, looking very sad, that the stuffed animal, Jesus, is gone.*) But, on the day of Pentecost, Jesus sent his spirit back to the people. (*Bring the stuffed animal back out and show it to the children.*) They did not get to see his body again, but his Spirit—the Holy Spirit— was with them, and they felt Jesus' love again!" (*Hug the stuffed animal tightly. And let the children clap and celebrate!*)

God, the Holy Spirit (Quiet and Prayer Time)

Say: "It is now time to pray. And for our prayer today, I am going to pass this stuffed animal around, and you can hug it and remember that Jesus' love is soft and warm and wonderful!" (*Pass the stuffed animal to each child.*)

Pray: "Dear God, thank you for sending the Holy Spirit on the Day of Pentecost, so that we can feel your love every day! In the name of Jesus, we pray. Amen."

(If using the extended Sacred Circle Time, stop here.)

A Time of Blessing

Explain that the symbol for today is a heart because Jesus loves us so much. Bless the children where they request, being sure to look them directly in their eyes. Thank them and say, "You are a blessing!"

Closing Time

Slowly put each Trinity symbol away.

Say: "And now we are finished with our Sacred Circle Time. We put away our symbol for God, the Creator. We put away our symbol for God, the Son. And we put away our symbol for God, the Holy Spirit."

Then quietly and gently put the sacred cloth away.

Conclude: "And we are all done with our Sacred Circle time. You did a great job. Yay!" Clap and celebrate a job well done.

Extended Format

(10 minutes) Begin with free-play time. Greet the children warmly and let them get used to the space. Have something in the free-play space for them to play with. Rotate each week:

Week One: Paper and crayons, markers, or paint.

Week Two: Clay, wire, pipe cleaners and beads, and tools to work the clay.

Week Three: Things to build with: blocks, Legos®, cans, boxes, or flat stones.

Week Four: Things that make noise.

(*3 minutes*) Transition Time. Let the children know that it is almost Sacred Circle Time. Say: "It is almost our Sacred Circle Time. I cannot wait to have sacred time with you today. Will you start to finish up? Then come join me for our special, holy time together."

Sit down in the Sacred Circle Time space and place your sacred basket in front of you.

(*10 minutes*) **Sacred Circle Time** (*Basic format*)—Use the Sacred Circle Basic Format, but do not include the blessing or closing.

(*10 minutes*) **Trinity Stations**

Explain the Trinity Stations procedure for new children and for those who might forget from time to time.

Walk with the children to the Trinity Stations and show them what they can do in the stations, but do not let them start until they have seen all three stations.

Tell the children that after the Trinity Stations, they will spend five minutes in quiet time thinking about the story and the activities they have completed. They will then return to the Sacred Circle Time space to draw pictures and talk about their activities.

Station One: God, the Creator (Wonder) Station

Walk with the children to this station and show them what they can do here. In addition to the suggested supplies (page 469), you might want to have some stuffed animals that have been "unstuffed." Let the children put the stuffing back in.

Station Two: God, the Son (Story) Station

Walk with the children to this station and show them what they can do here. In addition to the suggested supplies (page 469), you might want to add some stuffed animals for the children to play with.

Station Three: God, the Holy Spirit (Prayer) Station

Walk with the children to this station and show them what they can do here. In addition to the suggested supplies (page 469), you might want to have some soft objects for the children to touch and use as quiet prayer tools.

Begin Quiet Time

Say: "Let's begin five minutes of thinking about the Day of Pentecost and how Jesus sent his Spirit, so we can feel God's warm and wonderful love all the time. After five minutes, I will invite you to the Sacred Circle Time space to draw what you did or thought about."

(*2-minute transition time*) Place paper, crayons, and other materials in the circle. Invite the children, one at a time, to come and draw what they thought about or experienced.

(*10 minutes*) **Journal and Share Time**

Let them draw and journal as they gather. When most of the children have finished, let them begin to share. Remind the children that listening to one another is important.

Say: "Thank you for spending time with me in the Trinity Stations. I cannot wait to find out what you experienced today. Who would like to share?" (Give each child time to talk, and you should talk as well.)

Place their activities in individual folders; or if they are to take the folders home, place them behind them so they will not be distracted. This will keep you from having to correct the children's behavior.

10 minutes (snack or toy time)

A Time of Blessing

Explain that the symbol for today is a heart because Jesus loves us so much. Bless the children where they request, being sure to look them directly in their eyes. Thank them and say, "You are a blessing!"

Closing Time

Slowly put each Trinity symbol away.

Say: "And now we are finished with our Sacred Circle Time. We put away our symbol for God, the Creator. We put away our symbol for God, the Son. And we put away our symbol for God, the Holy Spirit."

Then quietly and gently put the sacred cloth away.

Conclude: "And we are all done with our Sacred Circle time. You did a great job. Yay!" Clap and celebrate a job well done.

About Ordinary Time in the Liturgical Calendar

The liturgical calendar is a calendar of seasons for the church. It begins with the life of Jesus as the central message: Advent, Christmas, events in his life, such as his baptism and temptation and then, of course his last supper, death, Resurrection, and ascension.

These special moments of his life are known as the high holy seasons and special Sundays. The rest of the year is called Ordinary Time. It is called Ordinary Time because the weeks are numbered (for example, First Sunday after Pentecost, Second Sunday after Pentecost, and so on). During this time, stories of all kinds are preached. The stories include some about Jesus and his teaching and ministry that are not included in the high holy season, many Old Testament stories, and the life and letters of Paul and the apostles. While these Sundays are referred to as Ordinary Time, they are hardly ordinary. Nothing in Scripture is ordinary. It is all holy and sacred.

In this resource, after the high holy season stories are used for Sacred Circle Time lessons, I have tried to move historically from the story of Creation through the Old Testament, introducing some of the main biblical figures. I have also included a few of the parables told by Jesus and some of the most central stories describing his ministry, such as the calming of the storm and the Last Supper. And I have included one story of Paul, the disciples, and the spread of Christianity throughout the world.

This is not an exhaustive journey through the Bible, but an introduction. Feel free to change the order of these stories as best fits with your own ministry setting. After you become more comfortable with the Sacred Circle format, you will be comfortable using it for any story you might want to include during the year.

Ordinary Time 1

Story: Creation (Part One . . . Light!)

Text: Genesis 1:1-5, NRSV

> In the beginning when God created the heavens and the earth, the earth was a formless void and darkness covered the face of the deep, while a wind from God swept over the face of the waters. Then God said, "Let there be light"; and there was light. And God saw that the light was good; and God separated the light from the darkness. God called the light Day, and the darkness he called Night. And there was evening and there was morning, the first day.

About the text: With all the heated discussions happening between those who believe that God literally created the world in seven days and those who believe that the world was created through billons of years of evolution, the Genesis text almost seems problematic to teach and, as a result, its powerful lessons risk being eliminated. We should not shy away from any Bible story because it is controversial, so I have included it here. The creation story is important because it asserts that from the very beginning, God's power and love was the source of all else. It also gives us a rich picture of God as the One who created people in God's own image and as such, our actions, deeds, and thoughts are meant to mirror God's love. It is such a central story that two lessons have been set aside to explore it.

The Sacred Circle Time Focus: The first time we explore this story, we will focus on the idea that everything comes from God. It is a central concept that is foundational as the children begin to grasp the power and awe of God.

Sacred Circle Time Basic Format

Sacred Circle basket and contents:

- Sacred space cloth
- Symbols for Creator (globe), Christ (cross), and Holy Spirit (bell or chimes)
- Small, unbreakable bottle to hold water or oil for the blessing
- A journal page (one per child)
- Crayons and/or markers
- A Bible bookmarked at Genesis 1:1-5
- Focused object from the Bible story: An empty box with a lid

The Lesson

Gathering

Sit down and place the sacred basket in front of you.

Pause so that the children notice it and begin to come closer.

Invite them to form a circle.

Sit quietly until they settle in and are quiet.

Say: "It is time for Sacred Circle Time. I am so glad that you are here today. I love learning our stories and experiencing God with you."

Creating the Sacred Space

Say: "First, we create our sacred space."

Slowly lay out the sacred cloth.

Slowly lift the globe (symbol of God, the Creator) and hold it at the eye level of the children. Say: "This is our symbol for God, the Creator." Carefully lay it on the sacred cloth. (*Pause.*)

Slowly lift the cross (symbol of God, the Son). Say: "This is our symbol for God, the Son." Carefully lay it on the sacred cloth. (*Pause.*)

Slowly lift the bell (symbol of God, the Holy Spirit). Say: "This is our symbol of God, the Holy Spirit." Carefully lay it on the sacred cloth. (*Pause.*)

Point to each symbol and say: "So we have God, the Creator; God, the Son; and God, the Holy Spirit. (*Pause.*) Our sacred space is ready. We are ready to begin our Sacred Circle Time together."

God, the Creator (A Time to Wonder)

Show the children the box with the lid on it. Ask, "What do you think is in the box?" (*Let them guess over and over. They will not guess that it is empty.*)

Say: "I will give you a hint. God used what I have in my box to make the whole world. What do you think God used?" (*They will guess lots of fun things.*)

God, the Son (Telling the Story)

Say: "Well, in our story today, which is found in (*open the Bible*) Genesis, chapter one, verses 1-5, we find God creating the whole world. And look . . . it is the very first story in the very first book in the Bible! It is an important story because it starts out the entire Bible!

"This important story begins with exactly what I have in this box. Nothing! It tells us that before the world was here, there were no people, no animals, no trees, no grass, no fish, no sun, no stars. There was only God and nothing else. Nothing!! This (*show them the empty box*) was all there was! And God took nothing and made everything!

"God was amazing and so powerful that God made everything out of nothing! I am going to try. Okay, what should I make?" (*Let the kids name something for you to make. Anything they say is fine.*)

271

Say: "Okay. I am going to use this nothing and make (*whatever they told you to make*)."

(*Pretend to make it.*)

Say: "Okay, I made (*whatever they told you to make*). What do you think?"

They will tell you that you didn't make anything.

Say: "Oh, you are right. I must have done something wrong. Let me try it again. What should I make this time?" (*Let the kids tell you, and try to make it.*)

Say: "You know what? I can't make something out of nothing. Only God could make something out of nothing. And God made the world. God made the trees, the sun, the moon, flowers, butterflies, children, food . . . God made everything out of nothing! God is so powerful and so amazing!"

God, the Holy Spirit (Quiet and Prayer Time)

Say: "It is now time to pray. For our prayer, we are going to do nothing except sit very still and be very quiet. This is called *contemplative prayer*, and it is a prayer time where we don't say anything. We just sit and see if we can feel God with us. So sit in a comfortable way and when I say, 'Dear God,' we will sit in silence for one minute."

"Dear God." (*Let them sit for about a minute.*)

Ask: "How did our contemplative prayer feel? Did any of you feel God near you?" (*Let them share.*)

Say: "God made the world out of nothing, and sometimes when we pray in silence and say nothing, we can feel God's love."

(**If using the extended Sacred Circle Time, stop here.**)

A Time of Blessing

Explain that the symbol for the story today is a world because God made the world out of nothing. Bless the children where they request, being sure to look them directly in their eyes. Thank them and say, "You are a blessing!"

Closing Time

Slowly put each Trinity symbol away.

Say: "And now we are finished with our Sacred Circle Time. We put away our symbol for God, the Creator. We put away our symbol for God, the Son. And we put away our symbol for God, the Holy Spirit."

Then quietly and gently put the sacred cloth away.

Conclude: "And we are all done with our Sacred Circle time. You did a great job. Yay!" Clap and celebrate a job well done.

Extended Format

(*10 minutes*) Begin with free-play time. Greet the children warmly and let them get used to the space. Have something in the free-play space for them to play with. Rotate each week:

Week One: Paper and crayons, markers, or paint.

Week Two: Clay, wire, pipe cleaners and beads, and tools to work the clay.

Week Three: Things to build with: blocks, Legos®, cans, boxes, or flat stones.

Week Four: Things that make noise.

(*3 minutes*) Transition Time. Let the children know that it is almost Sacred Circle Time. Say: "It is almost our Sacred Circle Time. I cannot wait to have sacred time with you today. Will you start to finish up? Then come join me for our special, holy time together."

Sit down in the Sacred Circle Time space and place your sacred basket in front of you.

(*10 minutes*) **Sacred Circle Time** (Basic Format)—Use the Sacred Circle Basic Format, but do not include the blessing or closing.

(*10 minutes*) **Trinity Stations**

Explain the Trinity Stations procedure for new children and for those who might forget from time to time.

Walk with the children to the Trinity Stations and show them what they can do in the stations, but do not let them start until they have seen all three stations.

Tell the children that after the Trinity Stations, they will spend five minutes in quiet time thinking about the story and the activities they have completed. They will then return to the Sacred Circle Time space to draw pictures and talk about their activities.

Station One: God, the Creator (Wonder) Station

Walk with the children to this station and show them what they can do here. In addition to the suggested supplies (page 469), you might want to add some boxes of all shapes and sizes or a globe for the children to look at.

Station Two: God, the Son (Story) Station

Walk with the children to this station and show them what they can do here. In addition to the suggested supplies (page 469), you might want to include clay so that the children can make the world.

Station Three: God, the Holy Spirit (Prayer) Station

Walk with the children to this station and show them what they can do here. In addition to the suggested supplies (page 469), you might want to add some nature items or pictures to help the children contemplate the wonder of God's world.

Begin Quiet Time

Say: "Let's begin five minutes of thinking about the story and how amazing and powerful God is to have created the entire world out of nothing. After five minutes, I will invite you to the Sacred Circle Time space to draw what you did or thought about, so we can all share together."

(*2-minute transition time*) Place paper, crayons, and other materials in the circle. Invite the children, one at a time, to come and draw what they thought about or experienced.

(*10 minutes*) **Journal and Share Time**

Let them draw and journal as they gather. When most of the children have finished, let them begin to share. Remind the children that listening to one another is important.

Say: "Thank you for spending time with me in the Trinity Stations. I cannot wait to find out what you experienced today. Who would like to share?" (Give each child time to talk, and you should talk as well.)

Place their activities in individual folders; or if they are to take the folders home, place them behind them so they will not be distracted. This will keep you from having to correct the children's behavior.

10 minutes (snack or toy time)

A Time of Blessing

Explain that the symbol for today is a world because God made the whole world out of nothing. Bless the children where they request, being sure to look them directly in their eyes. Thank them and say, "You are a blessing!"

Closing Time

Slowly put each Trinity symbol away.

Say: "And now we are finished with our Sacred Circle Time. We put away our symbol for God, the Creator. We put away our symbol for God, the Son. And we put away our symbol for God, the Holy Spirit."

Then quietly and gently put the sacred cloth away.

Conclude: "And we are all done with our Sacred Circle time. You did a great job. Yay!" Clap and celebrate a job well done.

Ordinary Time 2

Story: Creation (Part Two . . . Everything)

Text: Genesis 1:1-28, NRSV

In the beginning when God created the heavens and the earth, the earth was a formless void and darkness covered the face of the deep, while a wind from God swept over the face of the waters. Then God said, "Let there be light"; and there was light. And God saw that the light was good; and God separated the light from the darkness. God called the light Day, and the darkness he called Night. And there was evening and there was morning, the first day.

And God said, "Let there be a dome in the midst of the waters, and let it separate the waters from the waters." So God made the dome and separated the waters that were under the dome from the waters that were above the dome. And it was so. God called the dome Sky. And there was evening and there was morning, the second day.

And God said, "Let the waters under the sky be gathered together into one place, and let the dry land appear." And it was so. God called the dry land Earth, and the waters that were gathered together he called Seas. And God saw that it was good. Then God said, "Let the earth put forth vegetation: plants yielding seed, and fruit trees of every kind on earth that bear fruit with the seed in it." And it was so. The earth brought forth vegetation: plants yielding seed of every kind, and trees of every kind bearing fruit with the seed in it. And God saw that it was good. And there was evening and there was morning, the third day.

And God said, "Let there be lights in the dome of the sky to separate the day from the night; and let them be for signs and for seasons and for days and years, and let them be lights in the dome of the sky to give light upon the earth." And it was so. God made the two great lights—the greater light to rule the day and the lesser light to rule the night—and the stars. God set them in the dome of the sky to give light upon the earth, to rule over the day and over the night, and to separate the light from the darkness. And God saw that it was good. And there was evening and there was morning, the fourth day.

And God said, "Let the waters bring forth swarms of living creatures, and let birds fly above the earth across the dome of the sky." So God created the great sea monsters and every living creature that moves, of every kind, with which the waters swarm, and every winged bird of every kind. And God saw that it was good. God blessed them, saying, "Be fruitful and multiply and fill the waters in the seas, and let birds multiply on the earth." And there was evening and there was morning, the fifth day.

And God said, "Let the earth bring forth living creatures of every kind: cattle and creeping things and wild animals of the earth of every kind." And it was so. God made the wild animals of the earth of every kind, and the cattle of every kind, and everything that creeps upon the ground of every kind. And God saw that it was good.

Then God said, "Let us make humankind in our image, according to our likeness; and let them have dominion over the fish of the sea, and over the birds of the air, and over the cattle, and over all the wild animals of the earth, and over every creeping thing that creeps upon the earth."

So God created humankind in his image,
    in the image of God he created them;
    male and female he created them.

God blessed them, and God said to them, "Be fruitful and multiply, and fill the earth and subdue it; and have dominion over the fish of the sea and over the birds of the air and over every living thing that moves upon the earth."

About the text: The story of creation is a wonderful story because it shows the creative and playful side of God. Children delight in creating and playing, and they can relate well to this story. For many children, this will be their favorite Bible story and one they will remember for a very long time!

The Sacred Circle Time Focus: We will focus on the creativity and playfulness of God by creating together and enjoying and marveling about all that God has made.

Sacred Circle Time Basic Format

Sacred Circle basket and contents:

- Sacred space cloth
- Symbols for Creator (globe), Christ (cross), and Holy Spirit (bell or chimes)
- Small, unbreakable bottle to hold water or oil for the blessing
- A journal page (one per child)
- Crayons and/or markers
- A Bible bookmarked at Genesis 1:1-28
- Focused objects from the Bible story: Clay (several colors would be nice)

The Lesson

Gathering

Sit down and place the sacred basket in front of you.

Pause so that the children notice it and begin to come closer.

Invite them to form a circle.

Sit quietly until they settle in and are quiet.

Say: "It is time for Sacred Circle Time. I am so glad that you are here today. I love learning our stories and experiencing God with you."

Creating the Sacred Space

Say: "First, we create our sacred space."

Slowly lay out the sacred cloth.

Slowly lift the globe (symbol of God, the Creator) and hold it at the eye level of the children. Say: "This is our symbol for God, the Creator." Carefully lay it on the sacred cloth. (*Pause.*)

Slowly lift the cross (symbol of God, the Son). Say: "This is our symbol for God, the Son." Carefully lay it on the sacred cloth. (*Pause.*)

Slowly lift the bell (symbol of God, the Holy Spirit). Say: "This is our symbol of God, the Holy Spirit." Carefully lay it on the sacred cloth. (*Pause.*)

Point to each symbol and say: "So we have God, the Creator; God, the Son; and God, the Holy Spirit. (*Pause.*) Our sacred space is ready. We are ready to begin our Sacred Circle Time together."

God, the Creator (A Time to Wonder)

Begin by giving the children a small piece of the clay. Let them play with it. Ask them what they have made. Enjoy as they share what they have made with you.

Say: "You are so creative. I love all the fun and different things you made out of the clay. I am going to collect all the clay now and use it as I tell you our story for today."

God, the Son (Telling the Story)

Say: "In our story today, which is found in (*open the Bible*) Genesis, chapter one, verses 1-28, we find God creating the whole world. You remember how God made the world out of nothing? God had nothing; and out of that, God made the world! God is amazing and powerful!

"Today, I want to show you some of the things God made. I will make it, and you can guess it."

Make the following items: The world, a tree, a flower, a carrot, an apple, a dog, a bird, a fish, and a person. Do not worry about the quality of your artwork. The children will love guessing.

Say: "It took God six days to make everything that is in the world. God made the world. God made the trees. God made the flowers. God made vegetables. God made fruit. God made the fish. God made the birds. God made the animals and people. God made everything in the whole world in six days. And then do you know what God did? God took a nap. God worked so hard that God rested. And then God looked at everything God had made and said, 'It is good!' God made our good earth and everything in it."

God, the Holy Spirit (Quiet and Prayer Time)

Say: "It is now time to pray. For our prayer, we are going to thank God for the world. One at a time, I want you to say what you are thankful for. Then we will all say, 'Thank you God for (*whatever you said*).'"

Go around the circle and do this thankfulness prayer.

Pray: "Thank you, God, for the world and everything in it. You are so amazing and wonderful to have created everything. Thank you, God!"

(If using the extended Sacred Circle Time, stop here.)

A Time of Blessing

Explain that the symbol for today is a world because God made the world and everything in it. Bless the children where they request, being sure to look them directly in their eyes. Thank them and say, "You are a blessing!"

Closing Time

Slowly put each Trinity symbol away.

Say: "And now we are finished with our Sacred Circle Time. We put away our symbol for God, the Creator. We put away our symbol for God, the Son. And we put away our symbol for God, the Holy Spirit."

Then quietly and gently put the sacred cloth away.

Conclude: "And we are all done with our Sacred Circle time. You did a great job. Yay!" Clap and celebrate a job well done.

Extended Format

(*10 minutes*) Begin with free-play time. Greet the children warmly and let them get used to the space. Have something in the free-play space for them to play with. Rotate each week:

Week One: Paper and crayons, markers, or paint.

Week Two: Clay, wire, pipe cleaners and beads, and tools to work the clay.

Week Three: Things to build with: blocks, Legos®, cans, boxes, or flat stones.

Week Four: Things that make noise.

(*3 minutes*) Transition Time. Let the children know that it is almost Sacred Circle Time. Say: "It is almost our Sacred Circle Time. I cannot wait to have sacred time with you today. Will you start to finish up? Then come join me for our special, holy time together."

Sit down in the Sacred Circle Time space and place your sacred basket in front of you.

(*10 minutes*) **Sacred Circle Time** (*Basic Format*)—Use the Sacred Circle Basic Format, but do not include the blessing or closing.

(*10 minutes*) **Trinity Stations**

Explain the Trinity Stations procedure for new children and for those who might forget from time to time.

Walk with the children to the Trinity Stations and show them what they can do in the stations, but do not let them start until they have seen all three stations.

Tell the children that after the Trinity Stations, they will spend five minutes in quiet time thinking about the story and the activities they have completed. They will then return to the Sacred Circle Time space to draw pictures and talk about their activities.

Station One: God, the Creator (Wonder) Station

Walk with the children to this station and show them what they can do here. In addition to the suggested supplies (page 469), you might want to add some objects from nature (rock, sticks, leaves, shells) for the children to explore.

Station Two: God, the Son (Story) Station

Walk with the children to this station and show them what they can do here. In addition to the suggested supplies (page 469), you might want to include clay, so the children can make things that God would have made. Or they can pretend to be God and make crazy new things.

Station Three: God, the Holy Spirit (Prayer) Station

Walk with the children to this station and show them what they can do here. In addition to the suggested supplies (page 469), you might want to add some nature items or pictures for the children to contemplate the wonder of God's world.

Begin Quiet Time

Say: "Let's begin five minutes of thinking about the story and how amazing and powerful God is to have created the entire world out of nothing. After five minutes, I will invite to the Sacred Circle Time space to draw what you did or thought about."

(*2-minute transition time*) Place paper, crayons, and other material in the circle. Invite the children, one at a time, to come and draw what they did, thought about, or experienced.

(*10 minutes*) **Journal and Share Time**

Let them draw and journal as they gather. When most of the children have finished, let them begin to share. Remind the children that listening to one another is important.

Say: "Thank you for spending time with me in the Trinity Stations. I cannot wait to find out what you experienced today. Who would like to share?" (Give each child time to talk, and you should talk as well.)

Place their activities in individual folders; or if they are to take the folders home, place them behind them so they will not be distracted. This will keep you from having to correct the children's behavior.

10 minutes (snack or toy time)

A Time of Blessing

Explain that the symbol for today is a world because God made the whole world and everything in it. Bless the children where they request, being sure to look them directly in their eyes. Thank them and say, "You are a blessing!"

Closing Time

Slowly put each Trinity symbol away.

Say: "And now we are finished with our Sacred Circle Time. We put away our symbol for God, the Creator. We put away our symbol for God, the Son. And we put away our symbol for God, the Holy Spirit."

Then quietly and gently put the sacred cloth away.

Conclude: "And we are all done with our Sacred Circle time. You did a great job. Yay!" Clap and celebrate a job well done.

Ordinary Time 3

Story: Noah

Text: Genesis 6:18-22, NRSV

But I will establish my covenant with you; and you shall come into the ark, you, your sons, your wife, and your sons' wives with you. And of every living thing, of all flesh, you shall bring two of every kind into the ark, to keep them alive with you; they shall be male and female. Of the birds according to their kinds, and of the animals according to their kinds, of every creeping thing of the ground according to its kind, two of every kind shall come in to you, to keep them alive. Also take with you every kind of food that is eaten, and store it up; and it shall serve as food for you and for them." Noah did this; he did all that God commanded him.

About the Text: Whenever a story is long or told more than once in the Bible, it is a clue about its importance. The story of Noah is an important story. It is five chapters long, and it is told in two different versions. While we might never know what precisely happened during the great flood because of the two different versions, we know that this is an important story. It is one that we need to read, teach, and study. And while it is often considered a child's story, the destruction, anger of God, and corruption of the people of that time are not child-appropriate.

The Sacred Circle Time Focus: We will focus our Sacred Circle Time on Noah being obedient to God and working hard to follow God, and not so much on the evil or destruction that comes along with the telling of this story.

Sacred Circle Time Basic Format

Sacred Circle basket and contents:

- Sacred space cloth
- Symbols for Creator (globe), Christ (cross), and Holy Spirit (bell or chimes)
- Small, unbreakable bottle to hold water or oil for the blessing
- A journal page (one per child)
- Crayons and/or markers
- A Bible bookmarked at Genesis 6:18-22
- Focused objects from the Bible story: A bowl of water and several eye droppers. (If you don't have access to eye droppers, a large spoon will work as well.)

The Lesson

Gathering

Sit down and place the sacred basket in front of you.

Pause so that the children notice it and begin to come closer.

Invite them to form a circle.

Sit quietly until they settle in and are quiet.

Say: "It is time for Sacred Circle Time. I am so glad that you are here today. I love learning our stories and experiencing God with you."

Creating the Sacred Space

Say: "First, we create our sacred space."

Slowly lay out the sacred cloth.

Slowly lift the globe (symbol of God, the Creator) and hold it at the eye level of the children. Say: "This is our symbol for God, the Creator." Carefully lay it on the sacred cloth. (*Pause.*)

Slowly lift the cross (symbol of God, the Son). Say: "This is our symbol for God, the Son." Carefully lay it on the sacred cloth. (*Pause.*)

Slowly lift the bell (symbol of God, the Holy Spirit). Say: "This is our symbol of God, the Holy Spirit." Carefully lay it on the sacred cloth. (*Pause.*)

Point to each symbol and say: "So we have God, the Creator; God, the Son; and God, the Holy Spirit. (*Pause.*) Our sacred space is ready. We are ready to begin our Sacred Circle Time together."

God, the Creator (A Time to Wonder)

Place the bowl of water in front of you.

Ask: "What could we do with this water?"

Let the children think of all the things they could do: Drink it. Wash a pet in it. Mop the floor. Go swimming in it if they were very tiny. Listen and enjoy all the creative ideas they have.

Say: "All of those are such good ideas. I am going to use this water to make something. Watch and see what I make."

Get out the droppers, suck some of the water up, and drop the water back into the bowl.

Ask: "What is falling on the water?" (*Pause . . . they might guess and they might not.*) "Rain is falling on the water. Let's watch and see the ripples of the rain." (*Let them enjoy watching the rain drops fall into the bowl of water.*)

God, the Son (Telling the Story)

Say: "In our story today, which is found in (*open the Bible*) Genesis, the first book in the Bible, chapter six, verses 18-22, God decided to make rain fall for a long time on the earth. And God asked a man named Noah to build a big boat, called the ark. That boat was so big. And do you know why? God told Noah to make it big enough to hold two of every kind of animal on earth. That boat had to hold two elephants. Do you know how huge elephants are? That boat, the ark, had to hold two giraffes! What else did that big boat have to hold?" (*Let the children name as many animals as they can.*)

Say: "You are so smart to know about so many different kinds of animals! Now, do you think Noah had to work very long to build that ark? He did! Let's stand up and build an ark."

Do the following mime:

"First let's cut down trees." (*Have the children mime cutting down trees.*)

"Noah did what God asked him to do."

"Next, Let's make those trees into boards for the boat." (*Children mime doing this.*)

"Noah did what God asked him to do."

"Next, Let's hammer those boards together." (*Children mime hammering.*)

"Noah did what God asked him to do."

"Next, let's cover the boat with tar, so the water can't get in when the rain starts." (*Children mime covering the boat.*)

"Noah did what God asked him to do."

"Next, let's get all those animals. Let's get the little ones like mice and bugs!" (*Children mime gathering up little animals.*)

"Noah did what God asked him to do."

"Let's get the middle-sized ones, likes dogs and cats and monkeys and pigs and sheep and goats." (*Children mime gathering up these animals.*)

"Noah did what God asked him to do."

"Let's get the big animals now, like giraffes and elephants and hippopotamuses!" (*Children mime gathering up these animals.*)

"Noah did what God asked him to do."

"Oh, no . . . we have to get scary animals now, like tigers and mountain lions and snakes and big bears." (*Children mime gathering up these animals.*)

"Noah did what God asked him to do."

"Okay the boat is built, and everyone is on board." (*Have the children sit down.*)

"Noah did what God asked him to do."

God, the Holy Spirit (Quiet and Prayer Time)

Say: "It is now time to pray. Noah did what God asked him to do. And when he got on the boat and the rain started, he could relax and be still. I want you to just relax and be still for a few moments." (*Dip your hand in the water and let it drop, so that the sound of water helps the children relax.*)

Say: "God asked Noah to build the ark. Do you any of you feel that God is asking you to do anything?" (*Let them share.*)

Pray: "God, if you need us to help you with anything, please ask us just like you asked Noah. In the name of Christ, we pray. Amen."

(If using the extended Sacred Circle Time, stop here.)

A Time of Blessing

Explain that the symbol for today is water because the ark floated on the water for a long time. Bless the children where they request, being sure to look them directly in their eyes. Thank them and say, "You are a blessing!"

Extended Format

(*10 minutes*) Begin with free-play time. Greet the children warmly and let them get used to the space. Have something in the free-play space for them to play with. Rotate each week:

Week One: Paper and crayons, markers, or paint.

Week Two: Clay, wire, pipe cleaners and beads, and tools to work the clay.

Week Three: Things to build with: blocks, Legos®, cans, boxes, or flat stones.

Week Four: Things that make noise.

(*3 minutes*) Transition Time. Let the children know that it is almost Sacred Circle Time. Say: "It is almost our Sacred Circle Time. I cannot wait to have sacred time with you today. Will you start to finish up? Then come join me for our special, holy time together."

Sit down in the Sacred Circle Time space and place your sacred basket in front of you.

(*10 minutes*) **Sacred Circle Time** (*Basic Format*)—Use the Sacred Circle Basic Format, but not the blessing or closing.

(*10 minutes*) **Trinity Stations**

Explain the Trinity Stations procedure for new children and for those who might forget from time to time.

Walk with the children to the Trinity Stations and show them what they can do in the stations, but do not let them start until they have seen all three stations.

Tell the children that after the Trinity Stations, they will spend five minutes in quiet time thinking about the story and the activities they have completed. They will then return to the Sacred Circle Time space to draw pictures and talk about their activities.

Station One: God, the Creator (Wonder) Station

Walk with the children to this station and show them what they can do here. In addition to the suggested supplies (page 469), you might want to add a bowl of water and lots of cups, droppers, and spoons to allow the children to play in the water. Add some boats and things that either sink or float so that the children can experiment.

Station Two: God, the Son (Story) Station

Walk with the children to this station and show them what they can do here. In addition to the suggested supplies (page 469), you might want to include blocks or a big box to build a life-sized ark.

Station Three: God, the Holy Spirit (Prayer) Station

Walk with the children to this station and show them what they can do here. In addition to the suggested supplies (page 469), you might want to have some water and droppers, spoons, and cups to make soft noises as the children relax and spend time in prayer.

Begin Quiet Time

Say: "Let's begin five minutes of thinking about the story and how Noah did as God asked him and worked hard building that boat called an ark. After five minutes, I will invite you to the Sacred Circle Time space to draw what you did or thought about."

(2-minute transition time) Place paper, crayons, and other material in the circle. Invite the children, one at a time, to come and draw what they did, thought about, or experienced.

(10 minutes) **Journal and Share Time**

Let them draw and journal as they gather. When most of the children have finished, let them begin to share. Remind the children that listening to one another is important.

Say: "Thank you for spending time with me in the Trinity Stations. I cannot wait to find out what you experienced today. Who would like to share?" (Give each child time to talk, and you should talk as well.)

Place their activities in individual folders; or if they are to take the folders home, place them behind them so they will not be distracted. This will keep you from having to correct the children's behavior.

10 minutes (snack or toy time)

A Time of Blessing

Explain that the symbol for today is is water because the ark floated on the water for a long time. Bless the children where they request, being sure to look them directly in their eyes. Thank them and say, "You are a blessing!"

Closing Time

Slowly put each Trinity symbol away.

Say: "And now we are finished with our Sacred Circle Time. We put away our symbol for God, the Creator. We put away our symbol for God, the Son. And we put away our symbol for God, the Holy Spirit."

Then quietly and gently put the sacred cloth away.

Conclude: "And we are all done with our Sacred Circle time. You did a great job. Yay!" Clap and celebrate a job well done.

Ordinary Time 4

Story: Abraham and Sarah Are Called to Love God

Text: Genesis 12:1-5, NRSV

Now the LORD said to Abram, "Go from your country and your kindred and your father's house to the land that I will show you. I will make of you a great nation, and I will bless you, and make your name great, so that you will be a blessing. I will bless those who bless you, and the one who curses you I will curse; and in you all the families of the earth shall be blessed."

So Abram went, as the LORD had told him; and Lot went with him. Abram was seventy-five years old when he departed from Haran. Abram took his wife Sarah and his brother's son Lot, and all the possessions that they had gathered, and the persons whom they had acquired in Haran; and they set forth to go to the land of Canaan.

About the text: This story is central to our faith story because it becomes clear that God is the only God and that monotheism is what God requires. Abraham (Abram) and Sarah (Sarai) are asked to follow one God. They were asked to move to Canaan, a place known for worshiping many gods; and it is there that God asks them to live and begin worshiping the one true God.

The Sacred Circle Time Focus: We will focus on the idea that we have one God.

Sacred Circle Time Basic Format

Sacred Circle basket and contents:

- Sacred space cloth
- Symbols for Creator (globe), Christ (cross), and Holy Spirit (bell or chimes)
- Small, unbreakable bottle to hold water or oil for the blessing
- A journal page (one per child)
- Crayons and/or markers
- A Bible bookmarked at Genesis 12:1-5
- Focused object from the Bible story: A ball of clay

The Lesson

Gathering

Sit down and place the sacred basket in front of you.

Pause so that the children notice it and begin to come closer.

Invite them to form a circle.

Sit quietly until they settle in and are quiet.

Say: "It is time for Sacred Circle Time. I am so glad that you are here today. I love learning our stories and experiencing God with you."

Creating the Sacred Space

Say: "First, we create our sacred space."

Slowly lay out the sacred cloth.

Slowly lift the globe (symbol of God, the Creator) and hold it at the eye level of the children. Say: "This is our symbol for God, the Creator." Carefully lay it on the sacred cloth. (*Pause.*)

Slowly lift the cross (symbol of God, the Son). Say: "This is our symbol for God, the Son." Carefully lay it on the sacred cloth. (*Pause.*)

Slowly lift the bell (symbol of God, the Holy Spirit). Say: "This is our symbol of God, the Holy Spirit." Carefully lay it on the sacred cloth. (*Pause.*)

Point to each symbol and say: "So we have God, the Creator; God, the Son; and God, the Holy Spirit. (*Pause.*) Our sacred space is ready. We are ready to begin our Sacred Circle Time together."

God, the Creator (A Time to Wonder)

Use the ball of clay to do some simple math. Divide it in two halves and ask the children to count. Then divide it into more pieces, and have the children count the pieces. Keep dividing higher and higher and letting them count more and more pieces. The put the clay back together into one ball and have them count: one.

God, the Son (Telling the Story)

Say: "In our story today, which is found in (*open the Bible*) Genesis, chapter 12, verses 1-5, there are two people. One is named Abraham and one is named Sarah. And God tells them that they are to move to Canaan. Now Canaan was a beautiful place, but guess how many gods they had there?" (*Start dividing the clay ball into as many small pieces as you can. Make so many small pieces that the children cannot even count that high!*)

Say: "Canaan had this many gods . . . maybe even more! And Abraham and Sarah were asked to move there by God. And how many gods did Abraham and Sarah have?"

(*Gather all the clay back up into one ball.*)

"Abraham and Sarah had one God. The people who lived in Canaan thought there were many gods, but they were wrong. How many gods do we have?" (*Let the children say one God.*)

Shape the clay into a heart.

Say: "Abraham and Sarah had one God, and we still have one God; and God loves each of us so much!"

God, the Holy Spirit (Quiet and Prayer Time)

Say: "It is now time to pray. I am going to pass this heart around the circle. As you hold it, I want you to think about how much God, our one God, loves you and me and your friends and everyone in the whole world." (*Pass the heart to each child.*)

Pray: "God, thank you for loving everyone. Amen."

A Time of Blessing

Explain that the symbol for today is a heart because we have one God who loves us very much! Bless the children where they request, being sure to look them directly in their eyes.

Say: "Thank you for experiencing God with me today. You are a blessing!"

Extended Format

(*10 minutes*) Begin with free-play time. Greet the children warmly and let them get used to the space. Have something in the free-play space for them to play with. Rotate each week:

Week One: Paper and crayons, markers, or paint.

Week Two: Clay, wire, pipe cleaners and beads, and tools to work the clay.

Week Three: Things to build with: blocks, Legos®, cans, boxes, or flat stones.

Week Four: Things that make noise.

(*3 minutes*) Transition Time. Let the children know that it is almost Sacred Circle Time. Say: "It is almost our Sacred Circle Time. I cannot wait to have sacred time with you today. Will you start to finish up? Then come join me for our special, holy time together."

Sit down in the Sacred Circle Time space and place your sacred basket in front of you.

(*10 minutes*) **Sacred Circle Time** (*Basic Format*)—Use the Sacred Circle Basic Format, but do not include the blessing or closing.

(*10 minutes*) **Trinity Stations**

Explain the Trinity Stations procedure for new children and for those who might forget from time to time.

Walk with the children to the Trinity Stations and show them what they can do in the stations, but do not let them start until they have seen all three stations.

Tell the children that after the Trinity Stations, they will spend five minutes in quiet time thinking about the story and the activities they have completed. They will then return to the Sacred Circle Time space to draw pictures and talk about their activities.

Station One: God, the Creator (Wonder) Station

Walk with the children to this station and show them what they can do here. In addition to the suggested supplies (page 469), you might want to add clay, rolling pins, and cookie cutters and molds in different shapes.

Station Two: God, the Son (Story) Station

Walk with the children to this station and show them what they can do here. In addition to the suggested supplies (page 469), you might want to include some clay, so the children can use it to tell the story of Abraham and Sarah.

Station Three: God, the Holy Spirit (Prayer) Station

Walk with the children to this station and show them what they can do here. In addition to the suggested supplies (page 469), you might want to add some clay and some heart-shaped cookie cutters or heart objects to help the children reflect on God's love for them.

Begin Quiet Time

Say: "Let's begin five minutes of thinking about the story and how God asked Abraham and Sarah to go to Canaan, where there were so many gods. Think about how God is the only real God and how that same God loves us today. This is one God with so much love! After five minutes, I will invite you to the Sacred Circle Time space to draw what you did or thought about."

(2-minute transition time) Place paper, crayons, and other material in the circle. Invite the children, one at a time, to come and draw what they did, thought about, or experienced.

(10 minutes) **Journal and Share Time**

Let them draw and journal as they gather. When most of the children have finished, let them begin to share. Remind the children that listening to one another is important.

Say: "Thank you for spending time with me in the Trinity Stations. I cannot wait to find out what you experienced today. Who would like to share?" (Give each child time to talk, and you should talk as well.)

Place their activities in individual folders; or if they are to take the folders home, place them behind them so they will not be distracted. This will keep you from having to correct the children's behavior.

10 minutes (snack or toy time)

A Time of Blessing

Explain that the symbol for today is one heart because we have **one** God who loves us very much! Bless the children where they request, being sure to look them directly in their eyes.

Say: "Thank you for experiencing God with me today. You are a blessing!"

Closing Time

Slowly put each Trinity symbol away.

Say: "And now we are finished with our Sacred Circle Time. We put away our symbol for God, the Creator. We put away our symbol for God, the Son. And we put away our symbol for God, the Holy Spirit."

Then quietly and gently put the sacred cloth away.

Conclude: "And we are all done with our Sacred Circle time. You did a great job. Yay!" Clap and celebrate a job well done.

Ordinary Time 5

Story: Rebekah and Her Kindness

Text: Genesis 24:17-19, NRSV

Then the servant ran to meet her and said, "Please let me sip a little water from your jar." "Drink, my lord," she said, and quickly lowered her jar upon her hand and gave him a drink. When she had finished giving him a drink, she said, "I will draw for your camels also, until they have finished drinking."

About the text: Abraham and Sarah were blessed with a child in their old age, Isaac. As Abraham ages, it is important for Isaac to marry the right woman, because it is through their union that monotheism (belief in only one true God) will be passed on. The gift was given to Abraham and Sarah, and now it would be passed on through Rebekah and Isaac and then on and on.

The Sacred Circle Time Focus: Rebekah was chosen because of her kindness, thoughtfulness, and willingness to give to others.

Sacred Circle Time Basic Format

Sacred Circle basket and contents:

- Sacred space cloth
- Symbols for Creator (globe), Christ (cross), and Holy Spirit (bell or chimes)

- Small, unbreakable bottle to hold water or oil for the blessing
- A journal page (one per child)
- Crayons and/or markers
- A Bible bookmarked at Genesis 24:17-19
- Focused objects from the Bible story: A large bowl filled with water (about 10 cups) and one empty bowl; a cup; a picture of a camel or a toy stuffed camel

The Lesson

Gathering

Sit down and place the sacred basket in front of you.

Pause so that the children notice it and begin to come closer.

Invite them to form a circle.

Sit quietly until they settle in and are quiet.

Say: "It is time for Sacred Circle Time. I am so glad that you are here today. I love learning our stories and experiencing God with you."

Creating the Sacred Space

Say: "First, we create our sacred space."

Slowly lay out the sacred cloth.

Slowly lift the globe (symbol of God, the Creator) and hold it at the eye level of the children. Say: "This is our symbol for God, the Creator." Carefully lay it on the sacred cloth. (Pause.)

Slowly lift the cross (symbol of God, the Son). Say: "This is our symbol for God, the Son." Carefully lay it on the sacred cloth. (Pause.)

Slowly lift the bell (symbol of God, the Holy Spirit). Say: "This is our symbol of God, the Holy Spirit." Carefully lay it on the sacred cloth. (Pause.)

Point to each symbol and say: "So we have God, the Creator; God, the Son; and God, the Holy Spirit. (Pause.) Our sacred space is ready. We are ready to begin our Sacred Circle Time together."

God, the Creator (A Time to Wonder)

Show the children the stuffed camel and ask them what they know about camels. (*Let them tell you what they know.*)

Ask: "Do you know that there is a camel in the Bible?"

God, the Son (Telling the Story)

Say: "I am going to use this water, this cup, and the camel to tell you our Bible story (*open the Bible*), which is found in Genesis, chapter twenty-four, verses 17-19. Once there was a man named Abraham, who had son named Isaac. In those days, a daddy had to find the wife for his son to marry. So the daddy, Abraham, sent a servant out to find his son a very good wife! But the servant was scared because there were so many women to choose from. He wanted to find a very kind woman, but he was afraid he would not be able to tell who was kind and who was not kind. I mean, how would you know if someone was kind or not? Well, that is where the camel comes in. Did you know that camels drink a lot of water? They drink so much water! If we were going to give this camel a drink of water, he would not just drink one cup of water. He would drink so many cups of water! Count with me how many cups of water this camel drinks." (*One cup at a time, move the water from the full bowl to the empty one. Count as you go; be very dramatic as the camel "drinks" more and more water!!*)

"Wow, can you believe how much water a camel drinks? Now, back to our story. This servant needed to find a very kind woman who would be a very nice wife and mommy. And he did not know how he would know who was nice. But when he came to a city, there was a woman at a well with water in it. He was thirsty, so he asked, 'Will you please give me a drink of water?' And the woman gave him a drink. That was a kind thing to do, wasn't it? (*Let them respond.*) That was kind, but then she did something that was super kind. She said, 'I will also give your camel a drink of water.' And that was a lot of work for her . . . I mean, she had to give that camel so much water! And only a very kind woman would do that. And the servant knew because she gave the camel water that she was a very nice woman and a very kind woman and would be a very good wife and mommy. And her name was Rebekah. Because Rebekah gave the servant water, and because she also gave all of that water to the camel, the servant knew she had a very kind heart. And he chose her to marry Isaac."

God, the Holy Spirit (Quiet and Prayer Time)

Say: "Rebekah was very kind. And do you know what? You are very kind, as well. I see you do kind things for one another every time we are together. (*Name specific examples of kind things you have seen them do: share toys, clean up when you ask them to, come to Sacred Circle Time when asked, say 'thank you.' Be as specific as possible.*) You are very kind children. For our prayer time, I want to thank God for your kindness."

Look each child in the eye and say, "God, thank you for (*name of child*). He/she is very kind."

A Time of Blessing

Explain that the symbol for today is a heart because Rebekah had such a kind heart and the children have kind hearts as well. Bless the children where they request, being sure to look them directly in their eyes.

Say: "Thank you for experiencing God with me today. You are a blessing!"

Extended Format

(*10 minutes*) Begin with free-play time. Greet the children warmly and let them get used to the space. Have something in the free-play space for them to play with. Rotate each week:

Week One: Paper and crayons, markers, or paint.

Week Two: Clay, wire, pipe cleaners and beads, and tools to work the clay.

Week Three: Things to build with: blocks, Legos®, cans, boxes, or flat stones.

Week Four: Things that make noise.

(*3 minutes*) Transition Time. Let the children know that it is almost Sacred Circle Time. Say: "It is almost our Sacred Circle Time. I cannot wait to have sacred time with you today. Will you start to finish up? Then come join me for our special, holy time together."

Sit down in the Sacred Circle Time space and place your sacred basket in front of you.

(*10 minutes*) **Sacred Circle Time** (*Basic Format*)—Use the Sacred Circle Basic Format, but do not include the blessing or closing.

(*10 minutes*) **Trinity Stations**

Explain the Trinity Stations procedure for new children and for those who might forget from time to time.

Walk with the children to the Trinity Stations and show them what they can do in the stations, but do not let them start until they have seen all three stations.

Tell the children that after the Trinity Stations, they will spend five minutes in quiet time thinking about the story and the activities they have completed. They will then return to the Sacred Circle Time space to draw pictures and talk about their activities.

Station One: God, the Creator (Wonder) Station

Walk with the children to this station and show them what they can do here. In addition to the suggested supplies (page 469), you might want to have water and different sized bowls and cups for the children to fill.

Station Two: God, the Son (Story) Station

Walk with the children to this station and show them what they can do here. In addition to the suggested supplies (page 469), you might want to have a well (trash can) filled with water and a cup on a string to dip so that children can put water into the big bowl (labeled the camel bowl). This will help the children understand how hard Rebekah worked.

Station Three: God, the Holy Spirit Station

Walk with the children to this station and show them what they can do here. In addition to the suggested supplies (page 469), you might want to add pictures of people being kind to others and pictures of people not being kind to others. Let the children contemplate what kindness is.

Begin Quiet Time

Say: "Let's begin five minutes of thinking about the story and how the servant had to find a wife for Isaac and how he found Rebekah, who had a very kind heart. After five minutes, I will invite you, one at a time, to come to the Sacred Circle Time Space to draw what you did or thought about."

(*2-minute transition time*) Place paper, crayons, and other material in the circle. Invite the children, one at a time, to come and draw what they did, thought about, or experienced.

(*10 minutes*) Journal and Share Time

Let them draw and journal as they gather. When most of the children have finished, let them begin to share. Remind the children that listening to one another is important.

Say: "Thank you for spending time with me in the Trinity Stations. I cannot wait to find out what you experienced today. Who would like to share?" (Give each child time to talk, and you should talk as well.)

Place their activities in individual folders; or if they are to take the folders home, place them behind them so they will not be distracted. This will keep you from having to correct the children's behavior.

10 minutes (snack or toy time)

A Time of Blessing

Explain that the symbol for today is a heart because because Rebekah had such a kind heart and that the children are kind as well. Bless the children where they request, being sure to look them directly in their eyes.

Say: "Thank you for experiencing God with me today. You are a blessing!"

Closing Time

Slowly put each Trinity symbol away.

Say: "And now we are finished with our Sacred Circle Time. We put away our symbol for God, the Creator. We put away our symbol for God, the Son. And we put away our symbol for God, the Holy Spirit."

Then quietly and gently put the sacred cloth away.

Conclude: "And we are all done with our Sacred Circle time. You did a great job. Yay!" Clap and celebrate a job well done.

Ordinary Time 6

Story: Jacob's Ladder

Text: Genesis 28:10-19, NRSV

Jacob left Beersheba and went toward Haran. He came to a certain place and stayed there for the night, because the sun had set. Taking one of the stones of the place, he put it under his head and lay down in that place. And he dreamed that there was a ladder set up on the earth, the top of it reaching to heaven; and the angels of God were ascending and descending on it. And the LORD stood beside him and said, "I am the LORD, the God of Abraham your father and the God of Isaac; the land on which you lie I will give to you and to your offspring; and your off-spring shall be like the dust of the earth, and you shall spread abroad to the west and to the east and to the north and to the south; and all the families of the earth shall be blessed in you and in your offspring. Know that I am with you and will keep you wherever you go, and will bring you back to this land; for I will not leave you until I have done what I have promised you." Then Jacob woke from his sleep and said, "Surely the LORD is in this place—and I did not know it!" And he was afraid, and said, "How awesome is this place! This is none other than the house of God, and this is the gate of heaven."

So Jacob rose early in the morning, and he took the stone that he had put under his head and set it up for a pillar and poured oil on the top of it. He called that place Bethel; but the name of the city was Luz at the first.

About the text: In this story, Jacob is beginning his transformation from a man who does not really know God to someone who follows God. This is a powerful lesson for Jacob. His teacher was none other than God, who appeared to him in a dream. What was the lesson that Jacob learned through the dream? That God was with Jacob and would always be beside him. Since Jacob was such a rascal, we might expect that in the dream God would be correcting him. Instead, God assures him that God will always be near.

The Sacred Circle Time Focus: We will focus on God being with the children, just as God was with Jacob.

Sacred Circle Time Basic Format

Sacred Circle basket and contents:

- Sacred space cloth
- Symbols for Creator (globe), Christ (cross), and Holy Spirit (bell or chimes)
- Small, unbreakable bottle to hold water or oil for the blessing
- A journal page (one per child)
- Crayons and/or markers
- A Bible bookmarked at Genesis 28:10-19
- Focused objects from the Bible story: Assorted feathers

The Lesson

Gathering

Sit down and place the sacred basket in front of you.

Pause so that the children notice it and begin to come closer.

Invite them to form a circle.

Sit quietly until they settle in and are quiet.

Say: "It is time for Sacred Circle Time. I am so glad that you are here today. I love learning our stories and experiencing God with you."

Creating the Sacred Space

Say: "First, we create our sacred space."

Slowly lay out the sacred cloth.

Slowly lift the globe (symbol of God, the Creator) and hold it at the eye level of the children. Say: "This is our symbol for God, the Creator." Carefully lay it on the sacred cloth. (Pause.)

Slowly lift the cross (symbol of God, the Son). Say: "This is our symbol for God, the Son." Carefully lay it on the sacred cloth. (Pause.)

Slowly lift the bell (symbol of God, the Holy Spirit). Say: "This is our symbol of God, the Holy Spirit." Carefully lay it on the sacred cloth. (Pause.)

Point to each symbol and say: "So we have God, the Creator; God, the Son; and God, the Holy Spirit. (Pause.) Our sacred space is ready. We are ready to begin our Sacred Circle Time together."

God, the Creator (A Time to Wonder)

Show the children a feather and let them examine it. Talk about how gentle feathers are. Let the children rub the feather gently on their hands.

God, the Son (Telling the Story)

Say: "Our story today, which is found in (open the Bible) Genesis, chapter 28, verses 10-19, tells a story about a man named Jacob. Jacob was sort of naughty. He did things he was not supposed to do. He told lies. He tricked his brother. He was mean to his brother, and he ran away. And one night, he lay down and went to sleep, and he had a dream. And in the dream, a big ladder was beside him that stretched all the way into the sky, and angels were going up and down the ladder. (*Pretend that the feather is an angel going up and down a ladder.*) The angels went up the ladder and down the ladder . . .up and down . . . up and down. And then God was there right beside Jacob. And Jacob had been naughty and mean. What do you think God told him?" (*Let them guess.*)

"God wasn't mean to Jacob at all . . . even though Jacob had been naughty. God was gentle—as gentle as this feather. God said, 'Jacob I will always be with you.' And Jacob was so happy to be loved by God that he stopped being naughty, and he did what God told him to do."

God, the Holy Spirit (Quiet and Prayer Time)

Say: "It is now time to pray. God's love is very gentle. It is as gentle as a feather. I am going to pass this feather to each of you. When it is your turn, I want you to rub it very gently on your arm and remember how gentle God's love is for all of us." (*Pass the feather to each child.*)

Pray: "God, your love is so gentle. Thank you for loving us. Amen."

(If using the extended Sacred Circle Time format, stop here.)

A Time of Blessing

Say: "The symbol for the story today is a heart of love. Since God's love is so gentle, I am going to use the feather to gently bless you."

Ask: "Where would you like your blessing today?" (*Let them tell you.*)

Using the feather, make the symbol and look the children in their eyes.

Say: "Thank you for being here today and spending time experiencing God with me. You are a blessing!"

Extended Format

(*10 minutes*) Begin with free-play time. Greet the children warmly and let them get used to the space. Have something in the free-play space for them to play with. Rotate each week:

Week One: Paper and crayons, markers, or paint.

Week Two: Clay, wire, pipe cleaners and beads, and tools to work the clay.

Week Three: Things to build with: blocks, Legos®, cans, boxes, or flat stones.

Week Four: Things that make noise.

(*3 minutes*) Transition Time. Let the children know that it is almost Sacred Circle Time. Say: "It is almost our Sacred Circle Time. I cannot wait to have sacred time with you today. Will you start to finish up? Then come join me for our special, holy time together."

Sit down in the Sacred Circle Time space and place your sacred basket in front of you.

(*10 minutes*) **Sacred Circle Time** (*Basic Format*)—Use the Sacred Circle Basic Format, but do not include the blessing or closing.

(*10 minutes*) **Trinity Stations**

Explain the Trinity Stations procedure for new children and for those who might forget from time to time.

Walk with the children to the Trinity Stations and show them what they can do in the stations, but do not let them start until they have seen all three stations.

Tell the children that after the Trinity Stations, they will spend five minutes in quiet time thinking about the story and the activities they have completed. They will then return to the Sacred Circle Time space to draw pictures and talk about their activities.

Station One: God, the Creator (Wonder) Station

Walk with the children to this station and show them what they can do here. In addition to the suggested supplies (page 469), you might want to add some feathers and a magnifying glass and some bird books.

Station Two: God, the Son (Story) Station

Walk with the children to this station and show them what they can do here. In addition to the suggested supplies (page 469), you might want to include a stepladder for the children to climb and pretend to be the angels from the story.

Station Three: God, the Holy Spirit (Prayer) Station

Walk with the children to this station and show them what they can do here. In addition to the suggested supplies (page 469), you might have some soft objects (cotton ball, feathers, flowers) for the children to feel as they ponder the gentleness of God's love.

Begin Quiet Time

Say: "Let's begin five minutes of thinking about the story and how gentle God was to Jacob, even though Jacob had been very naughty. After five minutes, I will invite you to come to the Sacred Circle Time space to draw what you did or thought about."

(2-minute transition time) Place paper, crayons, and other material in the circle. Invite the children, one at a time, to come and draw what they did, thought about, or experienced.

(*10 minutes*) **Journal and Share Time**

Let them draw and journal as they gather. When most of the children have finished, let them begin to share. Remind the children that listening to one another is important.

Say: "Thank you for spending time with me in the Trinity Stations. I cannot wait to find out what you experienced today. Who would like to share?" (Give each child time to talk, and you should talk as well.)

Place their activities in individual folders; or if they are to take the folders home, place them behind them so they will not be distracted. This will keep you from having to correct the children's behavior.

10 minutes (snack or toy time)

A Time of Blessing

Explain that the symbol for today is a heart and that because God's love is so gentle you will use a feather to bless the children. Bless the children where they request, being sure to look them directly in their eyes.

Say: "Thank you for experiencing God with me today. You are a blessing!"

Closing Time

Slowly put each Trinity symbol away.

Say: "And now we are finished with our Sacred Circle Time. We put away our symbol for God, the Creator. We put away our symbol for God, the Son. And we put away our symbol for God, the Holy Spirit."

Then quietly and gently put the sacred cloth away.

Conclude: "And we are all done with our Sacred Circle time. You did a great job. Yay!" Clap and celebrate a job well done.

Ordinary Time 7

Story: Esau Forgives Jacob

Text: Genesis 33:1-4, NRSV

Now Jacob looked up and saw Esau coming, and four hundred men with him. So he divided the children among Leah and Rachel and the two maids. He put the maids with their children in front, then Leah with her children, and Rachel and Joseph last of all. He himself went on ahead of them, bowing himself to the ground seven times, until he came near his brother. But Esau ran to meet him, and embraced him, and fell on his neck and kissed him, and they wept.

About the text: Jacob, being second born, had no rights to his father's inheritance. It belonged to Esau, the oldest son. However, Jacob's mother and he came up with an elaborate plot; and Isaac accidentally gave his blessing to Jacob instead of Esau. Jacob was forced to run away because of Esau's anger. After living in a foreign land, Jacob wants to return home. He is afraid, though, because he is unsure of his brother's reaction. In this text, he is returning home to beg for his brother's forgiveness. It is a beautiful story of forgiveness.

The Sacred Circle Time Focus: We will focus on the ideas of anger and forgiveness.

Sacred Circle Time Basic Format

Sacred Circle basket and contents:

- Sacred space cloth
- Symbols for Creator (globe), Christ (cross), and Holy Spirit (bell or chimes)
- Small, unbreakable bottle to hold water or oil for the blessing
- A journal page (one per child)
- Crayons and/or markers
- A Bible bookmarked at Genesis 33:1-4

The Lesson

Gathering

Sit down and place the sacred basket in front of you.

Pause so that the children notice it and begin to come closer.

Invite them to form a circle.

Sit quietly until they settle in and are quiet.

Say: "It is time for Sacred Circle Time. I am so glad that you are here today. I love learning our stories and experiencing God with you."

Creating the Sacred Space

Say: "First, we create our sacred space."

Slowly lay out the sacred cloth.

Slowly lift the globe (symbol of God, the Creator) and hold it at the eye level of the children. Say: "This is our symbol for God, the Creator." Carefully lay it on the sacred cloth. (Pause.)

Slowly lift the cross (symbol of God, the Son). Say: "This is our symbol for God, the Son." Carefully lay it on the sacred cloth. (Pause.)

Slowly lift the bell (symbol of God, the Holy Spirit). Say: "This is our symbol of God, the Holy Spirit." Carefully lay it on the sacred cloth. (*Pause.*)

Point to each symbol and say: "So we have God, the Creator; God, the Son; and God, the Holy Spirit. (*Pause.*) Our sacred space is ready. We are ready to begin our Sacred Circle Time together."

God, the Creator (A Time to Wonder)

Ask: "What does a happy face look like? Can you show me by making one?" (*The children show their happy faces.*)

"What does a surprised face look like?" (*They children show you.*)

"What does a sad face look like?" (*The children show you.*)

"What does an angry face look like? (*They will show you.*)

"I mean a really angry face . . . Can you show me a really angry face? (*They will show you.*)

"Now . . . I want you to show me a REALLY, REALLY angry face!" (*They will show you.*)

God, the Son (Telling the Story)

Say: "In our story today, which is found in the book of Genesis (*open the Bible*), chapter 33, verses 1-4, we learn about two brothers named Jacob and Esau. Jacob did something terrible to his brother. He stole something very important called a birthright. And guess what? Esau got so mad at Jacob! Show me your angry faces. (*The children show their angry faces.*) No . . . he got much angrier than that. Show me your really, really angry faces. (*They show their angry faces again.*) Yes . . . Esau got THAT angry at Jacob, and Jacob ran away because he was so scared! And he stayed away for a very long time.

"While Jacob was away, he wondered if Esau was still mad. But he missed his brother and his family, and he was sorry. So he went home; and while he was walking home, he saw Esau far away.

"Now, do you remember how angry Esau was at his brother? Show me. (*They will make their very angry faces.*) Yes, you are right, Esau was that angry at Jacob. And Jacob came right up to Esau. They were very close. And do you know what Esau, who had been so angry, did? (*Let them guess.*) Esau had been so angry. Remember? Show me. (*Let them show you.*) And when Esau and Jacob were very close . . . Esau hugged Jacob and forgave him. And what do you think Esau's face looked like after he forgave his brother and gave him a big hug? Show me. (*Let them show you their happy faces.*) Yes, after Esau forgave his brother, he was very happy."

God, the Holy Spirit (Quiet and Prayer Time)

Say: "It is now time to pray. Let's begin by making our angry faces. (*Give them a few seconds of silence.*) God, when we get hurt and angry, help us to remember that forgiveness makes us smile." (*Give them a few seconds, and they will smile.*)

Pray: "God, please be close to all of us and those we love. In the name of Christ, we pray. Amen."

A Time of Blessing

Explain that the symbol for today is a smile because when we forgive, it makes us smile! Bless the children where they request, being sure to look them directly in their eyes.

Say: "Thank you for experiencing God with me today. You are a blessing!"

Extended Format

(*10 minutes*) Begin with free-play time. Greet the children warmly and let them get used to the space. Have something in the free-play space for them to play with. Rotate each week:

Week One: Paper and crayons, markers, or paint.

Week Two: Clay, wire, pipe cleaners and beads, and tools to work the clay.

Week Three: Things to build with: blocks, Legos®, cans, boxes, or flat stones.

Week Four: Things that make noise.

(*3 minutes*) Transition Time. Let the children know that it is almost Sacred Circle Time. Say: "It is almost our Sacred Circle Time. I cannot wait to have sacred time with you today. Will you start to finish up? Then come join me for our special, holy time together."

Sit down in the Sacred Circle Time space and place your sacred basket in front of you.

(*10 minutes*) **Sacred Circle Time** (*Basic Format*)—Use the Sacred Circle Basic Format, but do not include the blessing or closing.

(*10 minutes*) **Trinity Stations**

Explain the Trinity Stations procedure for new children and for those who might forget from time to time.

Walk with the children to the Trinity Stations and show them what they can do in the stations, but do not let them start until they have seen all three stations.

Tell the children that after the Trinity Stations, they will spend five minutes in quiet time thinking about the story and the activities they have completed. They will then return to the Sacred Circle Time space to draw pictures and talk about their activities.

Station One: God, the Creator (Wonder) Station

Walk with the children to this station and show them what they can do here. In addition to the suggested supplies (page 469), you might want to add mirrors so that the children can see how their faces change when they pretend to have different feelings.

Station Two: God, the Son (Story) Station

Walk with the children to this station and show them what they can do here. See the suggested supplies (page 469). Help the children act out the story of forgiveness.

Station Three: God, the Holy Spirit (Prayer) Station

Walk with the children to this station and show them what they can do here. In addition to the suggested supplies (page 469), you might want to include some pictures of people arguing and people hugging, so the children can think about anger and forgiveness.

Begin Quiet Time

Instruct the children to begin five minutes of quiet time to think about the Bible story. Explain that after the time has elapsed, you will invite them, one at a time, to the Sacred Circle Time space to draw what they did or thought about.

(2-minute transition time) Place paper, crayons, and other material in the circle. Invite the children, one at a time, to come and draw what they did, thought about, or experienced.

(10 minutes) **Journal and Share Time**

Let them draw and journal as they gather. When most of the children have finished, let them begin to share. Remind the children that listening to one another is important.

Say: "Thank you for spending time with me in the Trinity Stations. I cannot wait to find out what you experienced today. Who would like to share?" (Give each child time to talk, and you should talk as well.)

Place their activities in individual folders; or if they are to take the folders home, place them behind them so they will not be distracted. This will keep you from having to correct the children's behavior.

10 minutes (snack or toy time)

A Time of Blessing

Explain that the symbol for today is a smile because when we forgive, it makes us smile! Bless the children where they request, being sure to look them directly in their eyes.

Say: "Thank you for experiencing God with me today. You are a blessing!"

Closing Time

Slowly put each Trinity symbol away.

Say: "And now we are finished with our Sacred Circle Time. We put away our symbol for God, the Creator. We put away our symbol for God, the Son. And we put away our symbol for God, the Holy Spirit."

Then quietly and gently put the sacred cloth away.

Conclude: "And we are all done with our Sacred Circle time. You did a great job. Yay!" Clap and celebrate a job well done.

Ordinary Time 8

Story: Queen Esther

Text: Esther 7:1-4a, (NRSV)

> So the king and Haman went in to feast with Queen Esther. On the second day, as they were drinking wine, the king again said to Esther, "What is your petition, Queen Esther? It shall be granted you. And what is your request? Even to the half of my kingdom, it shall be fulfilled." Then Queen Esther answered, "If I have won your favor, O king, and if it pleases the king, let my life be given me—that is my petition—and the lives of my people—that is my request. For we have been sold, I and my people, to be destroyed, to be killed, and to be annihilated.

About the text: The book of Esther is a wonderful story, but it is much too long and confusing for young children to follow and understand. The heart of the story is that Haman hated Jews and wanted them to be annihilated. He convinced the king to follow his plan until Queen Esther, who was Jewish (the king did not know it), risked everything to save her people. She risked being killed by the king to save her own people. But the king loved her and spared her life and the lives of all the Jews in the kingdom.

The Sacred Circle Time Focus: We will focus on the bravery of Queen Esther to tell the truth.

Sacred Circle Time Basic Format

Sacred Circle basket and contents:

- Sacred space cloth
- Symbols for Creator (globe), Christ (cross), and Holy Spirit (bell or chimes)
- Small, unbreakable bottle to hold water or oil for the blessing
- A journal page (one per child)
- A Bible bookmarked at Esther 7:1-4a
- Focused object from the Bible story: Something broken

The Lesson

Gathering

Sit down and place the sacred basket in front of you.

Pause so that the children notice it and begin to come closer.

Invite them to form a circle.

Sit quietly until they settle in and are quiet.

Say: "It is time for Sacred Circle Time. I am so glad that you are here today. I love learning our stories and experiencing God with you."

Creating the Sacred Space

Say: "First, we create our sacred space."

Slowly lay out the sacred cloth.

Slowly lift the globe (symbol of God, the Creator) and hold it at the eye level of the children. Say: "This is our symbol for God, the Creator." Carefully lay it on the sacred cloth. *(Pause.)*

Slowly lift the cross (symbol of God, the Son). Say: "This is our symbol for God, the Son." Carefully lay it on the sacred cloth. *(Pause.)*

Slowly lift the bell (symbol of God, the Holy Spirit). Say: "This is our symbol of God, the Holy Spirit." Carefully lay it on the sacred cloth. (*Pause.*)

Point to each symbol and say: "So we have God, the Creator; God, the Son; and God, the Holy Spirit. (*Pause.*) Our sacred space is ready. We are ready to begin our Sacred Circle Time together."

God, the Creator (A Time to Wonder)

Say: "I have something to show you. (*Show them the broken object.*) Do you think I can fix this?" (*Let them look and try to help you fix it, while you act very worried.*)

Say: "This isn't mine. It belongs to someone else . . . should I tell my friend that I broke this? Should I tell the truth or just keep it a secret and hope my friend doesn't notice that I broke this?" (*Let the children give you advice. Just listen. Do not correct them.*)

God, the Son (Telling the Story)

Say: "In our story today, which is found (*open the Bible*) in Esther, chapter 7, verses 1-4a, there is a queen named Esther and a mean man named Haman who wants to kill Esther and her family. He was so mean. And Esther had a secret. She had never told her husband, the king, that she was Jewish. And if she told him the truth, she knew that the king might kill her. But if she kept her secret, the king might kill her family. What do you think Esther did? Do you think she kept the secret or told the truth? (*Let the children guess.*) Esther told the truth. And do you know that Queen Esther was very brave for telling the truth? She could have lied, but she told the truth. And the king saw how brave she was, and he loved her, so he did not kill her or her family. And Esther learned that telling the truth is a very good thing, but it takes lots of courage."

God, the Holy Spirit (Quiet and Prayer Time)

Say: "It is now time to pray. We are going to do a prayer called a "breath prayer," and we are going to breathe in courage and breathe out fear. You know, we all get scared sometimes; and this is good prayer to pray when we are scared. When you need courage, just breathe in courage and breathe out your fear." (*Do this prayer a few times. Breathe in courage and breathe out fear. Then sit in silence for a few moments.*)

Pray: "God, when we are afraid, help us to remember the courage of Queen Esther. She was very brave. Her courage helped her tell the truth. Amen."

(If using the extended Sacred Circle Time format, stop here.)

A Time of Blessing

Explain that the symbol for today is a cross, because Jesus—like Queen Esther—was very brave when he died for us. Bless the children where they request, being sure to look them directly in their eyes.

Say: "Thank you for experiencing God with me today. You are a blessing!"

Extended Format

(*10 minutes*) Begin with free-play time. Greet the children warmly and let them get used to the space. Have something in the free-play space for them to play with. Rotate each week:

Week One: Paper and crayons, markers, or paint.

Week Two: Clay, wire, pipe cleaners and beads, and tools to work the clay.

Week Three: Things to build with: blocks, Legos®, cans, boxes, or flat stones.

Week Four: Things that make noise.

(*3 minutes*) Transition Time. Let the children know that it is almost Sacred Circle Time. Say: "It is almost our Sacred Circle Time. I cannot wait to have sacred time with you today. Will you start to finish up? Then come join me for our special, holy time together."

Sit down in the Sacred Circle Time space and place your sacred basket in front of you.

(*10 minutes*) **Sacred Circle Time** (*Basic Format*)—Use the Sacred Circle Basic Format, but do not include the blessing or closing.

(*10 minutes*) **Trinity Stations**

Explain the Trinity Stations procedure for new children and for those who might forget from time to time.

Walk with the children to the Trinity Stations and show them what they can do in the stations, but do not let them start until they have seen all three stations.

Tell the children that after the Trinity Stations, they will spend five minutes in quiet time thinking about the story and the activities they have completed. They will then return to the Sacred Circle Time space to draw pictures and talk about their activities.

Station One: God, the Creator (Wonder) Station

Walk with the children to this station and show them what they can do here. In addition to the suggested supplies (page 469), you might want to add some broken things that the children can try to fix, such as broken toys, a broken vase, or a torn picture. Include supplies to make the repairs, such as a small hammer and nails, glue, and clear tape.

Station Two: God, the Son (Story) Station

Walk with the children to this station and show them what they can do here. In addition to the suggested supplies (page 469), you might want to include crowns so the children can pretend to be the king and Queen Esther.

Station Three: God, the Holy Spirit (Prayer) Station

Walk with the children to this station and show them what they can do here. In addition to the suggested supplies (page 469), you might want to have some paints and markers and instruct the children to draw what they think courage looks like.

Begin Quiet Time

Instruct the children to begin five minutes of quiet time to think about the Bible story. Explain that after the time has elapsed, you will invite them, one at a time, to the Sacred Circle Time space to draw what they did or thought about.

(2-minute transition time) Place paper, crayons, and other material in the circle. Invite the children, one at a time, to come and draw what they did, thought about, or experienced.

(10 minutes) Journal and Share Time

Let them draw and journal as they gather. When most of the children have finished, let them begin to share. Remind the children that listening to one another is important.

Say: "Thank you for spending time with me in the Trinity Stations. I cannot wait to find out what you experienced today. Who would like to share?" (Give each child time to talk, and you should talk as well.)

Place their activities in individual folders; or if they are to take the folders home, place them behind them so they will not be distracted. This will keep you from having to correct the children's behavior.

10 minutes (snack or toy time)

A Time of Blessing

Explain that the symbol for today is a cross, because Jesus—like Queen Esther—was very brave when he died for us. Bless the children where they request, being sure to look them directly in their eyes.

Say: "Thank you for experiencing God with me today. You are a blessing!"

Closing Time

Slowly put each Trinity symbol away.

Say: "And now we are finished with our Sacred Circle Time. We put away our symbol for God, the Creator. We put away our symbol for God, the Son. And we put away our symbol for God, the Holy Spirit."

Then quietly and gently put the sacred cloth away.

Conclude: "And we are all done with our Sacred Circle time. You did a great job. Yay!" Clap and celebrate a job well done.

Ordinary Time 9

Story: Joseph

Text: Genesis 37:3, NRSV

> Now Israel loved Joseph more than any other of his children, because he was the son of his old age; and he had made him a long robe with sleeves.

About the text: The story of Joseph is a great one, but it is very long and has a complex plot that includes favoritism, jealousy, a false accusation of sexual misconduct, slavery, and prison life. Much of this story is over the heads of young children, and it is much too long for Sacred Circle Time. However, it is important to mention Joseph because he is a central character in the Old Testament as one who kept his faith, even when perhaps he felt abandoned by God. Joseph was called by God and special to his father. He was very loved.

The Sacred Circle Time Focus: We will focus on God's love that is always there, even when we cannot see it.

Sacred Circle Time Basic Format

Sacred Circle basket and contents:

- Sacred space cloth
- Symbols for Creator (globe), Christ (cross), and Holy Spirit (bell or chimes)

- Small, unbreakable bottle to hold water or oil for the blessing
- A journal page (one per child)
- Crayons and/or markers
- A Bible bookmarked at Genesis 37:3
- Focused objects from the Bible story: A sheet of paper and crayons of all colors

The Lesson

Gathering

Sit down and place the sacred basket in front of you.

Pause so that the children notice it and begin to come closer.

Invite them to form a circle.

Sit quietly until they settle in and are quiet.

Say: "It is time for Sacred Circle Time. I am so glad that you are here today. I love learning our stories and experiencing God with you."

Creating the Sacred Space

Say: "First, we create our sacred space."

Slowly lay out the sacred cloth.

Slowly lift the globe (symbol of God, the Creator) and hold it at the eye level of the children. Say: "This is our symbol for God, the Creator." Carefully lay it on the sacred cloth. (Pause.)

Slowly lift the cross (symbol of God, the Son). Say: "This is our symbol for God, the Son." Carefully lay it on the sacred cloth. (Pause.)

Slowly lift the bell (symbol of God, the Holy Spirit). Say: "This is our symbol of God, the Holy Spirit." Carefully lay it on the sacred cloth. (Pause.)

Point to each symbol and say: "So we have God, the Creator; God, the Son; and God, the Holy Spirit. (Pause.) Our sacred space is ready. We are ready to begin our Sacred Circle Time together."

God, the Creator (A Time to Wonder)

Say: "I have box of crayons, and it has so many colors in it. I am going to color on this sheet of paper, and you can tell me what the colors are."

(Fill the sheet of paper with different colors, and let the children name the colors as you use them. Do this until the sheet of paper is filled with colors.)

"Wow . . . this is beautiful. Look at the colors."

God, the Son (Telling the Story)

Say: "Our story today, which is found in (open the Bible) Genesis, chapter 37, verse 3, is about a boy named Joseph who had a coat of many colors. His daddy had it made for him, and he felt very special in his coat. And he was special. But not because of his coat of many colors. He was special for the same reason you are special. He was special because he had a parent who loved him very much. Who loves you very much? (Let them share.)

"Poor Joseph. He felt so special in his coat, but life was hard on him. First of all, his brothers felt jealous of his coat, and they were mean to him (fold a little of the piece of paper so the colors are gone). And he ended up living far away from his family (fold a little more of the paper). And somebody told a lie about him (fold more of the paper). And he had to go to jail, even though he didn't do anything wrong (fold more of the paper). Poor Joseph. He did not feel special anymore. But he was! God was with him, and he got out jail (unfold some of the paper). And he got to be the boss of the kingdom (unfold more), and his brothers said they were sorry (unfold more), and he got to live with his daddy again" (unfold the paper so that all the colors show again).

God, the Holy Spirit (Quiet and Prayer Time)

Say: "It is now time to pray. Did you know that none of us will have a perfect life? Sad things will happen to all of us, and sometimes we might wonder if God still loves us. (Fold the paper so that none of the colors show.) But when you feel like this, remember

Joseph and that God always loved him. I am going to pass this paper around. As you hold it, the rest of us will say, 'God loves you and always will.'" (*Pass the paper to each child and have everyone say the phrase.*)

Pray: "God, thank you for always loving us. Amen."

A Time of Blessing

Explain that the symbol for today is a rainbow because the rainbow has so many colors in it just like Joseph's special coat. The rainbow reminds us that God will always love us.

Bless the children where they request, being sure to look them directly in their eyes.

Say: "Thank you for experiencing God with me today. You are a blessing!"

Extended Format

(*10 minutes*) Begin with free-play time. Greet the children warmly and let them get used to the space. Have something in the free-play space for them to play with. Rotate each week:

Week One: Paper and crayons, markers, or paint.

Week Two: Clay, wire, pipe cleaners and beads, and tools to work the clay.

Week Three: Things to build with: blocks, Legos®, cans, boxes, or flat stones.

Week Four: Things that make noise.

(*3 minutes*) Transition Time. Let the children know that it is almost Sacred Circle Time. Say: "It is almost our Sacred Circle Time. I cannot wait to have sacred time with you today. Will you start to finish up? Then come join me for our special, holy time together."

Sit down in the Sacred Circle Time space and place your sacred basket in front of you.

(*10 minutes*) **Sacred Circle Time** (*Basic Format*)—Use the Sacred Circle Basic Format, but do not include the blessing or closing.

(*10 minutes*) **Trinity Stations**

Explain the Trinity Stations procedure for new children and for those who might forget from time to time.

Walk with the children to the Trinity Stations and show them what they can do in the stations, but do not let them start until they have seen all three stations.

Tell the children that after the Trinity Stations, they will spend five minutes in quiet time thinking about the story and the activities they have completed. They will then return to the Sacred Circle Time space to draw pictures and talk about their activities.

Station One: God, the Creator (Wonder) Station

Walk with the children to this station and show them what they can do here. In addition to the suggested supplies (page 469), you you might want to add some water cups and food coloring, so that the children can experiment with changing colors in the water.

Station Two: God, the Son (Story) Station

Walk with the children to this station and show them what they can do here. In addition to the suggested supplies (page 469), you might want to provide a cloak and let the children tape colored patches on it to use as Joseph's coat.

Station Three: God, the Holy Spirit (Prayer) Station

Walk with the children to this station and show them what they can do here. In addition to the suggested supplies (page 469), you might want to have some crayons and paper for the children to draw colors on as they contemplate the love of God that always surrounds them.

Begin Quiet Time

Instruct the children to begin five minutes of quiet time to think about the Bible story. Explain that after the time has elapsed, you will invite them, one at a time, to the Sacred Circle Time space to draw what they did or thought about.

(2-minute transition time) Place paper, crayons, and other material in the circle. Invite the children, one at a time, to come and draw what they did, thought about, or experienced.

(10 minutes) **Journal and Share Time**

Let them draw and journal as they gather. When most of the children have finished, let them begin to share. Remind the children that listening to one another is important.

Say: "Thank you for spending time with me in the Trinity Stations. I cannot wait to find out what you experienced today. Who would like to share?" (Give each child time to talk, and you should talk as well.)

Place their activities in individual folders; or if they are to take the folders home, place them behind them so they will not be distracted. This will keep you from having to correct the children's behavior.

10 minutes (snack or toy time)

A Time of Blessing

Explain that the symbol for today is a rainbow because a rainbow has so many colors in it—just like Joseph's special coat. It reminds us that God will always love us.

Bless the children where they request, being sure to look them directly in their eyes.

Say: "Thank you for experiencing God with me today. You are a blessing!"

Closing Time

Slowly put each Trinity symbol away.

Say: "And now we are finished with our Sacred Circle Time. We put away our symbol for God, the Creator. We put away our symbol for God, the Son. And we put away our symbol for God, the Holy Spirit."

Then quietly and gently put the sacred cloth away.

Conclude: "And we are all done with our Sacred Circle time. You did a great job. Yay!" Clap and celebrate a job well done.

Ordinary Time 10

Story: God Takes Care of Moses

Text: Exodus 2:1-4, NRSV

Now a man from the house of Levi went and married a Levite woman. The woman conceived and bore a son; and when she saw that he was a fine baby, she hid him three months. When she could hide him no longer she got a papyrus basket for him, and plastered it with bitumen and pitch; she put the child in it and placed it among the reeds on the bank of the river. His sister stood at a distance, to see what would happen to him.

About the text: This story is the first in a series of stories in the Bible about the life of Moses. Moses is a major figure of the Jewish people, and many parallels can be found between the stories of Moses and the stories of the life of Jesus. We will have four lessons about the life of Moses because of this. While young children will not understand the parallels, this story is an important one for them to learn because concepts such as Passover, a baby being saved from the death decree of a king, and the 40-year time in the wilderness will have significance later in their learning, since much of Jesus' ministry will echo these themes.

The Sacred Circle Time Focus: We will focus on God's protection.

Sacred Circle Time Basic Format

Sacred Circle basket and contents:

- Sacred space cloth
- Symbols for Creator (globe), Christ (cross), and Holy Spirit (bell or chimes)
- Small, unbreakable bottle to hold water or oil for the blessing
- A journal page (one per child)
- Crayons and/or markers
- A Bible bookmarked at Exodus 2:1-4
- Focused objects from the Bible story: Three things we use to communicate with others. Some suggestions include a button; blue ribbon or paper cut into about a foot-long strip; a small thimble box or something tiny for the button to fit inside.

The Lesson

Gathering

Sit down and place the sacred basket in front of you.

Pause so that the children notice it and begin to come closer.

Invite them to form a circle.

Sit quietly until they settle in and are quiet.

Say: "It is time for Sacred Circle Time. I am so glad that you are here today. I love learning our stories and experiencing God with you."

Creating the Sacred Space

Say: "First, we create our sacred space." Slowly lay out the sacred cloth.

Slowly lift the globe (symbol of God, the Creator) and hold it at the eye level of the children. Say: "This is our symbol for God, the Creator." Carefully lay it on the sacred cloth. (Pause.)

Slowly lift the cross (symbol of God, the Son). Say: "This is our symbol for God, the Son." Carefully lay it on the sacred cloth. (*Pause.*)

Slowly lift the bell (symbol of God, the Holy Spirit). Say: "This is our symbol of God, the Holy Spirit." Carefully lay it on the sacred cloth. (*Pause.*)

Point to each symbol and say: "So we have God, the Creator; God, the Son; and God, the Holy Spirit. (*Pause.*) Our sacred space is ready. We are ready to begin our Sacred Circle Time together."

God, the Creator (A Time to Wonder)

Begin by showing the children the button, thimble, and ribbon.

Ask: "What can we make out of these? Any ideas?" (*Let them share their ideas. Enjoy the clever things they come up with.*)

Say: "Those are great ideas! But right now, I am going to use them to tell you a very special story."

God, the Son (Telling the Story)

Say: "Our story today, which is in (open the Bible) Exodus, chapter two, verses 1-4, talks about a tiny baby named Moses." (*Hold the tiny button in your hand and pretend that it is a baby. Gaze at it and rock it. If you pretend it is a baby, the children will enjoy pretending that you have a tiny baby, as they like tiny things very much.*)

Say: "Moses was so loved. His mommy loved him, his daddy loved him, and his sister loved him! But there was a king who hated babies, and he ordered that all the Jewish babies should be killed. Poor little Moses!! Luckily, Moses had a very smart mommy who decided that she would put Moses in a basket (put the button in the thimble) and float him down the river (*lay out the ribbon*) to see what happened. There was only one problem: The river was dangerous. There were crocodiles and snakes, and the basket might tip over; and if that happened, poor little baby Moses might drown or maybe even be eaten by one of the crocodiles. Do you think little Moses got eaten?" (*Let them answer.*)

"We will see. His mommy put him in the basket and floated him down the Nile River. (*Slowly move him along the ribbon.*) And . . . whew!!! He made it safely! God took good care of Moses and protected him."

God, the Holy Spirit (Quiet and Prayer Time)

Say: "It is now time to pray. For our prayer time, I want you to take your arms and wrap yourself up just like Baby Moses was wrapped up in that basket. (*Have the children pull their knees up tight and wrap their arms around them making a little cocoon of their bodies.*) Now I want you to sit here and feel God holding you tight and protecting you." (*Give them a few seconds of silence.*)

Pray: "God, thank you for protecting us and keeping us safe when we need you. Amen."

A Time of Blessing

Explain that the symbol for today is a river because God kept Moses safe in the River Nile. Bless the children where they request, being sure to look them directly in their eyes.

Say: "Thank you for experiencing God with me today. You are a blessing!"

Extended Format

(*10 minutes*) Begin with free-play time. Greet the children warmly and let them get used to the space. Have something in the free-play space for them to play with. Rotate each week:

Week One: Paper and crayons, markers, or paint.
Week Two: Clay, wire, pipe cleaners and beads, and tools to work the clay.
Week Three: Things to build with: blocks, Legos®, cans, boxes, or flat stones.
Week Four: Things that make noise.

(*3 minutes*) Transition time. Let the children know that it is almost Sacred Circle Time. Say: "It is almost our Sacred Circle Time. I cannot wait to have sacred time with you today. Will you start to finish up? Then come join me for our special, holy time together."

Sit down in the Sacred Circle Time space and place your sacred basket in front of you.

(*10 minutes*) **Sacred Circle Time** (*Basic Format*)—Use the Sacred Circle Basic Format, but do not include the blessing or closing.

(*10 minutes*) **Trinity Stations**

Explain the Trinity Stations procedure for new children and for those who might forget from time to time.

Walk with the children to the Trinity Stations and show them what they can do in the stations, but do not let them start until they have seen all three stations.

Tell the children that after the Trinity Stations, they will spend five minutes in quiet time thinking about the story and the activities they have completed. They will then return to the Sacred Circle Time space to draw pictures and talk about their activities.

Station One: God, the Creator (Wonder) Station

Walk with the children to this station and show them what they can do here. In addition to the suggested supplies (page 469), you might want to provide some pictures and plastic or rubber crocodiles, snakes, and spiders for the children to examine.

Station Two: God, the Son (Story) Station

Walk with the children to this station and show them what they can do here. In addition to the suggested supplies (page 469), you might want to include a baby doll, basket, and blue blanket to shape into a river so that the children can act out the story.

Station Three: God, the Holy Spirit (Prayer) Station

Walk with the children to this station and show them what they can do here. In addition to the suggested supplies (page 469), you might want want to add some water in a large bowl, a small basket that floats, and straws to blow the basket around in the water.

Begin Quiet Time

Instruct the children to begin five minutes of quiet time to think about the Bible story. Explain that after the time has elapsed, you will invite them, one at a time, to the Sacred Circle Time space to draw what they did or thought about.

(2-minute transition time) Place paper, crayons, and other material in the circle. Invite the children, one at a time, to come and draw what they did, thought about, or experienced.

(10 minutes) **Journal and Share Time**

Let them draw and journal as they gather. When most of the children have finished, let them begin to share. Remind the children that listening to one another is important.

Say: "Thank you for spending time with me in the Trinity Stations. I cannot wait to find out what you experienced today. Who would like to share?" (Give each child time to talk, and you should talk as well.)

Place their activities in individual folders; or if they are to take the folders home, place them behind them so they will not be distracted. This will keep you from having to correct the children's behavior.

10 minutes (snack or toy time)

A Time of Blessing

Explain that the symbol for today is a river because God kept Moses safe in the River Nile. Bless the children where they request, being sure to look them directly in their eyes.

Say: "Thank you for experiencing God with me today. You are a blessing!"

Closing Time

Slowly put each Trinity symbol away.

Say: "And now we are finished with our Sacred Circle Time. We put away our symbol for God, the Creator. We put away our symbol for God, the Son. And we put away our symbol for God, the Holy Spirit."

Then quietly and gently put the sacred cloth away.

Conclude: "And we are all done with our Sacred Circle time. You did a great job. Yay!" Clap and celebrate a job well done.

Ordinary Time 11

Story: Moses and His Family

Text: Exodus 2:5-11, NRSV

The daughter of Pharaoh came down to bathe at the river, while her attendants walked beside the river. She saw the basket among the reeds and sent her maid to bring it. When she opened it, she saw the child. He was crying, and she took pity on him. "This must be one of the Hebrews' children," she said. Then his sister said to Pharaoh's daughter, "Shall I go and get you a nurse from the Hebrew women to nurse the child for you?" Pharaoh's daughter said to her, "Yes." So the girl went and called the child's mother. Pharaoh's daughter said to her, "Take this child and nurse it for me, and I will give you your wages." So the woman took the child and nursed it. When the child grew up, she brought him to Pharaoh's daughter, and she took him as her son. She named him Moses, "because," she said, "I drew him out of the water."

About the text: This is the story of Moses's adoption by Pharaoh's daughter. She draws him out of the water and then finds a woman (Moses's mother) to care for him. This is one of the first examples of a blended family in the Bible. Many children today live in some kind of blended family arrangement (children of divorced homes, children in remarried homes, children being raised by grandparents, foster children, adopted children), so this story is a great one for these children to *see themselves* in and to realize that God provides for our care in many different ways.

The Sacred Circle Time Focus: This is an important story to help young children begin to see their caretakers as gifts from God. And that the way we are cared for, by those who love us, is much like the love God has for us.

Sacred Circle Time Basic Format

Sacred Circle basket and contents:

- Sacred space cloth
- Symbols for Creator (globe), Christ (cross), and Holy Spirit (bell or chimes)
- Small, unbreakable bottle to hold water or oil for the blessing
- A journal page (one per child)
- Crayons and/or markers
- A Bible bookmarked at Exodus 2:5-11
- Focused objects from the Bible story:
  - 4 paper cups labeled "Mommy," "Pharaoh's daughter," "Miriam," and "God."
  - A small ball or object with a face drawn on it (it should be small enough to fit inside the cups)

The Lesson

Gathering

Sit down and place the sacred basket in front of you.

Pause so that the children notice it and begin to come closer.

Invite them to form a circle.

Sit quietly until they settle in and are quiet. Say: "It is time for Sacred Circle Time. I am so glad that you are here today. I love learning our stories and experiencing God with you."

Creating the Sacred Space

Say: "First, we create our sacred space."

Slowly lay out the sacred cloth.

Slowly lift the globe (symbol of God, the Creator) and hold it at the eye level of the children. Say: "This is our symbol for God, the Creator." Carefully lay it on the sacred cloth. (*Pause.*)

Slowly lift the cross (symbol of God, the Son). Say: "This is our symbol for God, the Son." Carefully lay it on the sacred cloth. (*Pause.*)

Slowly lift the bell (symbol of God, the Holy Spirit). Say: "This is our symbol of God, the Holy Spirit." Carefully lay it on the sacred cloth. (*Pause.*)

Point to each symbol and say: "So we have God, the Creator; God, the Son; and God, the Holy Spirit. (*Pause.*) Our sacred space is ready. We are ready to begin our Sacred Circle Time together."

God, the Creator (A Time to Wonder)

Begin by showing the children the ball and three cups. Do not use the "God" cup until later.

Say: "Let's play a little game. I am going to place this ball under one of these cups. I will move the cups around, and I want you to try to guess which cup the little ball is under." (*Do this several times. Let them guess and enjoy this little game.*)

"That was a fun game. But I did not bring these cups and this little ball just to play games. I brought them to tell you a story."

God, the Son (Telling the Story)

Say: "In our story today, which is in (*open the Bible*) Exodus, chapter 2, verses 5-11, there is a baby named Moses (*show them the ball*) and a very mean pharaoh who wanted to kill him. Moses's mommy (*show them the cup labeled 'Mommy'*) took good care of him by putting him in a little basket and placing it in the Nile River. (*Place the* ball—Moses—into the mommy cup). Baby Moses floated down the river where the pharaoh's daughter (show them the cup marked 'Pharaoh's daughter') found him and pulled him out of the water. And she loved him. And she took care of him. (Take Moses out of the mommy cup and place him in the Pharaoh's daughter cup.) And then Moses's sister Miriam took care of Moses. (Remove Moses from the cup marked 'Pharaoh's daughter' and put him in the cup labeled, 'Miriam.') Miriam ran to the pharaoh's daughter and said, 'Do you need help taking care of the baby? My mother (who was Moses's mother too) can help you.' And the pharaoh's daughter thought that was a great idea; so while Moses grew up, he had three people taking care of him: The pharaoh's daughter loved Moses and took care of him. (Place Moses in the Pharaoh's daughter cup.) His sister Miriam loved and took care of Moses. (Place Moses in the Miriam cup.) And his mommy loved him and took care of him. (Place Moses in the Mommy cup.) And do you know who else loved Moses and took care of him? God. God loved Moses and took care of him. (Get out the cup labeled "God.") God loved Moses's mommy. (Stack the Mommy cup inside the God cup.) God loved and took care of Pharaoh's daughter. (Stack the Pharaoh's daughter cup inside the other two cups.) God loved and took care of Miriam. (Stack Miriam's cup inside the others.) God loved and took care of Moses." (Place Moses—the ball—inside the cups.)

God, the Holy Spirit (Quiet and Prayer Time)

Say: "It is now time to pray. I am going to pass our Baby Moses (get the ball out) around the circle again. As I do, I want you to tell us who loves and takes care of you."

Pass the ball to the children and invite them to share the names of those who love and care for them. After each child has spoken, say: "Those people do care for you, and God loves and cares for you, too."

Pray: "God, thank you for all the people who love and care for us, and thank you for also loving and caring for us. Amen."

A Time of Blessing

Explain that the symbol for today is a heart because the children are loved and cared for, just as Moses was. Bless the children where they request, being sure to look them directly in their eyes.

Say: "Thank you for experiencing God with me today. You are a blessing!"

Extended Format

(*10 minutes*) Begin with free-play time. Greet the children warmly and let them get used to the space. Have something in the free-play space for them to play with. Rotate each week:

Week One: Paper and crayons, markers, or paint.

Week Two: Clay, wire, pipe cleaners and beads, and tools to work the clay.

Week Three: Things to build with: blocks, Legos®, cans, boxes, or flat stones.

Week Four: Things that make noise.

(*3 minutes*) Transition Time. Let the children know that it is almost Sacred Circle Time. Say: "It is almost our Sacred Circle Time. I cannot wait to have sacred time with you today. Will you start to finish up? Then come join me for our special, holy time together."

Sit down in the Sacred Circle Time space and place your sacred basket in front of you.

(*10 minutes*) **Sacred Circle Time** (*Basic Format*)—Use the Sacred Circle Basic Format, but do not include the blessing or closing.

(*10 minutes*) **Trinity Stations**

Explain the Trinity Stations procedure for new children and for those who might forget from time to time.

Walk with the children to the Trinity Stations and show them what they can do in the stations, but do not let them start until they have seen all three stations.

Tell the children that after the Trinity Stations, they will spend five minutes in quiet time thinking about the story and the activities they have completed. They will then return to the Sacred Circle Time space to draw pictures and talk about their activities.

Station One: God, the Creator (Wonder) Station

Walk with the children to this station and show them what they can do here. In addition to the suggested supplies (page 469), you might want to add the cups and the ball that you used in the story.

Station Two: God, the Son (Story) Station

Walk with the children to this station and show them what they can do here. In addition to the suggested supplies (page 469), you might want to include some dolls, blankets, and diapers so that the children can care for Baby Moses.

Station Three: God, the Holy Spirit Station

Walk with the children to this station and show them what they can do here. In addition to the suggested supplies (page 469), you might want to add some baby blankets that the children can use as prayer shawls.

Begin Quiet Time

Instruct the children to begin five minutes of quiet time to think about the Bible story. Explain that after the time has elapsed, you will invite them, one at a time, to the Sacred Circle Time space to draw what they did or thought about.

(*2-minute transition time*) Place paper, crayons, and other material in the circle. Invite the children, one at a time, to come and draw what they did, thought about, or experienced.

(10 minutes) **Journal and Share Time**

Let them draw and journal as they gather. When most of the children have finished, let them begin to share. Remind the children that listening to one another is important.

Say: "Thank you for spending time with me in the Trinity Stations. I cannot wait to find out what you experienced today. Who would like to share?" (Give each child time to talk, and you should talk as well.)

Place their activities in individual folders; or if they are to take the folders home, place them behind them so they will not be distracted. This will keep you from having to correct the children's behavior.

10 minutes (snack or toy time)

A Time of Blessing

Explain that the symbol for today is a heart because the children are loved and cared for just as Moses was. Bless the children where they request, being sure to look them directly in their eyes.

Say: "Thank you for experiencing God with me today. You are a blessing!"

Closing Time

Slowly put each Trinity symbol away.

Say: "And now we are finished with our Sacred Circle Time. We put away our symbol for God, the Creator. We put away our symbol for God, the Son. And we put away our symbol for God, the Holy Spirit."

Then quietly and gently put the sacred cloth away.

Conclude: "And we are all done with our Sacred Circle time. You did a great job. Yay!" Clap and celebrate a job well done.

Ordinary Time 12

Story: Moses and the Burning Bush

Text: Exodus 3:1-11, NRSV

Moses was keeping the flock of his father-in-law Jethro, the priest of Midian; he led his flock beyond the wilderness, and came to Horeb, the mountain of God. There the angel of the LORD appeared to him in a flame of fire out of a bush; he looked, and the bush was blazing, yet it was not consumed. Then Moses said, "I must turn aside and look at this great sight, and see why the bush is not burned up." When the LORD saw that he had turned aside to see, God called to him out of the bush, "Moses, Moses!" And he said, "Here I am." Then he said, "Come no closer! Remove the sandals from your feet, for the place on which you are standing is holy ground." He said further, "I am the God of your father, the God of Abraham, the God of Isaac, and the God of Jacob." And Moses hid his face, for he was afraid to look at God.

Then the LORD said, "I have observed the misery of my people who are in Egypt; I have heard their cry on account of their taskmasters. Indeed, I know their sufferings, and I have come down to deliver them from the Egyptians, and to bring them up out of that land to a good and broad land, a land flowing with milk and honey, to the country of the Canaanites, the Hittites, the Amorites, the Perizzites, the Hivites, and the Jebusites. The cry of the Israelites has now come to me; I have also seen how the Egyptians oppress them. So come, I will send you to Pharaoh to bring my people, the Israelites, out of Egypt." But Moses said to God, "Who am I that I should go to Pharaoh, and bring the Israelites out of Egypt?"

About the text: This is the story of the call of Moses. It is often called the story of the burning bush because God appeared to Moses in a burning bush, asking Moses to go and free God's people. This is surprising because, at the time God appears, Moses has had to flee from Egypt, after killing a man who was beating a Jewish man. In the story, Moses cannot understand why God would call him. He is not being falsely modest, but rather, genuinely unsure that he should be the one called to God's work. This is a powerful story because it reminds us all that God calls us and can use our gifts, even if we do not feel worthy. This is a powerful story for the children to learn because it will give them the opportunity to begin thinking about their spiritual gifts. The sooner children begin to identify their gifts, the sooner they will be able to understand that they can serve God with the gifts they have been given.

The Sacred Circle Time Focus: We will focus on our spiritual gifts and being called by God.

Sacred Circle Time Basic Format

Sacred Circle basket and contents:

- Sacred space cloth
- Symbols for Creator (globe), Christ (cross), and Holy Spirit (bell or chimes)
- Small, unbreakable bottle to hold water or oil for the blessing
- A journal page (one per child)
- Crayons and/or markers
- A Bible bookmarked at Exodus 3:1-11
- Focused objects from the Bible story: A red crepe paper strip about a foot long for each child; a small branch

The Lesson

Gathering

Sit down and place the sacred basket in front of you.

Pause so that the children notice it and begin to come closer.

Invite them to form a circle.

Sit quietly until they settle in and are quiet.

Say: "It is time for Sacred Circle Time. I am so glad that you are here today. I love learning our stories and experiencing God with you."

Creating the Sacred Space

Say: "First, we create our sacred space."

Slowly lay out the sacred cloth.

Slowly lift the globe (symbol of God, the Creator) and hold it at the eye level of the children. Say: "This is our symbol for God, the Creator." Carefully lay it on the sacred cloth. (Pause.)

Slowly lift the cross (symbol of God, the Son). Say: "This is our symbol for God, the Son." Carefully lay it on the sacred cloth. (Pause.)

Slowly lift the bell (symbol of God, the Holy Spirit). Say: "This is our symbol of God, the Holy Spirit." Carefully lay it on the sacred cloth. (Pause.)

Point to each symbol and say: "So we have God, the Creator; God, the Son; and God, the Holy Spirit. (Pause.) Our sacred space is ready. We are ready to begin our Sacred Circle Time together."

God, the Creator (A Time to Wonder)

Give each child a strip of the red crepe paper to play with. Just let them play. They will stretch it, blow it, and twist it. Let them enjoy it. You might want to play some music or sounds from nature and let them dance and move using the streamers.

Ask: "Do you like the way the streamers move in the air? (*Let them respond.*) I would like for you to sit down and lay your streamer out in front of you. We will be using it for our story."

God, the Son (Telling the Story)

Say: "In our story today, which is found in (*open the Bible*) Exodus, chapter 3, verses 1-11, there is a story about a bush. Let's pretend that this is the bush. (*Show the children the branch.*) Moses was sitting beside the bush and watching his sheep. Remember Moses? He was the baby who floated down the Nile River and was cared for by his mommy and his sister and Pharaoh's daughter. Well, Moses got into trouble and had to leave his home, and he was working as a shepherd taking care of sheep. And that is when something happened to the bush." (*Quietly, tie each of the red streamers to the branch and then begin to gently wave the branch.*)

Say: "The bush began to burn, but it was not a fire. It was the voice of God saying, 'Moses, I have an important job for you to do. I need you to work for me and go help my children in Egypt leave. The pharaoh is very mean. I need you to help me!' And Moses could not believe that he was special to God. But he was. He had a job to do for God. A very important job! And God spoke to Moses in a burning bush."

God, the Holy Spirit (Quiet and Prayer Time)

Say: "It is now time to pray. I am going to pass the burning bush to each of you; and as you hold it, I am going to tell you something very important."

Pass the bush to each child and let each wave it, and as he or she waves it, say: "(*Name of child*), you are very special, and someday you will do a very important job for God. I don't know what God will ask you to do. But you are so special, and someday God will use you to help others."

Pray: "God, when it is time, show us what special job we are to do for you. For you have called us by our names, and we belong to you. Amen."

A Time of Blessing

Explain that the symbol for today is a flame because God spoke to Moses from a burning bush. Bless the children where they request, being sure to look them directly in their eyes.

Say: "Thank you for experiencing God with me today. You are a blessing!"

Extended Format

(*10 minutes*) Begin with free-play time. Greet the children warmly and let them get used to the space. Have something in the free-play space for them to play with. Rotate each week:

Week One: Paper and crayons, markers, or paint.

Week Two: Clay, wire, pipe cleaners and beads, and tools to work the clay.

Week Three: Things to build with: blocks, Legos®, cans, boxes, or flat stones.

Week Four: Things that make noise.

(*3 minutes*) Transition Time. Let the children know that it is almost Sacred Circle Time. Say: "It is almost our Sacred Circle Time. I cannot wait to have sacred time with you today. Will you start to finish up? Then come join me for our special, holy time together."

Sit down in the Sacred Circle Time space and place your sacred basket in front of you.

(*10 minutes*) **Sacred Circle Time** (*Basic Format*)—Use the Sacred Circle Basic Format, but do not include the blessing or closing.

(*10 minutes*) **Trinity Stations**

Explain the Trinity Stations procedure for new children and for those who might forget from time to time.

Walk with the children to the Trinity Stations and show them what they can do in the stations, but do not let them start until they have seen all three stations.

Tell the children that after the Trinity Stations, they will spend five minutes in quiet time thinking about the story and the activities they have completed. They will then return to the Sacred Circle Time space to draw pictures and talk about their activities.

God, the Creator (Wonder) Station

Walk with the children to this station and show them what they can do here. In addition to the suggested supplies (page 469), you might want to add a few branches and more streamers, red ribbon, and string to allow the children to be creative.

Station Two: God, the Son (Story) Station

Walk with the children to this station and show them what they can do here. In addition to the suggested supplies (page 469), you might want to include the burning bush from the Sacred Circle Time.

Station Three: God, the Holy Spirit (Prayer) Station

Walk with the children to this station and show them what they can do here. In addition to the suggested supplies (page 469), you might want to add some pictures of people doing jobs, so the children can ponder what God might be calling them to do.

Begin Quiet Time

Instruct the children to begin five minutes of quiet time to think about the Bible story. Explain that after the time has elapsed, you will invite them, one at a time, to the Sacred Circle Time space to draw what they did or thought about.

(*2-minute transition time*) Place paper, crayons, and other material in the circle. Invite the children, one at a time, to come and draw what they did, thought about, or experienced.

(10 minutes) **Journal and Share Time**

Let them draw and journal as they gather. When most of the children have finished, let them begin to share. Remind the children that listening to one another is important.

Say: "Thank you for spending time with me in the Trinity Stations. I cannot wait to find out what you experienced today. Who would like to share?" (Give each child time to talk, and you should talk as well.)

Place their activities in individual folders; or if they are to take the folders home, place them behind them so they will not be distracted. This will keep you from having to correct the children's behavior.

10 minutes (snack or toy time)

A Time of Blessing

Explain that the symbol for today is a flame because God spoke to Moses from a burning bush. Bless the children where they request, being sure to look them directly in their eyes.

Say: "Thank you for experiencing God with me today. You are a blessing!"

Closing Time

Slowly put each Trinity symbol away.

Say: "And now we are finished with our Sacred Circle Time. We put away our symbol for God, the Creator. We put away our symbol for God, the Son. And we put away our symbol for God, the Holy Spirit."

Then quietly and gently put the sacred cloth away.

Conclude: "And we are all done with our Sacred Circle time. You did a great job. Yay!" Clap and celebrate a job well done.

Ordinary Time 13

Story: Moses Frees the Israelites

Text: Exodus 14:15-21, NRSV

Then the LORD said to Moses, "Why do you cry out to me? Tell the Israelites to go forward. But you lift up your staff, and stretch out your hand over the sea and divide it, that the Israelites may go into the sea on dry ground. Then I will harden the hearts of the Egyptians so that they will go in after them; and so I will gain glory for myself over Pharaoh and all his army, his chariots, and his chariot drivers. And the Egyptians shall know that I am the LORD, when I have gained glory for myself over Pharaoh, his chariots, and his chariot drivers."

The angel of God who was going before the Israelite army moved and went behind them; and the pillar of cloud moved from in front of them and took its place behind them. It came between the army of Egypt and the army of Israel. And so the cloud was there with the darkness, and it lit up the night; one did not come near the other all night.

Then Moses stretched out his hand over the sea. The LORD drove the sea back by a strong east wind all night, and turned the sea into dry land; and the waters were divided.

About the text: The text directly before this and this text tell the story of God leading the Israelites out of Egypt by parting the Red Sea. The plagues and death of firstborns are difficult texts and should not be introduced to young children. However, this part of the story captures the essence of the Passover . . . that God will save God's people. This story is critical for children to learn so that they can understand the symbolism and parallels between it and the death, Resurrection, and promise of life eternal through Christ, as they grow older. This is also an important text because we know that Jesus would have heard this story told each year as his family celebrated Passover.

The Sacred Circle Time Focus: We will focus on the fact that God made a miracle and saved the people from Pharaoh.

Sacred Circle Time Basic Format

Sacred Circle basket and contents:

- Sacred space cloth
- Symbols for Creator (globe), Christ (cross), and Holy Spirit (bell or chimes)
- Small, unbreakable bottle to hold water or oil for the blessing
- A journal page (one per child)
- Crayons and/or markers
- A Bible bookmarked at Exodus 14:15-21
- Focused objects from the Bible story: A cake pan of water and some spoons, paper, and cups

The Lesson

Gathering

Sit down and place the sacred basket in front of you.

Pause so that the children notice it and begin to come closer.

Invite them to form a circle.

Sit quietly until they settle in and are quiet.

Say: "It is time for Sacred Circle Time. I am so glad that you are here today. I love learning our stories and experiencing God with you."

Creating the Sacred Space

Say: "First, we create our sacred space."

Slowly lay out the sacred cloth.

Slowly lift the globe (symbol of God, the Creator) and hold it at the eye level of the children. Say: "This is our symbol for God, the Creator." Carefully lay it on the sacred cloth. *(Pause.)*

Slowly lift the cross (symbol of God, the Son). Say: "This is our symbol for God, the Son." Carefully lay it on the sacred cloth. (*Pause.*)

Slowly lift the bell (symbol of God, the Holy Spirit). Say: "This is our symbol of God, the Holy Spirit." Carefully lay it on the sacred cloth. (*Pause.*)

Point to each symbol and say: "So we have God, the Creator; God, the Son; and God, the Holy Spirit. (*Pause.*) Our sacred space is ready. We are ready to begin our Sacred Circle Time together."

God, the Creator (A Time to Wonder)

Let the children play in the water with the cake pan, cups, and spoons; then ask:

"Can you help me divide the water. I need half of it on this side and the other half on this side and a dry strip in the middle." (*Let them try.*)

God, the Son (Telling the Story)

Say: "You know, it is impossible to divide the water, isn't it? Well at least it is for us. But in our story today, which is found in (*open the Bible*) Exodus, chapter 14, verses 15-21, there is story where the water divides in half. Moses was called by God to save his family, the Israelites. Can you say that word? (*Have them try.*) The Israelites were the children of God, and Moses was an Israelite. Anyway, the Pharaoh was very mean to the Israelites. He made them work in the hot sun, did not give them enough food to eat, and beat them when they were too tired to work. He was very mean, and God did not want God's children to be Pharaoh's slaves anymore. So God called

Moses through the burning bush to go and save the Israelites. It took a long time and Pharaoh, the mean king, did not want to let them go. But finally, he told the people that they could leave. So they packed all their things and walked out of Egypt as fast as they could. But Pharaoh changed his mind and chased them to bring them back. And the Israelites had a problem. They needed to cross the sea to get away from Pharaoh. And the sea was very big and very deep. (*Put your hands together, laced in the front with your arms making a big circle, as if you were holding an invisible basketball.*) The sea was this big. It was huge! And the people had to cross it. But they didn't have a boat. And it was too deep to swim across. And they were trapped. The sea was in front of them, and Pharaoh was coming to get them. But God called to Moses and said, 'Moses, what are you waiting for? Take a step!' And when Moses took a step, the water parted in half. (*Open your arms.*) It was a miracle, and all of the people walked on dry land right through the water. And then it closed back up (*clasp your hands together again forming the sea with your arms*), so that Pharaoh could not cross the water and bring the Israelites back into slavery. Can you believe God could part the water? It was a miracle! God took care of the Israelites."

God, the Holy Spirit (Quiet and Prayer Time)

Say: "It is now time to pray. I want you to put your hands together, and I want you to slowly open your hands and remember the miracle of God parting the water. (*Have them use their own hands to form a sea as you did during the story.*) Do this a few times on your own and just thank God for making that special miracle." (*Give them a few seconds of silence as they part the water and reflect on the grandeur of God's miracle.*)

"God took care of Moses and the Israelites by parting the water, and God takes care of us too."

Pray: "God, thank you for the special miracle when you parted the water and thank you for taking care of all your children. Amen."

A Time of Blessing

Explain that the symbol for today is a water drop because God parted the water and made a miracle and took care of God's children, the Israelites. Bless the children where they request, being sure to look them directly in their eyes.

Say: "Thank you for experiencing God with me today. You are a blessing!"

Extended Format

(*10 minutes*) Begin with free-play time. Greet the children warmly and let them get used to the space. Have something in the free-play space for them to play with. Rotate each week:

Week One: Paper and crayons, markers, or paint.

Week Two: Clay, wire, pipe cleaners and beads, and tools to work the clay.

Week Three: Things to build with: blocks, Legos®, cans, boxes, or flat stones.

Week Four: Things that make noise.

(*3 minutes*) Transition Time. Let the children know that it is almost Sacred Circle Time. Say: "It is almost our Sacred Circle Time. I cannot wait to have sacred time with you today. Will you start to finish up? Then come join me for our special, holy time together."

Sit down in the Sacred Circle Time space and place your sacred basket in front of you.

(*10 minutes*) **Sacred Circle Time** (*Basic Format*)—Use the Sacred Circle Basic Format, but do not include the blessing or closing.

(*10 minutes*) **Trinity Stations**

Explain the Trinity Stations procedure for new children and for those who might forget from time to time.

Walk with the children to the Trinity Stations and show them what they can do in the stations, but do not let them start until they have seen all three stations.

Tell the children that after the Trinity Stations, they will spend five minutes in quiet time thinking about the story and the activities they have completed. They will then return to the Sacred Circle Time space to draw pictures and talk about their activities.

Station One: God, the Creator (Wonder) Station

Walk with the children to this station and show them what they can do here. In addition to the suggested supplies (page 469), you might want to add the bowl of water and cups from the Sacred Circle Time.

Station Two: God, the Son (Story) Station

Walk with the children to this station and show them what they can do here. In addition to the suggested supplies (page 469), you might want to include two large boxes or chairs with blue fabric over them so that they can be placed side by side. These can represent the sea, and the children can "part the water" by moving them apart and walking through them.

Station Three: God, the Holy Spirit (Prayer) Station

Walk with the children to this station and show them what they can do here. In addition to the suggested supplies (page 469), you might want to add some watercolors and paint, so that the children can paint a prayer.

Begin Quiet Time

Instruct the children to begin five minutes of quiet time to think about the Bible story. Explain that after the time has elapsed, you will invite them, one at a time, to the Sacred Circle Time space to draw what they did or thought about.

(2-minute transition time) Place paper, crayons, and other material in the circle. Invite the children, one at a time, to come and draw what they did, thought about, or experienced.

(10 minutes) **Journal and Share Time**

Let them draw and journal as they gather. When most of the children have finished, let them begin to share. Remind the children that listening to one another is important.

Say: "Thank you for spending time with me in the Trinity Stations. I cannot wait to find out what you experienced today. Who would like to share?" (Give each child time to talk, and you should talk as well.)

Place their activities in individual folders; or if they are to take the folders home, place them behind them so they will not be distracted. This will keep you from having to correct the children's behavior.

10 minutes (snack or toy time)

A Time of Blessing

Explain that the symbol for today is is a water drop because God parted the water and took care of God's children, the Israelites. Bless the children where they request, being sure to look them directly in their eyes.

Say: "Thank you for experiencing God with me today. You are a blessing!"

Closing Time

Slowly put each Trinity symbol away.

Say: "And now we are finished with our Sacred Circle Time. We put away our symbol for God, the Creator. We put away our symbol for God, the Son. And we put away our symbol for God, the Holy Spirit."

Then quietly and gently put the sacred cloth away.

Conclude: "And we are all done with our Sacred Circle time. You did a great job. Yay!" Clap and celebrate a job well done.

Ordinary Time 14

Story: Moses and the Ten Commandments

Text: Exodus 20:1-17, NRSV

Then God spoke all these words:

I am the LORD your God, who brought you out of the land of Egypt, out of the house of slavery; you shall have no other gods before me.

You shall not make for yourself an idol, whether in the form of anything that is in heaven above, or that is on the earth beneath, or that is in the water under the earth. You shall not bow down to them or worship them; for I the LORD your God am a jealous God, punishing children for the iniquity of parents, to the third and the fourth generation of those who reject me, but showing steadfast love to the thousandth generation of those who love me and keep my commandments.

You shall not make wrongful use of the name of the LORD your God, for the LORD will not acquit anyone who misuses his name.

Remember the Sabbath day, and keep it holy. Six days you shall labor and do all your work. But the seventh day is a Sabbath to the LORD your God; you shall not do any work—you, your son or your daughter, your male or female slave, your livestock, or the alien resident in your towns. For in six days the LORD made heaven and earth, the sea, and all that is in them, but rested the seventh day; therefore the LORD blessed the Sabbath day and consecrated it.

Honor your father and your mother, so that your days may be long in the land that the LORD your God is giving you.

You shall not murder.

You shall not commit adultery.

You shall not steal.

You shall not bear false witness against your neighbor.

You shall not covet your neighbor's house; you shall not covet your neighbor's wife, or male or female slave, or ox, or donkey, or anything that belongs to your neighbor.

About the text: After being slaves in Egypt for such a long time, the people had forgotten what people of God should act like and how they should treat one another. In Egypt, they had been told what to do and when to do it. But now, in the wilderness, they had to manage their own affairs and remember what it was to be children of God. The Ten Commandments were the foundation for remembering how to treat one another. They seem simple enough for a child, but they are quite challenging. This lesson introduces them to the children. However, the details of them do not need to be discussed at length because many of the commandments do not apply to young children.

The Sacred Circle Time Focus: We will focus on God making rules to help people.

Sacred Circle Time Basic Format

Sacred Circle basket and contents:

- Sacred space cloth
- Symbols for Creator (globe), Christ (cross), and Holy Spirit (bell or chimes)
- Small, unbreakable bottle to hold water or oil for the blessing
- A journal page (one per child)
- Crayons and/or markers
- A Bible bookmarked at Exodus 20:1-17
- Focused objects from the Bible story: Large paper and a marker

The Lesson

Gathering

Sit down and place the sacred basket in front of you.

Pause so that the children notice it and begin to come closer.

Invite them to form a circle.

Sit quietly until they settle in and are quiet.

Say: "It is time for Sacred Circle Time. I am so glad that you are here today. I love learning our stories and experiencing God with you."

Creating the Sacred Space

Say: "First, we create our sacred space."

Slowly lay out the sacred cloth.

Slowly lift the globe (symbol of God, the Creator) and hold it at the eye level of the children. Say: "This is our symbol for God, the Creator." Carefully lay it on the sacred cloth. (*Pause.*)

Slowly lift the cross (symbol of God, the Son). Say: "This is our symbol for God, the Son." Carefully lay it on the sacred cloth. (*Pause.*)

Slowly lift the bell (symbol of God, the Holy Spirit). Say: "This is our symbol of God, the Holy Spirit." Carefully lay it on the sacred cloth. (*Pause.*)

Point to each symbol and say: "So we have God, the Creator; God, the Son; and God, the Holy Spirit. (*Pause.*) Our sacred space is ready. We are ready to begin our Sacred Circle Time together."

God, the Creator (A Time to Wonder)

Say: "Today, we are going to think about rules. I am going to write a rule on my board, and you can tell me why we have that rule.

"Rule 1: You must brush your teeth." (*Draw a toothbrush.*)

"Why do we have that rule?" (*Let them answer.*)

"Rule 2: You must not jump into the swimming pool without an adult with you." (*Draw a pool.*)

"Why do we have that rule?" (*Let them tell you.*)

"Rule 3: You must hold the hand of an adult when you cross the street." (*Draw a street.*)

"Why do we have that rule?"

"Who can think of another rule?" (*Give them time to think of rules and follow each rule with asking why we have that rule.*)

Explain: "Rules keep us safe. Your parents make rules so that you will be safe. They make rules because they love you!"

God, the Son (Telling the Story)

Say: "In our story today, which is found in (*open the Bible*) Exodus, chapter 20, verses 1-17, God knew that God's children needed some rules to keep them safe. And so God told Moses to climb up a very tall mountain. When Moses climbed all the way up that mountain, God told him to write down some rules. God gave these rules to Moses to keep the people safe. How many rules do you think God gave to Moses? (*Let them guess.*) Let's count and see . . . (*Using your fingers, let them count to ten with you.*) God gave the people ten rules, and they are called the Ten Commandments; ten rules (*count to ten again*) to keep the children of God, the Israelites, safe. I am going to read the ten rules to you. (*Read the commandments, holding up a finger for each rule, in this simplified form and do not try to explain them. The children will learn their meaning later. For now, let them simply hear that there are ten rules*):

Rule Number One: You must love only one God.

Rule Number Two: You must not worship anything besides God.

Rule Number Three: You must not use God's name to say naughty things.

Rule Number Four: You must keep one day during the week for rest and worship.

Rule Number Five: You must love and listen to your parents.

Rule Number Six: You must not kill anyone.

Rule Number Seven: You must not commit adultery.

Rule Number Eight: You must not steal.

Rule Number Nine: You must not lie.

Rule Number Ten: You must not want things that belong to someone else.

"There are ten rules, the Ten Commandments, that God told Moses to give to the people so that they would be safe."

God, the Holy Spirit (Quiet and Prayer Time)

Say: "It is now time to pray. We are going to be still for ten seconds because there are Ten Commandments in our story. Let's be very quiet and just be with God for ten seconds of silent prayer." (*Silently count to ten using your fingers to mark the time.*)

Pray: "God, thank you for the rules, the Ten Commandments, which were given to us to keep us safe. Amen."

A Time of Blessing

Explain that the symbol for today is the number ten because there are Ten Commandments. Bless the children where they request, being sure to look them directly in their eyes.

Say: "Thank you for experiencing God with me today. You are a blessing!"

Extended Format

(*10 minutes*) Begin with free-play time. Greet the children warmly and let them get used to the space. Have something in the free-play space for them to play with. Rotate each week:

Week One: Paper and crayons, markers, or paint.

Week Two: Clay, wire, pipe cleaners and beads, and tools to work the clay.

Week Three: Things to build with: blocks, Legos®, cans, boxes, or flat stones.

Week Four: Things that make noise.

(*3 minutes*) Transition Time. Let the children know that it is almost Sacred Circle Time. Say: "It is almost our Sacred Circle Time. I cannot wait to have sacred time with you today. Will you start to finish up? Then come join me for our special, holy time together."

Sit down in the Sacred Circle Time space and place your sacred basket in front of you.

(*10 minutes*) **Sacred Circle Time** (*Basic Format*)—Use the Sacred Circle Basic Format, but do not include the blessing or closing.

(*10 minutes*) **Trinity Stations**

Explain the Trinity Stations procedure for new children and for those who might forget from time to time.

Walk with the children to the Trinity Stations and show them what they can do in the stations, but do not let them start until they have seen all three stations.

Tell the children that after the Trinity Stations, they will spend five minutes in quiet time thinking about the story and the activities they have completed. They will then return to the Sacred Circle Time space to draw pictures and talk about their activities.

Station One: God, the Creator (Wonder) Station

Walk with the children to this station and show them what they can do here. In addition to the suggested supplies (page 469), you might want to add some counting beads to string or blocks to stack and count.

Station Two: God, the Son (Story) Station

Walk with the children to this station and show them what they can do here. In addition to the suggested supplies (page 469), you might include some clay and small sticks. Explain that Moses did not write the Ten Commandments on paper, but carved them out of stone. Clay and small sticks will allow the children to carve the commandments as Moses did.

Station Three: God, the Holy Spirit (Prayer) Station

Walk with the children to this station and show them what they can do here. In addition to the suggested supplies (page 469), you might provide a dish of ten small beads or prayer beads in sets of ten for the children to use as they pray.

Begin Quiet Time

Instruct the children to begin five minutes of quiet time to think about the Bible story. Explain that after the time has elapsed, you will invite them, one at a time, to the Sacred Circle Time space to draw what they did or thought about.

(2-minute transition time) Place paper, crayons, and other material in the circle. Invite the children, one at a time, to come and draw what they did, thought about, or experienced.

(10 minutes) **Journal and Share Time**

Let them draw and journal as they gather. When most of the children have finished, let them begin to share. Remind the children that listening to one another is important.

Say: "Thank you for spending time with me in the Trinity Stations. I cannot wait to find out what you experienced today. Who would like to share?" (Give each child time to talk, and you should talk as well.)

Place their activities in individual folders; or if they are to take the folders home, place them behind them so they will not be distracted. This will keep you from having to correct the children's behavior.

10 minutes (snack or toy time)

A Time of Blessing

Explain that the symbol for today is the number ten because there are Ten Commandments. Bless the children where they request, being sure to look them directly in their eyes.

Say: "Thank you for experiencing God with me today. You are a blessing!"

Closing Time

Slowly put each Trinity symbol away.

Say: "And now we are finished with our Sacred Circle Time. We put away our symbol for God, the Creator. We put away our symbol for God, the Son. And we put away our symbol for God, the Holy Spirit."

Then quietly and gently put the sacred cloth away.

Conclude: "And we are all done with our Sacred Circle time. You did a great job. Yay!" Clap and celebrate a job well done.

Ordinary Time 15

Story: Ruth

Text: Ruth 2:11-13

All that you have done for your mother-in-law since the death of your husband has been fully told me, and how you left your father and mother and your native land and came to a people that you did not know before. May the LORD reward you for your deeds, and may you have a full reward from the LORD, the God of Israel, under whose wings you have come for refuge!" Then she said, "May I continue to find favor in your sight, my lord, for you have comforted me and spoken kindly to your servant, even though I am not one of your servants."

About the text: At the time of this story, widows often starved to death after the death of a husband when they had no family to care for them. Women were not able to work and, as a result, widows were at the mercy of their families to care for them. Ruth and her mother-in-law are both widows, and Ruth would have normally left her mother-in-law to care for herself, returned to her own home, and been taken care of by her own family. But Ruth was not like other women. She cared so deeply for her mother-in-law that she did not leave her, but vowed to follow her. Because of her kindness, God warms the heart of Boaz, and he cares for Ruth by allowing her to glean in his field and eventually to marry him. He cares for both Ruth and Naomi; and because of his kindness, the foremother of Jesus survives. Ruth is an important part of the genealogy of Jesus.

The Sacred Circle Time Focus: We will focus on kindness toward others.

Sacred Circle Time Basic Format

Sacred Circle basket and contents:

- Sacred space cloth
- Symbols for Creator (globe), Christ (cross), and Holy Spirit (bell or chimes)
- Small, unbreakable bottle to hold water or oil for the blessing
- A journal page (one per child)
- Crayons and/or markers
- A Bible bookmarked at Ruth 2:11-13
- Focused objects from the Bible story: A small bag with three flat stones. The stones should be blank on one side with a small heart drawn on the other side. If you don't have stones handy, use beans, paper squares, or anything flat.

The Lesson

Gathering

Sit down and place the sacred basket in front of you.

Pause so that the children notice it and begin to come closer.

Invite them to form a circle.

Sit quietly until they settle in and are quiet.

Say: "It is time for Sacred Circle Time. I am so glad that you are here today. I love learning our stories and experiencing God with you."

Creating the Sacred Space

Say: "First, we create our sacred space."

Slowly lay out the sacred cloth.

Slowly lift the globe (symbol of God, the Creator) and hold it at the eye level of the children. Say: "This is our symbol for God, the Creator." Carefully lay it on the sacred cloth. (*Pause.*)

Slowly lift the cross (symbol of God, the Son). Say: "This is our symbol for God, the Son." Carefully lay it on the sacred cloth. (*Pause.*)

Slowly lift the bell (symbol of God, the Holy Spirit). Say: "This is our symbol of God, the Holy Spirit." Carefully lay it on the sacred cloth. (*Pause.*)

Point to each symbol and say: "So we have God, the Creator; God, the Son; and God, the Holy Spirit. (*Pause.*) Our sacred space is ready. We are ready to begin our Sacred Circle Time together."

God, the Creator (A Time to Wonder)

Show the children the small bag. Shake it gently, and ask: "What do you think I have in this bag?" (*Let them guess.*) Slowly take the stones out, one at a time, and have the children count them with you. Place the stones with the hearts facing down.

God, the Son (Telling the Story)

Say: "In our story today, which is found in (*open the Bible*) Ruth, chapter 2, verses 11-13, we learn about three people: Ruth, Naomi, and Boaz. This is Naomi. (*Point to the first stone.*) Naomi's son marred Ruth. (*Point to the second stone.*) Naomi was very kind to Ruth. (*Turn the stone over and reveal the heart.*) When Naomi's son and Ruth's husband died, Ruth could have left Naomi and gone home. But Ruth remembered how kind Naomi had been to her, so she stayed. Ruth was very kind to Naomi. (*Turn Ruth's stone over and reveal the heart.*) Now these two kind women needed food and a nice place to live; but they did not have a house, and they did not have food. They might have died, but guess what? Boaz (*point to the third stone*) heard about how kind Naomi had been to Ruth and how kind Ruth had been to Naomi, and he decided to be kind to them. (*Turn his stone over to reveal the heart.*) Naomi was kind to Ruth; Ruth was kind to Naomi; and Boaz was kind to Ruth and Naomi. This is a story about kindness."

God, the Holy Spirit (Quiet and Prayer Time)

Say: "It is now time to pray. I am going to pass one of these kindness stones around; and as you hold it, share one kind thing you have done." (*Pass the stone and have each child share.*)

Pray: "God, thank you for kindness. May we always try to be kind. In the name of Christ, we pray. Amen."

A Time of Blessing

Explain that the symbol for today is a smile because when we are kind to others, we make them very happy. Bless the children where they request, being sure to look them directly in their eyes.

Say: "Thank you for experiencing God with me today. You are a blessing!"

Extended Format

(*10 minutes*) Begin with free-play time. Greet the children warmly and let them get used to the space. Have something in the free-play space for them to play with. Rotate each week:

Week One: Paper and crayons, markers, or paint.

Week Two: Clay, wire, pipe cleaners and beads, and tools to work the clay.

Week Three: Things to build with: blocks, Legos®, cans, boxes, or flat stones.

Week Four: Things that make noise.

(*3 minutes*) Transition Time. Let the children know that it is almost Sacred Circle Time. Say: "It is almost our Sacred Circle Time. I cannot wait to have sacred time with you today. Will you start to finish up? Then come join me for our special, holy time together."

Sit down in the Sacred Circle Time space and place your sacred basket in front of you.

(*10 minutes*) **Sacred Circle Time** (*Basic Format*)—Use the Sacred Circle Basic Format, but do not include the blessing or closing.

(*10 minutes*) **Trinity Stations**

Explain the Trinity Stations procedure for new children and for those who might forget from time to time.

Walk with the children to the Trinity Stations and show them what they can do in the stations, but do not let them start until they have seen all three stations.

Tell the children that after the Trinity Stations, they will spend five minutes in quiet time thinking about the story and the activities they have completed. They will then return to the Sacred Circle Time space to draw pictures and talk about their activities.

Station One: God, the Creator (Wonder) Station

Walk with the children to this station and show them what they can do here. In addition to the suggested supplies (page 469), you you might want to add paper, blocks, and stones to enable the children to create hearts.

Station Two: God, the Son (Story) Station

Walk with the children to this station and show them what they can do here. In addition to the suggested supplies (page 469), you might want to include hearts for the children to pass around as they show one another kindness.

Station Three: God, the Holy Spirit (Prayer) Station

Walk with the children to this station and show them what they can do here. In addition to the suggested supplies (page 469), you might want to have pictures of people being kind or people who need kindness so that the children can contemplate kind responses.

Begin Quiet Time

Instruct the children to begin five minutes of quiet time to think about the Bible story. Explain that after the time has elapsed, you will invite them, one at a time, to the Sacred Circle Time space to draw what they did or thought about.

(2-minute transition time) Place paper, crayons, and other material in the circle. Invite the children, one at a time, to come and draw what they did, thought about, or experienced.

(10 minutes) **Journal and Share Time**

Let them draw and journal as they gather. When most of the children have finished, let them begin to share. Remind the children that listening to one another is important.

Say: "Thank you for spending time with me in the Trinity Stations. I cannot wait to find out what you experienced today. Who would like to share?" (Give each child time to talk, and you should talk as well.)

Place their activities in individual folders; or if they are to take the folders home, place them behind them so they will not be distracted. This will keep you from having to correct the children's behavior.

10 minutes (snack or toy time)

A Time of Blessing

Explain that the symbol for today is a smile because when we are kind to others, we make them very happy. Bless the children where they request, being sure to look them directly in their eyes.

Say: "Thank you for experiencing God with me today. You are a blessing!"

Closing Time

Slowly put each Trinity symbol away.

Say: "And now we are finished with our Sacred Circle Time. We put away our symbol for God, the Creator. We put away our symbol for God, the Son. And we put away our symbol for God, the Holy Spirit."

Then quietly and gently put the sacred cloth away.

Conclude: "And we are all done with our Sacred Circle time. You did a great job. Yay!" Clap and celebrate a job well done.

Ordinary Time 16

Story: David as a Shepherd Boy

Text: Psalm 23, NRSV

The LORD IS MY SHEPHERD, I SHALL NOT WANT.
He makes me lie down in green pastures;
he leads me beside still waters;
he restores my soul.
He leads me in right paths
    for his name's sake.
Even though I walk through the darkest valley,
    I fear no evil;
for you are with me;
    your rod and your staff—
    they comfort me.
You prepare a table before me
    in the presence of my enemies;
you anoint my head with oil;
    my cup overflows.
Surely goodness and mercy shall follow me
    all the days of my life,
and I shall dwell in the house of the LORD
    my whole life long.

About the text: This Psalm is called "The Psalm of David," and David is credited with writing it. We know that his early years were spent as a shepherd and that his life as a shepherd shaped his understanding of God. David imagined God as a great shepherd who cares greatly for his sheep. This psalm also reminds us of our Good Shepherd, Jesus.

The Sacred Circle Time Focus: We will focus on Jesus as a shepherd who cares for us.

Sacred Circle Time Basic Format

Sacred Circle basket and contents:

- Sacred space cloth
- Symbols for Creator (globe), Christ (cross), and Holy Spirit (bell or chimes)
- Small, unbreakable bottle to hold water or oil for the blessing
- A journal page (one per child)
- Crayons and/or markers
- A Bible bookmarked at Psalm 23
- Focused symbols from the Bible story: Bring in different sweaters or things made from yarn or wool. Also bring sheep's wool if you have any, but do not worry if you do not.

The Lesson

Gathering

Sit down and place the sacred basket in front of you.

Pause so that the children notice it and begin to come closer.

Invite them to form a circle.

Sit quietly until they settle in and are quiet.

Say: "It is time for Sacred Circle Time. I am so glad that you are here today. I love learning our stories and experiencing God with you."

Creating the Sacred Space

Say: "First, we create our sacred space."

Slowly lay out the sacred cloth.

Slowly lift the globe (symbol of God, the Creator) and hold it at the eye level of the children. Say: "This is our symbol for God, the Creator." Carefully lay it on the sacred cloth. *(Pause.)*

Slowly lift the cross (symbol of God, the Son). Say: "This is our symbol for God, the Son." Carefully lay it on the sacred cloth. (*Pause.*)

Slowly lift the bell (symbol of God, the Holy Spirit). Say: "This is our symbol of God, the Holy Spirit." Carefully lay it on the sacred cloth. (*Pause.*)

Point to each symbol and say: "So we have God, the Creator; God, the Son; and God, the Holy Spirit. (*Pause.*) Our sacred space is ready. We are ready to begin our Sacred Circle Time together."

God, the Creator (A Time to Wonder)

Begin by showing the children the different yarns and sweaters. Let them feel how some are soft and others are scratchy. Some are dyed pink and others are dyed black. Let them enjoy feeling the different textures and noticing the differences.

After they have had time to explore, say: "Sheep grow very long wool. Once a year, people take big scissors and cut the wool off and use it to make yarn to make sweaters and other clothes. And did you know that sheep are in the Bible?"

God, the Son (Telling the Story)

Say: "In the Bible, there is a book of Psalms (*open the Bible to the Psalms*). Psalms were poems and songs written by special people who loved God very much. One of those people was a little boy named David, who became a great king. But when he was a young boy, he was a shepherd. A shepherd is a person who takes care of sheep. And he wrote a psalm, Psalm 23, that is right here in our Bible (*open to Psalm 23*). This psalm is all about how shepherds take care of their sheep. Instead of telling you about the psalm, we are going to act it out."

Say: "I am going to be the shepherd, and you are my sheep. Shepherds take good care of their sheep. So follow me little sheep."

Invite the children to pretend to be sheep. They can crawl or walk and say "baa-baa." Walk ahead of the sheep around the room.

Say: "Little, sheep I want you to drink some water. Here is the water."

Tell the children to pretend to drink water and then walk some more.

Say: "Okay, little sheep, here is a nice place to rest. Take a little nap." (*Let them pretend to sleep and then walk some more.*)

Say: "Oh no, little sheep, a big wolf is coming to try and eat you. Get very close to me and I will protect you." (*Let them gather around you.*)

Say: "Little sheep, we have had a long day. Let's go back to our Sacred Circle seats." (*Lead them back to the Sacred Circle.*)

Say: "David wrote a psalm about what good care a shepherd takes of his sheep. And Jesus is often called our Good Shepherd. Why do you think Jesus is called our Good Shepherd?" (*Let them ponder and answer.*)

Say: "The shepherd takes good care of and loves the sheep, and Jesus takes good care of us and loves us like a shepherd loves and cares for the sheep."

God, the Holy Spirit (Quiet and Prayer Time)

Say: "It is now time to pray. I am going to lead our prayer. I want you to do what I do." (*Trace a big heart in the air very slowly. Have the children follow you as if in a mirror.*)

Pray: "God, thank you for loving us and caring for us like a shepherd cares for his sheep. Amen."

A Time of Blessing

Explain that the symbol for today is a heart because because our Good Shepherd cares for us. Bless the children where they request, being sure to look them directly in their eyes.

Say: "Thank you for experiencing God with me today. You are a blessing!"

Extended Format

(*10 minutes*) Begin with free-play time. Greet the children warmly and let them get used to the space. Have something in the free-play space for them to play with. Rotate each week:

Week One: Paper and crayons, markers, or paint.

Week Two: Clay, wire, pipe cleaners and beads, and tools to work the clay.

Week Three: Things to build with: blocks, Legos®, cans, boxes, or flat stones.

Week Four: Things that make noise.

(*3 minutes*) Transition time. Let the children know that it is almost Sacred Circle Time. Say: "It is almost our Sacred Circle Time. I cannot wait to have sacred time with you today. Will you start to finish up? Then come join me for our special, holy time together."

Sit down in the Sacred Circle Time space and place your sacred basket in front of you.

(*10 minutes*) **Sacred Circle Time** (*Basic Format*)—Use the Sacred Circle Basic Format, but do not include the blessing or closing.

(*10 minutes*) **Trinity Stations**

Explain the Trinity Stations procedure for new children and for those who might forget from time to time.

Walk with the children to the Trinity Stations and show them what they can do in the stations, but do not let them start until they have seen all three stations.

Tell the children that after the Trinity Stations, they will spend five minutes in quiet time thinking about the story and the activities they have completed. They will then return to the Sacred Circle Time space to draw pictures and talk about their activities.

Station One: God, the Creator (Wonder) Station

Walk with the children to this station and show them what they can do here. In addition to the suggested supplies (page 469), you might want to add some yarn and simple weaving looms made of cardboard.

Station Two: God, the Son (Story) Station

Walk with the children to this station and show them what they can do here. In addition to the suggested supplies (page 469), you might want to include a cane or a large stick to serve as a shepherd's staff and have the children take turns leading the "sheep."

Station Three: God, the Holy Spirit (Prayer) Station

Walk with the children to this station and show them what they can do here. In addition to the suggested supplies (page 469), you might want to provide some wool or knitted blankets for the children to use as prayer shawls.

Begin Quiet Time

Instruct the children to begin five minutes of quiet time to think about the Bible story. Explain that after the time has elapsed, you will invite them, one at a time, to the Sacred Circle Time space to draw what they did or thought about.

(2-minute transition time) Place paper, crayons, and other material in the circle. Invite the children, one at a time, to come and draw what they did, thought about, or experienced.

(10 minutes) **Journal and Share Time**

Let them draw and journal as they gather. When most of the children have finished, let them begin to share. Remind the children that listening to one another is important.

Say: "Thank you for spending time with me in the Trinity Stations. I cannot wait to find out what you experienced today. Who would like to share?" (Give each child time to talk, and you should talk as well.)

Place their activities in individual folders; or if they are to take the folders home, place them behind them so they will not be distracted. This will keep you from having to correct the children's behavior.

10 minutes (snack or toy time)

A Time of Blessing

Explain that the symbol for today is a heart because because our Good Shepherd cares for us. Bless the children where they request, being sure to look them directly in their eyes.

Say: "Thank you for experiencing God with me today. You are a blessing!"

Closing Time

Slowly put each Trinity symbol away.

Say: "And now we are finished with our Sacred Circle Time. We put away our symbol for God, the Creator. We put away our symbol for God, the Son. And we put away our symbol for God, the Holy Spirit."

Then quietly and gently put the sacred cloth away.

Conclude: "And we are all done with our Sacred Circle time. You did a great job. Yay!" Clap and celebrate a job well done.

Ordinary Time 17

Story: David Makes Music

Text: I Samuel 16:14-23, NRSV

Now the spirit of the LORD departed from Saul, and an evil spirit from the LORD tormented him. And Saul's servants said to him, "See now, an evil spirit from God is tormenting you. Let our lord now command the servants who attend you to look for someone who is skillful in playing the lyre; and when the evil spirit from God is upon you, he will play it, and you will feel better." So Saul said to his servants, "Provide for me someone who can play well, and bring him to me." One of the young men answered, "I have seen a son of Jesse the Bethlehemite who is skillful in playing, a man of valor, a warrior, prudent in speech, and a man of good presence; and the LORD is with him." So Saul sent messengers to Jesse, and said, "Send me your son David who is with the sheep." Jesse took a donkey loaded with bread, a skin of wine, and a kid, and sent them by his son David to Saul. And David came to Saul, and entered his service. Saul loved him greatly, and he became his armor-bearer. Saul sent to Jesse, saying, "Let David remain in my service, for he has found favor in my sight." And whenever the evil spirit from God came upon Saul, David took the lyre and played it with his hand, and Saul would be relieved and feel better, and the evil spirit would depart from him.

About the text: David was a musician, and music was always a part of his prayer life. His music brought healing to King Saul, who suffered from some kind of mental illness. David wrote some of the psalms, and he hired musicians as part of his court. Music can help us praise God when words are not enough.

The Sacred Circle Time Focus: We will make prayers of music!

Sacred Circle Time Basic Format

Sacred Circle basket and contents:

- Sacred space cloth
- Symbols for Creator (globe), Christ (cross), and Holy Spirit (bell or chimes)
- Small, unbreakable bottle to hold water or oil for the blessing
- A journal page (one per child)
- Crayons and/or markers
- A Bible bookmarked at I Samuel 16:14-23
- Focused objects from the Bible story: Items that can make music—bells, drums, sticks—anything that the children can play and enjoy. These items may be bought or made.

The Lesson

Gathering

Sit down and place the sacred basket in front of you.

Pause so that the children notice it and begin to come closer.

Invite them to form a circle.

Sit quietly until they settle in and are quiet.

Say: "It is time for Sacred Circle Time. I am so glad that you are here today. I love learning our stories and experiencing God with you."

Creating the Sacred Space

Say: "First, we create our sacred space."

Slowly lay out the sacred cloth.

Slowly lift the globe (symbol of God, the Creator) and hold it at the eye level of the children. Say: "This is our symbol for God, the Creator." Carefully lay it on the sacred cloth. *(Pause.)*

Slowly lift the cross (symbol of God, the Son). Say: "This is our symbol for God, the Son." Carefully lay it on the sacred cloth. (*Pause.*)

Slowly lift the bell (symbol of God, the Holy Spirit). Say: "This is our symbol of God, the Holy Spirit." Carefully lay it on the sacred cloth. (*Pause.*)

Point to each symbol and say: "So we have God, the Creator; God, the Son; and God, the Holy Spirit. (*Pause.*) Our sacred space is ready. We are ready to begin our Sacred Circle Time together."

God, the Creator (A Time to Wonder)

Get out the bells, drums, and other music instruments, and let the children play. You might play music for them to play along with, or just allow them to have fun making their own music. Encourage them to trade and share after they have used one instrument for a few minutes, so that everyone gets to play all the instruments. Collect the instruments after the children have time to play. You will want quiet before the story.

God, the Son (Telling the Story)

Say: "Music is fun isn't it? Did you know that music can also be used to heal people and to pray to God? Well, in our story today, which is found in (*open the Bible*) I Samuel, chapter 16, and verses 14-23, David is a little boy who was asked to come and live with King Saul to play music for him. King Saul was very sick, but when David played music for him, he felt better. David loved music. When he grew up, he wrote songs and filled his kingdom with musicians playing music. And he even wrote prayers and sang them to God. David loved music and prayed to God with music and songs."

God, the Holy Spirit (Quiet and Prayer Time)

Say: "It is now time to pray."

For the prayer time, play a song on a CD player or teach the children a song that you like or that is used in your faith community. Or sing to them. Let them enjoy the music as they listen, or have them sing along or play along with the music makers.

Pray: "God, our song is our prayer. Amen."

(If using the extended Sacred Circle Time, stop here.)

A Time of Blessing

Explain that the symbol for today is a music note because David taught us to sing as prayer. Bless the children where they request, being sure to look them directly in their eyes.

Say: "Thank you for experiencing God with me today. You are a blessing!"

Extended Format

(10 minutes) Begin with free-play time. Greet the children warmly and let them get used to the space. Have something in the free-play space for them to play with. Rotate each week:

Week One: Paper and crayons, markers, or paint.

Week Two: Clay, wire, pipe cleaners and beads, and tools to work the clay.

Week Three: Things to build with: blocks, Legos®, cans, boxes, or flat stones.

Week Four: Things that make noise.

(3 minutes) Transition Time. Let the children know that it is almost Sacred Circle Time.

Say: "It is almost our Sacred Circle Time. I cannot wait to have sacred time with you today. Will you start to finish up? Then come join me for our special, holy time together."

Sit down in the Sacred Circle Time space and place your sacred basket in front of you.

(*10 minutes*) **Sacred Circle Time** (*Basic Format*)—Use the Sacred Circle Basic Format, but do not include the blessing or closing.

(*10 minutes*) **Trinity Stations**

Explain the Trinity Stations procedure for new children and for those who might forget from time to time.

Walk with the children to the Trinity Stations and show them what they can do in the stations, but do not let them start until they have seen all three stations.

Tell the children that after the Trinity Stations, they will spend five minutes in quiet time thinking about the story and the activities they have completed. They will then return to the Sacred Circle Time space to draw pictures and talk about their activities.

Station One: God, the Creator (Wonder) Station

Walk with the children to this station and show them what they can do here. In addition to the suggested supplies (page 469), you might want to add some materials that the children can use to create their own musical instruments: string, pipe, small boxes, rocks and rubber bands, tin cans, spoons, and so on.

Station Two: God, the Son (Story) Station

Walk with the children to this station and show them what they can do here. In addition to the suggested supplies (page 469), you might want to include the music instruments from the Sacred Circle (Wonder) Time.

Station Three: God, the Holy Spirit (Prayer) Station

Walk with the children to this station and show them what they can do here. In addition to the suggested supplies (page 469), you might want to have an old guitar or autoharp for the children to play as they pray. Or you might want to provide paper for them to write a song on or a tape recorder for them to sing, tape, and listen to the song they have written.

Begin Quiet Time

Instruct the children to begin five minutes of quiet time to think about the Bible story. Explain that after the time has elapsed, you will invite them, one at a time, to the Sacred Circle Time space to draw what they did or thought about.

(2-minute transition time) Place paper, crayons, and other material in the circle. Invite the children, one at a time, to come and draw what they did, thought about, or experienced.

(10 minutes) **Journal and Share Time**

Let them draw and journal as they gather. When most of the children have finished, let them begin to share. Remind the children that listening to one another is important.

Say: "Thank you for spending time with me in the Trinity Stations. I cannot wait to find out what you experienced today. Who would like to share?" (Give each child time to talk, and you should talk as well.)

Place their activities in individual folders; or if they are to take the folders home, place them behind them so they will not be distracted. This will keep you from having to correct the children's behavior.

10 minutes (snack or toy time)

A Time of Blessing

Explain that the symbol for today is a music note because David taught us to sing as prayer. Bless the children where they request, being sure to look them directly in their eyes.

Say: "Thank you for experiencing God with me today. You are a blessing!"

Closing Time

Slowly put each Trinity symbol away.

Say: "And now we are finished with our Sacred Circle Time. We put away our symbol for God, the Creator. We put away our symbol for God, the Son. And we put away our symbol for God, the Holy Spirit."

Then quietly and gently put the sacred cloth away.

Conclude: "And we are all done with our Sacred Circle time. You did a great job. Yay!" Clap and celebrate a job well done.

Ordinary Time 18

Story: David Is Brave

Text: I Samuel 17:45-47, NRSV

But David said to the Philistine, "You come to me with sword and spear and javelin; but I come to you in the name of the LORD of hosts, the God of the armies of Israel, whom you have defied. This very day the LORD will deliver you into my hand, and I will strike you down and cut off your head; and I will give the dead bodies of the Philistine army this very day to the birds of the air and to the wild animals of the earth, so that all the earth may know that there is a God in Israel, and that all this assembly may know that the LORD does not save by sword and spear; for the battle is the Lords and he will give you into our hand."

About the text: The story of David slaying the giant is a great story for children, since the hero of the story is a child. Not only is the hero a child, but he is a child who loves God. Children have many heroes in their lives, but not many who love God. Sometimes we shy away from this story because it has violence. With this in mind, this telling of the story focuses more on the bravery of David and less on the death of Goliath. All children face difficulties in life. This story will remind them that God is always with us, no matter what kind of "giants" or "battles" we are faced with.

The Sacred Circle Time Focus: We will focus on David being brave as he faced Goliath. He was brave because he knew that God was with him.

Sacred Circle Time Basic Format

Sacred Circle basket and contents:

- Sacred space cloth
- Symbols for Creator (globe), Christ (cross), and Holy Spirit (bell or chimes)
- Small, unbreakable bottle to hold water or oil for the blessing
- A journal page (one per child)
- Crayons and/or markers
- A Bible bookmarked at I Samuel 17:45-47
- Focused objects from the Bible story: Blocks or anything that can be stacked high

The Lesson

Gathering

Sit down and place the sacred basket in front of you.

Pause so that the children notice it and begin to come closer.

Invite them to form a circle.

Sit quietly until they settle in and are quiet.

Say: "It is time for Sacred Circle Time. I am so glad that you are here today. I love learning our stories and experiencing God with you."

Creating the Sacred Space

Say: "First, we create our sacred space."

Slowly lay out the sacred cloth.

Slowly lift the globe (symbol of God, the Creator) and hold it at the eye level of the children. Say: "This is our symbol for God, the Creator." Carefully lay it on the sacred cloth. (Pause.)

Slowly lift the cross (symbol of God, the Son). Say: "This is our symbol for God, the Son." Carefully lay it on the sacred cloth. (*Pause.*)

Slowly lift the bell (symbol of God, the Holy Spirit). Say: "This is our symbol of God, the Holy Spirit." Carefully lay it on the sacred cloth. (*Pause.*)

Point to each symbol and say: "So we have God, the Creator; God, the Son; and God, the Holy Spirit. (*Pause.*) Our sacred space is ready. We are ready to begin our Sacred Circle Time together."

God, the Creator (A Time to Wonder)

Get the blocks out, and let the children make shapes with them. Then make the letter "D." Have the children guess what letter it is.

God, the Son (Telling the Story)

Say: "I made the letter 'D' because that is the first letter of the name of our Bible character today. His name was David, and David was a little boy. In (*open the Bible*) I Samuel, chapter 17, there is a great story about David. But before I get to the part about David, I have to tell you that there was a giant named Goliath that everyone was afraid of. The king was afraid of him. The soldiers were afraid of him. Everyone was afraid of him because he was a big giant. Except for one person. (*Point to the letter 'D.'*) David was not afraid of Goliath. And someone had to fight Goliath. So David offered, and off he went to fight the giant. All he had was a slingshot and a five little stones. And Goliath was big. This big. (*Stack all but one of the blocks on top of one another.*) And David was a little boy, only this big. (*Point to the one small block.*) Who do you think will win? (*Let them answer.*) Well, little David went right up to big Goliath and said, 'I am not afraid of your sword or how big you are. I have called on God, and God will help me win this battle!' And David did win the battle, and Goliath lost. (*Knock the stack of blocks over.*) And why did David win? Because he had God to help him! And knowing that God was with him made him feel very brave!"

God, the Holy Spirit (Quiet and Prayer Time)

Say: "It is now time to pray. I am going to make another letter out of the blocks. This time I am making the letter 'G.' Do you know what name starts with 'G?' God. For our prayer time, I want you sit silently for a few moments and think about God and how God is always with you, just like God was with David." (*Give them a few seconds of silence.*)

Pray: "God, thank you for always being with us. Amen."

(If using the extended Sacred Circle Time, stop here.)

A Time of Blessing

Explain that the symbol for today is the letter "G" because God is always with us.

Bless the children where they request, being sure to look them directly in their eyes.

Say: "Thank you for experiencing God with me today. You are a blessing!"

Extended Format

(*10 minutes*) Begin with free-play time. Greet the children warmly and let them get used to the space. Have something in the free-play space for them to play with. Rotate each week:

Week One: Paper and crayons, markers, or paint.

Week Two: Clay, wire, pipe cleaners and beads, and tools to work the clay.

Week Three: Things to build with: blocks, Legos®, cans, boxes, or flat stones.

Week Four: Things that make noise.

(*3 minutes*) Transition time. Let the children know that it is almost Sacred Circle Time. Say: "It is almost our Sacred Circle Time. I cannot wait to have sacred time with you today. Will you start to finish up? Then come join me for our special, holy time together."

Sit down in the Sacred Circle Time space and place your sacred basket in front of you.

(*10 minutes*) **Sacred Circle Time** (*Basic Format*)—Use the Sacred Circle Basic Format, but do not include the blessing or closing.

(*10 minutes*) **Trinity Stations**

Explain the Trinity Stations procedure for new children and for those who might forget from time to time.

Walk with the children to the Trinity Stations and show them what they can do in the stations, but do not let them start until they have seen all three stations.

Tell the children that after the Trinity Stations, they will spend five minutes in quiet time thinking about the story and the activities they have completed. They will then return to the Sacred Circle Time space to draw pictures and talk about their activities.

Station One: God the Creator (Wonder) Station

Walk with the children to this station and show them what they can do here. In addition to the suggested supplies (page 469), you might want to add the blocks from the Sacred Circle Time.

Station Two: God, the Son (Story) Station

Walk with the children to this station and show them what they can do here. In addition to the suggested supplies (page 469), you might want to include some big boxes to stack up and pretend they are a giant, so that the children can act out the story.

Station Three: God, the Holy Spirit (Prayer) Station

Walk with the children to this station and show them what they can do here. In addition to the suggested supplies (page 469), you might provide a mirror so the children can reflect on how brave and wonderfully made they are (very much like David)!

Begin Quiet Time

Instruct the children to begin five minutes of quiet time to think about the Bible story. Explain that after the time has elapsed, you will invite them, one at a time, to the Sacred Circle Time space to draw what they did or thought about.

(*2-minute transition time*) Place paper, crayons, and other material in the circle. Invite the children, one at a time, to come and draw what they did, thought about, or experienced.

(*10 minutes*) **Journal and Share Time**

Let them draw and journal as they gather. When most of the children have finished, let them begin to share. Remind the children that listening to one another is important.

Say: "Thank you for spending time with me in the Trinity Stations. I cannot wait to find out what you experienced today. Who would like to share?" (Give each child time to talk, and you should talk as well.)

Place their activities in individual folders; or if they are to take the folders home, place them behind them so they will not be distracted. This will keep you from having to correct the children's behavior.

10 minutes (snack or toy time)

A Time of Blessing

Explain that the symbol for today is the letter "G" because God is always with us.

Bless the children where they request, being sure to look them directly in their eyes.

Say: "Thank you for experiencing God with me today. You are a blessing!"

Closing Time

Slowly put each Trinity symbol away.

Say: "And now we are finished with our Sacred Circle Time. We put away our symbol for God, the Creator. We put away our symbol for God, the Son. And we put away our symbol for God, the Holy Spirit."

Then quietly and gently put the sacred cloth away.

Conclude: "And we are all done with our Sacred Circle time. You did a great job. Yay!" Clap and celebrate a job well done.

Ordinary Time 19

Story: David Is a Good King

Text: I Samuel 16:11-13, NRSV

Samuel said to Jesse, "Are all your sons here?" And he said, "There remains yet the youngest, but he is keeping the sheep." And Samuel said to Jesse, "Send and bring him; for we will not sit down until he comes here." He sent and brought him in. Now he was ruddy, and had beautiful eyes, and was handsome. The LORD said, "Rise and anoint him; for this is the one." Then Samuel took the horn of oil, and anointed him in the presence of his brothers; and the spirit of the Lord came mightily upon David from that day forward. Samuel then set out and went to Ramah.

About the text: The people wanted a king because others had a king. They had cried out and begged God for a king, so God heard their prayers and selected Saul as the first king. The people wanted a king who would protect them. But of course, God is the only true protection we have, so God chose men to be kings who would follow God. Thus, the people would have the protection of God through the leadership of their king. Saul was the first king, but he lost his will to follow God, and God lost favor in him. In this story, God sends Samuel to anoint a new king. He finds David, still a young boy, and anoints him the new king. King David, while not perfect, loved God and served God faithfully; and it is from his lineage that Jesus was born.

The Sacred Circle Time Focus: We will focus on David being anointed king and loving God all his life.

Sacred Circle Time Basic Format

Sacred Circle basket and contents:

- Sacred space cloth
- Symbols for Creator (globe), Christ (cross), and Holy Spirit (bell or chimes)
- Small, unbreakable bottle to hold water or oil for the blessing
- A journal page (one per child)
- Crayons and/or markers
- A Bible bookmarked at I Samuel 16:11-13
- Focused objects from the Bible story: A small amount of oil on a cotton ball placed in a small bowl

The Gathering

Sit down and place the sacred basket in front of you.

Pause so that the children notice it and begin to come closer.

Invite them to form a circle.

Sit quietly until they settle in and are quiet.

Say: "It is time for Sacred Circle Time. I am so glad that you are here today. I love learning our stories and experiencing God with you."

Creating the Sacred Space

Say: "First, we create our sacred space."

Slowly lay out the sacred cloth.

Slowly lift the globe (symbol of God, the Creator) and hold it at the eye level of the children. Say: "This is our symbol for God, the Creator." Carefully lay it on the sacred cloth. (*Pause.*)

Slowly lift the cross (symbol of God, the Son). Say: "This is our symbol for God, the Son." Carefully lay it on the sacred cloth. (*Pause.*)

Slowly lift the bell (symbol of God, the Holy Spirit). Say: "This is our symbol of God, the Holy Spirit." Carefully lay it on the sacred cloth. (*Pause.*)

Point to each symbol and say: "So we have God, the Creator; God, the Son; and God, the Holy Spirit. (*Pause.*) Our sacred space is ready. We are ready to begin our Sacred Circle Time together."

God, the Creator (A Time to Wonder)

Say: "Today, I want us to pretend. Let's pretend that we are babies. (*Let them act as if they are babies.*) Now, let's pretend that we are big kids. (*Let them walk around acting as if they are big!*) Now let's act like we mommies and daddies. (*Let them walk around pretending to be grown.*) And now, let's pretend to be very old." (*Let them pretend to be old people.*)

Say: "You are very good at pretending. Let's be ourselves again now and sit and listen to our story." (*Give them a few seconds to settle down after having fun.*)

God, the Son (Telling the Story)

Say: "In our story today, which is found (*open the Bible*) in I Samuel, chapter 16, verses 11-13, God sends a helper named Samuel to find a new king. God wants Samuel to find a person who will love God and listen to God, not just when he is a baby, or a little child, or a daddy, but for his entire life. God wants people to love God and listen to God for their entire lives! So Samuel goes to the house where David, the little shepherd boy lives. After meeting all of David's older brothers, Samuel gets to meet David. And when he meets David, God tells Samuel to make David the king. And he takes some special oil, like this (*show them your oil*), and rubs it on David's face. This oil meant that God had chosen David to be the king. God knew that David would love

God for his entire life, so God made him king by asking Samuel to rub special oil on him. David became the king, and do you know what? He loved God for his whole life! He loved God when he was a boy, when he was a daddy, and when he was very old."

God, the Holy Spirit (Quiet and Prayer Time)

Say: "It is now time to pray. For our prayer, I am going to place a tiny bit of oil on your hand or your head as a prayer that you, like David, will love God for your whole life."

Anoint each child. Ask the children if they would like the oil on their face or hand before you anoint them.

As you place the oil on each child, say: "(*Name of Child*), I pray that you love God every day of your entire life."

Pray: "God, You love us, and we love you. Amen."

(If using the extended Sacred Circle Time, stop here.)

A Time of Blessing

Explain that the symbol for today is a crown because, the children, like David, are very special to God! Bless the children where they request, being sure to look them directly in their eyes.

Say: "Thank you for experiencing God with me today. You are a blessing!"

Extended Format

(*10 minutes*) Begin with free-play time. Greet the children warmly and let them get used to the space. Have something in the free-play space for them to play with. Rotate each week:

Week One: Paper and crayons, markers, or paint.

Week Two: Clay, wire, pipe cleaners and beads, and tools to work the clay.

Week Three: Things to build with: blocks, Legos®, cans, boxes, or flat stones.

Week Four: Things that make noise.

(*3 minutes*) Transition Time. Let the children know that it is almost Sacred Circle Time. Say: "It is almost our Sacred Circle Time. I cannot wait to have sacred time with you today. Will you start to finish up? Then come join me for our special, holy time together."

Sit down in the Sacred Circle Time space and place your sacred basket in front of you.

(*10 minutes*) **Sacred Circle Time** (*Basic Format*)—Use the Sacred Circle Basic Format, but do not include the blessing or closing.

(*10 minutes*) **Trinity Stations**

Explain the Trinity Stations procedure for new children and for those who might forget from time to time.

Walk with the children to the Trinity Stations and show them what they can do in the stations, but do not let them start until they have seen all three stations.

Tell the children that after the Trinity Stations, they will spend five minutes in quiet time thinking about the story and the activities they have completed. They will then return to the Sacred Circle Time space to draw pictures and talk about their activities.

Station One: God, the Creator (Wonder) Station

Walk with the children to this station and show them what they can do here. In addition to the suggested supplies (page 469), you you might want to add some play gems like a king or queen would have on his or her crown and a magnifying glass so the children may look at them closely.

Station Two: God, the Son (Story) Station

Walk with the children to this station and show them what they can do here. In addition to the suggested supplies (page 469), you might want to include the king's attire and oil from the Sacred Circle Time for the children to act out the story.

Station Three: God, the Holy Spirit (Prayer) Station

Walk with the children to this station and show them what they can do here. In addition to the suggested supplies (page 469), you might also want to provide some water and colored oils that the children may use during prayer time as they contemplate God's love for them.

Begin Quiet Time

Instruct the children to begin five minutes of quiet time to think about the Bible story. Explain that after the time has elapsed, you will invite them, one at a time, to the Sacred Circle Time space to draw what they did or thought about.

(*2-minute transition time*) Place paper, crayons, and other material in the circle. Invite the children, one at a time, to come and draw what they did, thought about, or experienced.

(*10 minutes*) **Journal and Share Time**

Let them draw and journal as they gather. When most of the children have finished, let them begin to share. Remind the children that listening to one another is important.

Say: "Thank you for spending time with me in the Trinity Stations. I cannot wait to find out what you experienced today. Who would like to share?" (Give each child time to talk, and you should talk as well.)

Place their activities in individual folders; or if they are to take the folders home, place them behind them so they will not be distracted. This will keep you from having to correct the children's behavior.

10 minutes (snack or toy time)

A Time of Blessing

Explain that the symbol for today is a crown because the children, like David, are very special to God! Bless the children where they request, being sure to look them directly in their eyes.

Say: "Thank you for experiencing God with me today. You are a blessing!"

Closing Time

Slowly put each Trinity symbol away.

Say: "And now we are finished with our Sacred Circle Time. We put away our symbol for God, the Creator. We put away our symbol for God, the Son. And we put away our symbol for God, the Holy Spirit."

Then quietly and gently put the sacred cloth away.

Conclude: "And we are all done with our Sacred Circle time. You did a great job. Yay!" Clap and celebrate a job well done.

Ordinary Time 20

Story: Daniel in the Lions' Den

Text: Daniel 6:16-24, NRSV

Then the king gave the command, and Daniel was brought and thrown into the den of lions. The king said to Daniel, "May your God, whom you faithfully serve, deliver you!" A stone was brought and laid on the mouth of the den, and the king sealed it with his own signet and with the signet of his lords, so that nothing might be changed concerning Daniel. Then the king went to his palace and spent the night fasting; no food was brought to him, and sleep fled from him.

Then, at break of day, the king got up and hurried to the den of lions. When he came near the den where Daniel was, he cried out anxiously to Daniel, "O Daniel, servant of the living God, has your God whom you faithfully serve been able to deliver you from the lions?" Daniel then said to the king, "O king, live forever! My God sent his angel and shut the lions' mouths so that they would not hurt me, because I was found blameless before him; and also before you, O king, I have done no wrong." Then the king was exceedingly glad and commanded that Daniel be taken up out of the den. So Daniel was taken up out of the den, and no kind of harm was found on him, because he had trusted in his God.

About the text: Daniel in the Lions' Den is a great story for children because Daniel is a young person when taken to serve the king, yet he demonstrates great maturity and determination to serve God no matter what trials he had to endure. This is one of the most famous of stories about Daniel and a great one for young children to learn.

The Sacred Circle Time Focus: We will focus on Daniel, who refused to stop worshiping God and who was protected by God in the lions' den.

Sacred Circle Time Basic Format

Sacred Circle basket and contents:

- Sacred space cloth
- Symbols for Creator (globe), Christ (cross), and Holy Spirit (bell or chimes)
- Small, unbreakable bottle to hold water or oil for the blessing
- A journal page (one per child)
- Crayons and/or markers
- A Bible bookmarked at Daniel 6:16-24
- Focused objects from the Bible story: A toothbrush and toothpaste and mirror

The Lesson

Gathering

Sit down and place the sacred basket in front of you.

Pause so that the children notice it and begin to come closer.

Invite them to form a circle.

Sit quietly until they settle in and are quiet.

Say: "It is time for Sacred Circle Time. I am so glad that you are here today. I love learning our stories and experiencing God with you."

Creating the Sacred Space

Say: "First, we create our sacred space."

Slowly lay out the sacred cloth.

Slowly lift the globe (symbol of God, the Creator) and hold it at the eye level of the children. Say: "This is our symbol for God, the Creator." Carefully lay it on the sacred cloth. (*Pause.*)

Slowly lift the cross (symbol of God, the Son). Say: "This is our symbol for God, the Son." Carefully lay it on the sacred cloth. (*Pause.*)

Slowly lift the bell (symbol of God, the Holy Spirit). Say: "This is our symbol of God, the Holy Spirit." Carefully lay it on the sacred cloth. (*Pause.*)

Point to each symbol and say: "So we have God, the Creator; God, the Son; and God, the Holy Spirit. (*Pause.*) Our sacred space is ready. We are ready to begin our Sacred Circle Time together."

God, the Creator (A Time to Wonder)

Begin by showing the children your teeth and talking about why we take care of our teeth. We need our teeth so that we can eat. Let the children look at their own teeth in the mirror. Kids love teeth and will find this fascinating.

God, the Son (Telling the Story)

Say: "You know, there are teeth in our story today, which is found in (*open the Bible*) Daniel, chapter 6, verses 16-24. The story begins with a boy named Daniel who loved God so much! The king told Daniel that he was not allowed to pray to God anymore. But Daniel loved God, and he would not stop praying to God. So the king decided to throw Daniel in a lions' den and let the lions eat him. I told you this story was about teeth . . . big lion teeth. Now you know how big your teeth are. How big do you think a lion's teeth are? (*Let them share.*) Yes, lions have very big and very sharp teeth. The king got so mad at Daniel because he would not stop praying to God that he decided to put

Daniel in a big cave where lions lived. He was going to let those lions with their great big teeth eat poor Daniel! Poor Daniel was thrown into the lions' den. Do you think those lions ate him? (*Let them guess.*) No. They did not eat him. God shut the mouths of those lions, and they did not eat poor Daniel. God protected Daniel. Daniel loved God, and Daniel trusted God. And God took care of Daniel."

God, the Holy Spirit (Quiet and Prayer Time)

"Say: It is now time to pray. But before we do, I am going to pass this toothbrush around, and as you think about those big lion teeth and how scared poor Daniel was in the lions' den, I want you to share something you are afraid of. We are all afraid of something." (*You should speak first, so that they do not feel embarrassed. Then have the children speak.*)

Pray: "God, all of us are afraid of something. Please remind us that you care for us just like you cared for Daniel in the lions' den. Amen."

(If using the extended Sacred Circle Time, stop here.)

A Time of Blessing

Explain that the symbol for today is a lion because God protected Daniel from the lions in the lions' den. Bless the children where they request, being sure to look them directly in their eyes.

Say: "Thank you for experiencing God with me today. You are a blessing!"

Extended Format

(*10 minutes*) Begin with free-play time. Greet the children warmly and let them get used to the space. Have something in the free-play space for them to play with. Rotate each week:

Week One: Paper and crayons, markers, or paint.

Week Two: Clay, wire, pipe cleaners and beads, and tools to work the clay.

Week Three: Things to build with: blocks, Legos®, cans, boxes, or flat stones.

Week Four: Things that make noise.

(*3 minutes*) Transition Time. Let the children know that it is almost Sacred Circle Time. Say: "It is almost our Sacred Circle Time. I cannot wait to have sacred time with you today. Will you start to finish up? Then come join me for our special, holy time together."

Sit down in the Sacred Circle Time space and place your sacred basket in front of you.

(*10 minutes*) **Sacred Circle Time** (*Basic Format*)—Use the Sacred Circle Basic Format, but do not include the blessing or closing.

(*10 minutes*) **Trinity Stations**

Explain the Trinity Stations procedure for new children and for those who might forget from time to time.

Walk with the children to the Trinity Stations and show them what they can do in the stations, but do not let them start until they have seen all three stations.

Tell the children that after the Trinity Stations, they will spend five minutes in quiet time thinking about the story and the activities they have completed. They will then return to the Sacred Circle Time space to draw pictures and talk about their activities.

Station One: God, the Creator (Wonder) Station

Walk with the children to this station and show them what they can do here. In addition to the suggested supplies (page 469), you might want to add some real animal teeth or plastic animals with their teeth showing. Include some mirrors so that the children can examine their own teeth.

Station Two: God, the Son (Story) Station

Walk with the children to this station and show them what they can do here. In addition to the suggested supplies (page 469), you might want to include a large box filled with stuffed lions or paper to make lions so that the children can act out the story.

Station Three: God, the Holy Spirit (Prayer) Station

Walk with the children to this station and show them what they can do here. In addition to the suggested supplies (page 469), you might want to include a flashlight to remind the children that God is always with them, even in dark times.

Begin Quiet Time

Instruct the children to begin five minutes of quiet time to think about the Bible story. Explain that after the time has elapsed, you will invite them, one at a time, to the Sacred Circle Time space to draw what they did or thought about.

(*2-minute transition time*) Place paper, crayons, and other material in the circle. Invite the children, one at a time, to come and draw what they did, thought about, or experienced.

(*10 minutes*) **Journal and Share Time**

Let them draw and journal as they gather. When most of the children have finished, let them begin to share. Remind the children that listening to one another is important.

Say: "Thank you for spending time with me in the Trinity Stations. I cannot wait to find out what you experienced today. Who would like to share?" (Give each child time to talk, and you should talk as well.)

Place their activities in individual folders; or if they are to take the folders home, place them behind them so they will not be distracted. This will keep you from having to correct the children's behavior.

10 minutes (snack or toy time)

A Time of Blessing

Explain that the symbol for today is a lion because God protected Daniel from the lions in the lions' den. Bless the children where they request, being sure to look them directly in their eyes.

Say: "Thank you for experiencing God with me today. You are a blessing!"

Closing Time

Slowly put each Trinity symbol away.

Say: "And now we are finished with our Sacred Circle Time. We put away our symbol for God, the Creator. We put away our symbol for God, the Son. And we put away our symbol for God, the Holy Spirit."

Then quietly and gently put the sacred cloth away.

Conclude: "And we are all done with our Sacred Circle time. You did a great job. Yay!" Clap and celebrate a job well done.

Ordinary Time 21

Story: Parable of the Lost Sheep

Text: Luke 15:3-7, NRSV

So he told them this parable: "Which one of you, having a hundred sheep and losing one of them, does not leave the ninety-nine in the wilderness and go after the one that is lost until he finds it? When he has found it, he lays it on his shoulders and rejoices. And when he comes home, he calls together his friends and neighbors, saying to them, 'Rejoice with me, for I have found my sheep that was lost.' Just so, I tell you, there will be more joy in heaven over one sinner who repents than over ninety-nine righteous persons who need no repentance.

About the text: Jesus often taught through parables. He used symbolic language to describe a spiritual reality that is often difficult to capture with words. Teaching a parable to young children is difficult because they cannot make the leap between the symbolic language used and how the story "really" means something about God. However, this parable, where Jesus talks about a good shepherd, is one that young children can relate to, partly because they love animals and partly because they understand what it is to need to be cared for. This parable should be taught over and over. Knowing that Jesus cares for us, even when we get lost, is a foundational lesson. This image of Jesus as the Good Shepherd was also used in Psalm 23, and we are using it again because it is such a central image of Jesus. Repetition of images is good for young children.

The Sacred Circle Time Focus: We will focus on Jesus being our shepherd who knows and loves us.

Sacred Circle Time Basic Format

Sacred Circle basket and contents:

- Sacred space cloth
- Symbols for Creator (globe), Christ (cross), and Holy Spirit (bell or chimes)
- Small, unbreakable bottle to hold water or oil for the blessing
- A journal page (one per child)
- Crayons and/or markers
- A Bible bookmarked at Luke 15:3-7
- Focused objects from the Bible story: Three things we use to communicate with others. Some suggestions are 39 cotton balls in a basket and one cotton ball hidden somewhere.

The Lesson

Gathering

Sit down and place the sacred basket in front of you.

Pause so that the children notice it and begin to come closer.

Invite them to form a circle.

Sit quietly until they settle in and are quiet.

Say: "It is time for Sacred Circle Time. I am so glad that you are here today. I love learning our stories and experiencing God with you."

Creating the Sacred Space

Say: "First, we create our sacred space."

Slowly lay out the sacred cloth.

Slowly lift the globe (symbol of God, the Creator) and hold it at the eye level of the children. Say: "This is our symbol for God, the Creator." Carefully lay it on the sacred cloth. (*Pause.*)

Slowly lift the cross (symbol of God, the Son). Say: "This is our symbol for God, the Son." Carefully lay it on the sacred cloth. (*Pause.*)

Slowly lift the bell (symbol of God, the Holy Spirit).

Say: "This is our symbol of God, the Holy Spirit." Carefully lay it on the sacred cloth. (*Pause.*)

Point to each symbol and say: "So we have God, the Creator; God, the Son; and God, the Holy Spirit. (*Pause.*) Our sacred space is ready. We are ready to begin our Sacred Circle Time together."

God, the Creator (A Time to Wonder)

Show the children the cotton balls. Ask, "Why do you think I have a basket of cotton balls? What could we do with these?" (*Let them come up with lots of ideas.*)

God, the Son (Telling the Story)

Say: "In our story today, which is found in (*open the Bible*) Luke, chapter 15, verses 3-7, there is a story about a good shepherd who loved his sheep and took good care of them. I was wondering if you want to be shepherds to my sheep. These cotton balls are my tiny sheep. I have 40 sheep. Would you like to help me care for them? (*The children will be very excited about the sheep.*) Okay, we are the shepherds, and we will need to feed our sheep, and make sure they get enough food and water. And we must take care of all 40 of them. And each day, we must count our sheep to make sure they are all here. So will you help me count my sheep?"

Count the sheep one at a time. The Bible has 99 sheep, but young children will lose interest if you have 100 sheep (cotton balls). Forty is a large number, and they will get the point of the parable. When you find out that you have only 39 sheep, act upset.

Say: "Oh, no! I cannot believe one of our sheep is missing, and we are the shepherds. It is our job to take care of all the sheep. And one is not here. She won't be able to eat or drink, and she might be hurt. We have to find her! Little shepherds, help me find the sheep! (*Let them search and search. The cotton ball sheep should be hidden well so that it is not easily found. When it is found, get very excited and start clapping!*)

"We found the sheep . . . we found the sheep!!!! (*You might want to start a chant of 'The lost sheep was lost and now is found' while you return it to its basket.*) We love all our sheep. When one is missing, we will not stop until we find it!! Thank you for helping me find my little sheep. She was lost but now she is found, and I am so very happy!"

"Our story for today is about a good shepherd who lost his sheep. He loved that sheep so much that he looked and looked until he found it; then he was so excited, just like we were! Do any of you know who *our* Good Shepherd is? Who it is that watches over and cares for us? Jesus. He loves you like the little sheep was loved!"

God, the Holy Spirit (Quiet and Prayer Time)

Say: "It is now time to pray. I am going to give each of you a little sheep to hold.

(*Place a cotton ball in each of their hands.*) I want you to close your eyes and imagine that you are this little sheep and that the loving hands of Jesus are holding you. Image how tenderly and lovingly he holds you, my little sheep." (*Give them a few seconds of silence.*)

Pray: "God, thank you for Jesus, our Good Shepherd, who loves us all so much. In his name, we pray. Amen."

(If using the extended Sacred Circle Time, stop here.)

A Time of Blessing

Explain that the symbol for today is a little sheep because the children are like little sheep, and Jesus is our shepherd and he loves and cares for us. Bless the children where they request, being sure to look them directly in their eyes.

Say: "Thank you for experiencing God with me today. You are a blessing!"

Extended Format

(*10 minutes*) Begin with free-play time. Greet the children warmly and let them get used to the space. Have something in the free-play space for them to play with. Rotate each week:

Week One: Paper and crayons, markers, or paint.

Week Two: Clay, wire, pipe cleaners and beads, and tools to work the clay.

Week Three: Things to build with: blocks, Legos®, cans, boxes, or flat stones.

Week Four: Things that make noise.

(*3 minutes*) Transition Time. Let the children know that it is almost Sacred Circle Time. Say: "It is almost our Sacred Circle Time. I cannot wait to have sacred time with you today. Will you start to finish up? Then come join me for our special, holy time together."

Sit down in the Sacred Circle Time space and place your sacred basket in front of you.

(*10 minutes*) **Trinity Stations**

Explain the Trinity Stations procedure for new children and for those who might forget from time to time.

Walk with the children to the Trinity Stations and show them what they can do in the stations, but do not let them start until they have seen all three stations.

Tell the children that after the Trinity Stations, they will spend five minutes in quiet time thinking about the story and the activities they have completed. They will then return to the Sacred Circle Time space to draw pictures and talk about their activities.

Station One: God, the Creator (Wonder) Station

Walk with the children to this station and show them what they can do here. In addition to the suggested supplies (page 469), you might want to add some books that have hidden objects and encourage the children to try to find them. You can also make simple hide-and-find toys by hiding small objects inside clear plastic bottles filled with rice. The children can turn and twist the bottles around, shifting the rice until they discover the hidden items.

Station Two: God, the Son (Story) Station

Walk with the children to this station and show them what they can do here. In addition to the suggested supplies (page 469), you might want to include a shepherd's staff or cane and some stuffed animals so that the children can pretend to be shepherds. Or provide cotton balls that the children can use as their sheep.

Station Three: God, the Holy Spirit (Prayer) Station

Walk with the children to this station and show them what they can do here. In addition to the suggested supplies (page 469), you might want to provide cotton balls and paint and encourage the children to paint a picture prayer of the care of the Good Shepherd.

Begin Quiet Time

Instruct the children to begin five minutes of quiet time to think about the Bible story. Explain that after the time has elapsed, you will invite them, one at a time, to the Sacred Circle Time space to draw what they did or thought about.

(2-minute transition time) Place paper, crayons, and other material in the circle. Invite the children, one at a time, to come and draw what they did, thought about, or experienced.

(10 minutes) **Journal and Share Time**

Let them draw and journal as they gather. When most of the children have finished, let them begin to share. Remind the children that listening to one another is important.

Say: "Thank you for spending time with me in the Trinity Stations. I cannot wait to find out what you experienced today. Who would like to share?" (Give each child time to talk, and you should talk as well.)

Place their activities in individual folders; or if they are to take the folders home, place them behind them so they will not be distracted. This will keep you from having to correct the children's behavior.

10 minutes (snack or toy time)

A Time of Blessing

Explain that the symbol for today is a little sheep because the children are like little sheep, and Jesus is our shepherd and he loves and cares for us. Bless the children where they request, being sure to look them directly in their eyes.

Say: "Thank you for experiencing God with me today. You are a blessing!"

Closing Time

Slowly put each Trinity symbol away.

Say: "And now we are finished with our Sacred Circle Time. We put away our symbol for God, the Creator. We put away our symbol for God, the Son. And we put away our symbol for God, the Holy Spirit."

Then quietly and gently put the sacred cloth away.

Conclude: "And we are all done with our Sacred Circle time. You did a great job. Yay!" Clap and celebrate a job well done.

Ordinary Time 22

Story: Parable of the Lost Son

Text: Luke 15:11-25, NRSV

Then Jesus said, "There was a man who had two sons. The younger of them said to his father, 'Father, give me the share of the property that will belong to me.' So he divided his property between them. A few days later the younger son gathered all he had and traveled to a distant country, and there he squandered his property in dissolute living. When he had spent everything, a severe famine took place throughout that country, and he began to be in need. So he went and hired himself out to one of the citizens of that country, who sent him to his fields to feed the pigs. He would gladly have filled himself with the pods that the pigs were eating; and no one gave him anything. But when he came to himself he said, 'How many of my father's hired hands have bread enough and to spare, but here I am dying of hunger. I will get up and go to my father, and I will say to him, "Father, I have sinned against heaven and before you; I am no longer worthy to be called your son; treat me like one of your hired hands."' So he set off and went to his father. But while he was still far off, his father saw him and was filled with compassion; he ran and put his arms around him and kissed him. Then the son said to him, 'Father, I have sinned against heaven and before you; I am no longer worthy to be called your son.' But the father said to his slaves,

'Quickly, bring out a robe—the best one—and put it on him; put a ring on his finger and sandals on his feet. And get the fatted calf and kill it, and let us eat and celebrate; for this son of mine was dead and is alive again; he was lost and is found!' And they began to celebrate.

About the text: Forgiveness is one of the first theological concepts young children grasp. Being able to tell another person that you are sorry and being able to receive forgiveness is a lesson Jesus taught in many different parables. This parable is a story of forgiveness and great love. There is no need to discuss sin or trespasses at this age. The first step in looking for forgiveness is awareness that we have a parent who loves us and always welcomes us home.

The Sacred Circle Time Focus: We will focus on forgiveness and the knowledge that that God is always happy to see us.

Sacred Circle Time Basic Format

Sacred Circle basket and contents:

- Sacred space cloth
- Symbols for Creator (globe), Christ (cross), and Holy Spirit (bell or chimes)
- Small, unbreakable bottle to hold water or oil for the blessing
- A journal page (one per child)
- Crayons and/or markers
- A Bible bookmarked at Luke 15:11-25
- Focused object from the Bible story: A hand mirror

The Lesson

Gathering

Sit down and place the sacred basket in front of you.

Pause so that the children notice it and begin to come closer.

420

Invite them to form a circle.

Sit quietly until they settle in and are quiet.

Say: "It is time for Sacred Circle Time. I am so glad that you are here today. I love learning our stories and experiencing God with you."

Creating the Sacred Space

Say: "First, we create our sacred space."

Slowly lay out the sacred cloth.

Slowly lift the globe (symbol of God, the Creator) and hold it at the eye level of the children. Say: "This is our symbol for God, the Creator." Carefully lay it on the sacred cloth. *(Pause.)*

Slowly lift the cross (symbol of God, the Son). Say: "This is our symbol for God, the Son." Carefully lay it on the sacred cloth. *(Pause.)*

Slowly lift the bell (symbol of God, the Holy Spirit). Say: "This is our symbol of God, the Holy Spirit." Carefully lay it on the sacred cloth. *(Pause.)*

Point to each symbol and say: "So we have God, the Creator; God, the Son; and God, the Holy Spirit. *(Pause.)* Our sacred space is ready. We are ready to begin our Sacred Circle Time together."

God, the Creator (A Time to Wonder)

Make faces and have the children guess the emotion you are expressing. Have the children take turns making faces and letting the other children guess what emotions they are feeling. Pass around the mirror so that each child can see his or her own face.

God, the Son (Telling the Story)

Say: "In our story today, which is found in (*open the Bible*) Luke, chapter 15, verses 11-25, there was a daddy who loved his son very much. One day his son came and said, 'I wish you were dead, so I could have lots of things.' How do you think the daddy felt when his son said that? Can you show me your saddest face?" (*Let them show you.*)

"Yes, the daddy felt so sad because his son then moved far away, and the daddy worried about his son. Show me your worry faces. (*Let them show you.*) The daddy was sad and wished his son had not left him. Can you show me your sad faces? (*Let them show you.*) Yes, that is how sad the daddy felt. And as time went on, he felt sadder and sadder. Can you make your faces look sadder? (*Let them.*) Oh, yes, that is how sad the daddy was. And the son was gone for a very long time! And the daddy kept feeling sad, every day! But one day, the daddy was looking for his son, and he felt surprised. Can you show me your surprised faces? (*Let them.*) The daddy was surprised because when he looked down the road, he thought he saw his son! And he did! It was his son!! Now . . .what do you think the daddy's face looked like? Do you think it was sad? (*They will tell you that he looked happy.*) Yes, you are correct, the daddy was very, very happy! Let me see your happiest faces! (*They will show you.*) The daddy was so sad when his son went away, but so happy when his son came home. Did you know that the daddy in this story is like God? And did you know that when God sees you, God is so happy. Just like the daddy in the story was when he saw his son. God loves you so much and will always be happy to see you."

God, the Holy Spirit (Quiet and Prayer Time)

Say: "It is now time to pray. I want you to make your saddest face and think about how sad God would be without you. And now I want you to make your happiest face and think about happy God is because you are you! Now just sit here for a few seconds knowing that God loves you." (*Give them a few seconds of silence.*)

Pray: "God, thank you for always loving us. In the name of Christ, we pray. Amen."
(If using the extended Sacred Circle Time, stop here.)

A Time of Blessing

Explain that the symbol for today is a smile because God loves us so much!

Bless the children where they request, being sure to look them directly in their eyes.

Say: "Thank you for experiencing God with me today. You are a blessing!"

Extended Format

(*10 minutes*) Begin with free-play time. Greet the children warmly and let them get used to the space. Have something in the free-play space for them to play with. Rotate each week:

Week One: Paper and crayons, markers, or paint.
Week Two: Clay, wire, pipe cleaners and beads, and tools to work the clay.
Week Three: Things to build with: blocks, Legos®, cans, boxes, or flat stones.
Week Four: Things that make noise.

(*3 minutes*) Transition Time. Let the children know that it is almost Sacred Circle Time. Say: "It is almost our Sacred Circle Time. I cannot wait to have sacred time with you today. Will you start to finish up? Then come join me for our special, holy time together."

Sit down in the Sacred Circle Time space and place your sacred basket in front of you.

(*10 minutes*) **Sacred Circle Time** (*Basic Format*)—Use the Sacred Circle Basic Format, but do not include the blessing or closing.

(*10 minutes*) **Trinity Stations**

Explain the Trinity Stations procedure for new children and for those who might forget from time to time.

Walk with the children to the Trinity Stations and show them what they can do in the stations, but do not let them start until they have seen all three stations.

Tell the children that after the Trinity Stations, they will spend five minutes in quiet time thinking about the story and the activities they have completed. They will then return to the Sacred Circle Time space to draw pictures and talk about their activities.

Station One: God, the Creator (Wonder) Station

Walk with the children to this station and show them what they can do here. In addition to the suggested supplies (page 469), you might want to add some mirrors so that the children can make faces and see themselves.

Station Two: God, the Son (Story) Station

Walk with the children to this station and show them what they can do here. In addition to the suggested supplies (page 469), you might want to include a storybook with the story of the prodigal son.

Station Three: God, the Holy Spirit (Prayer) Station

Walk with the children to this station and show them what they can do here. In addition to the suggested supplies (page 469), you might want to include pictures of people showing different emotions to help the children think about different emotions.

Begin Quiet Time

Instruct the children to begin five minutes of quiet time to think about the Bible story. Explain that after the time has elapsed, you will invite them, one at a time, to the Sacred Circle Time space to draw what they did or thought about.

(2-minute transition time) Place paper, crayons, and other material in the circle. Invite the children, one at a time, to come and draw what they did, thought about, or experienced.

(*10 minutes*) **Journal and Share Time**

Let them draw and journal as they gather. When most of the children have finished, let them begin to share. Remind the children that listening to one another is important.

Say: "Thank you for spending time with me in the Trinity Stations. I cannot wait to find out what you experienced today. Who would like to share?" (Give each child time to talk, and you should talk as well.)

Place their activities in individual folders; or if they are to take the folders home, place them behind them so they will not be distracted. This will keep you from having to correct the children's behavior.

10 minutes (snack or toy time)

A Time of Blessing

Explain that the symbol for today is a smile because God loves us so much!

Bless the children where they request, being sure to look them directly in their eyes.

Say: "Thank you for experiencing God with me today. You are a blessing!"

Closing Time

Slowly put each Trinity symbol away.

Say: "And now we are finished with our Sacred Circle Time. We put away our symbol for God, the Creator. We put away our symbol for God, the Son. And we put away our symbol for God, the Holy Spirit."

Then quietly and gently put the sacred cloth away.

Conclude: "And we are all done with our Sacred Circle time. You did a great job. Yay!" Clap and celebrate a job well done.

Ordinary Time 23

Story: Parable of the Mustard Seed

Text: Matthew 13:31-32, NRSV

> He put before them another parable: "The kingdom of heaven is like a mustard seed that someone took and sowed in his field; it is the smallest of all the seeds, but when it has grown it is the greatest of shrubs and becomes a tree, so that the birds of the air come and make nests in its branches."

About the text: This parable is an important one for children to know because it impresses upon them that God creates amazing things. It fits perfectly with a young child's sense of wonder that things grow and that God makes them grow. For young children, this parable will remain on a concrete level. Seeds grow huge with God's love; but as the children grow older, their wonder at the growth of this tiny seed will lay the foundation for them to wonder at all of God's works.

The Sacred Circle Time Focus: We will focus on how amazing the works of God truly are and how God's love makes amazing things grow from the smallest seeds.

Sacred Circle Time Basic Format

Sacred Circle basket and contents:

- Sacred space cloth
- Symbols for Creator (globe), Christ (cross), and Holy Spirit (bell or chimes)

- Small, unbreakable bottle to hold water or oil for the blessing
- A journal page (one per child)
- Crayons and/or markers
- A Bible bookmarked at Matthew 13:31-32
- Focused objects from the Bible story: Many different seed packets; a mustard seed for each child. (Have extras because they will drop and lose them.)

The Lesson

Gathering

Sit down and place the sacred basket in front of you.

Pause so that the children notice it and begin to come closer.

Invite them to form a circle.

Sit quietly until they settle in and are quiet.

Say: "It is time for Sacred Circle Time. I am so glad that you are here today. I love learning our stories and experiencing God with you."

Creating the Sacred Space

Say: "First, we create our sacred space."

Slowly lay out the sacred cloth.

Slowly lift the globe (symbol of God, the Creator) and hold it at the eye level of the children. Say: "This is our symbol for God, the Creator." Carefully lay it on the sacred cloth. (*Pause.*)

Slowly lift the cross (symbol of God, the Son). Say: "This is our symbol for God, the Son." Carefully lay it on the sacred cloth. (*Pause.*)

Slowly lift the bell (symbol of God, the Holy Spirit). Say: "This is our symbol of God, the Holy Spirit." Carefully lay it on the sacred cloth. (*Pause.*)

Point to each symbol and say: "So we have God, the Creator; God, the Son; and God, the Holy Spirit. (*Pause.*) Our sacred space is ready. We are ready to begin our Sacred Circle Time together."

God, the Creator (A Time to Wonder)

Begin by showing the children a seed and then having them guess what the seed will become. Then show them the picture from the front of the seed packet. If it is summer or fall and you have a garden nearby, it would be great to show them a small seed and then go outside and see something actually growing. Then give each child a mustard seed.

Say: "This seed is special because it is found in the Bible."

God, the Son (Telling the Story)

Say: "In our story today, which is found in (*open the Bible*) Matthew, chapter 13, verses 31-32, Jesus talks about this tiny seed. This tiny little seed grows so big! Did you know that it grows so big that birds build nests in its tall branches? Let me show you. I want you to get down and pretend to be a tiny seed. (*The children will crouch down into tiny balls.*) Okay little seeds, God's love touches you, and you grow so tall. Let's grow tall! (*The children will pretend to grow tall by placing their arms over their heads.*) In this story, Jesus tells us that God makes this little seed grow tall and that God makes everything grow big. Love starts out tiny, and it gets bigger. Our tiny hopes and dreams grow bigger with God's love. God is amazing, just like this little seed growing into a tall bush is amazing."

God, the Holy Spirit (Quiet and Prayer Time)

Say: "It is now time to pray. For our prayer, I want us to remember how amazing God is. Let's get into tiny seeds and grow again. Let's crouch down. (*Children crouch down.*

428

Pause for a few seconds.) Now God's love touches us, and we grow so tall. God is amazing! Let's sit here for a moment and just think about how amazing God really is."

(*Give them a few seconds of silence.*)

Pray: "God, your love makes a little seed grow so tall. That is amazing. Your love makes everything better. That is amazing! Thank you for loving us. In the name of Christ, we pray. Amen."

(If using the extended Sacred Circle Time, stop here.)

A Time of Blessing

Explain that the symbol for today is a tall mustard plant because God's love is so amazing! Bless the children where they request, being sure to look them directly in their eyes.

Say: "Thank you for experiencing God with me today. You are a blessing!"

Extended Format

(*10 minutes*) Begin with free-play time. Greet the children warmly and let them get used to the space. Have something in the free-play space for them to play with. Rotate each week:

Week One: Paper and crayons, markers, or paint.
Week Two: Clay, wire, pipe cleaners and beads, and tools to work the clay.
Week Three: Things to build with: blocks, Legos®, cans, boxes, or flat stones.
Week Four: Things that make noise.

(*3 minutes*) Transition time. Let the children know that it is almost Sacred Circle Time. Say: "It is almost our Sacred Circle Time. I cannot wait to have sacred time with you today. Will you start to finish up? Then come join me for our special, holy time together."

Sit down in the Sacred Circle Time space and place your sacred basket in front of you.

(*10 minutes*) **Sacred Circle Time** (*Basic Format*)—Use the Sacred Circle Basic Format, but do not include the blessing or closing.

(*10 minutes*) **Trinity Stations**

Explain the Trinity Stations procedure for new children and for those who might forget from time to time.

Walk with the children to the Trinity Stations and show them what they can do in the stations, but do not let them start until they have seen all three stations.

Tell the children that after the Trinity Stations, they will spend five minutes in quiet time thinking about the story and the activities they have completed. They will then return to the Sacred Circle Time space to draw pictures and talk about their activities.

Station One: God the Creator (Wonder) Station

Walk with the children to this station and show them what they can do here. In addition to the suggested supplies (page 469), you might want to add some seeds and soil and cups to plant the seeds. Or you might want to have some potatoes to place in water to watch the roots grow. Or you might have seeds of all kinds for the children to explore and marvel at.

Station Two: God, the Son (Story) Station

Walk with the children to this station and show them what they can do here. In addition to the suggested supplies (page 469), you might want to have some blocks or paper tubes or old newspapers that the children can use to create a pretend tall mustard plant.

Station Three: God, the Holy Spirit (Prayer) Station

Walk with the children to this station and show them what they can do here. In addition to the suggested supplies (page 469), you also want to have some seeds, paper, and glue for the children to use to create prayer designs.

Begin Quiet Time

Instruct the children to begin five minutes of quiet time to think about the Bible story. Explain that after the time has elapsed, you will invite them, one at a time, to the Sacred Circle Time space to draw what they did or thought about.

(2-minute transition time) Place paper, crayons, and other material in the circle. Invite the children, one at a time, to come and draw what they did, thought about, or experienced.

(10 minutes) **Journal and Share Time**

Let them draw and journal as they gather. When most of the children have finished, let them begin to share. Remind the children that listening to one another is important.

Say: "Thank you for spending time with me in the Trinity Stations. I cannot wait to find out what you experienced today. Who would like to share?" (Give each child time to talk, and you should talk as well.)

Place their activities in individual folders; or if they are to take the folders home, place them behind them so they will not be distracted. This will keep you from having to correct the children's behavior.

10 minutes (snack or toy time)

A Time of Blessing

Explain that the symbol for today is a tall mustard plant because God's love is so amazing! Bless the children where they request, being sure to look them directly in their eyes.

Say: "Thank you for experiencing God with me today. You are a blessing!"

Closing Time

Slowly put each Trinity symbol away.

Say: "And now we are finished with our Sacred Circle Time. We put away our symbol for God, the Creator. We put away our symbol for God, the Son. And we put away our symbol for God, the Holy Spirit."

Then quietly and gently put the sacred cloth away.

Conclude: "And we are all done with our Sacred Circle time. You did a great job. Yay!" Clap and celebrate a job well done.

Ordinary Time 24

Story: Jesus Is Lost in Jerusalem

Text: Luke 2:41-52, NRSV

Now every year his parents went to Jerusalem for the festival of the Passover. And when he was twelve years old, they went up as usual for the festival. When the festival was ended and they started to return, the boy Jesus stayed behind in Jerusalem, but his parents did not know it. Assuming that he was in the group of travelers, they went a day's journey. Then they started to look for him among their relatives and friends. When they did not find him, they returned to Jerusalem to search for him. After three days they found him in the temple, sitting among the teachers, listening to them and asking them questions. And all who heard him were amazed at his understanding and his answers. When his parents saw him they were astonished; and his mother said to him, "Child, why have you treated us like this? Look, your father and I have been searching for you in great anxiety." He said to them, "Why were you searching for me? Did you not know that I must be in my Father's house?" But they did not understand what he said to them. Then he went down with them and came to Nazareth, and was obedient to them. His mother treasured all these things in her heart.

And Jesus increased in wisdom and in years, and in divine and human favor.

About the text: This is great story to use if there is a week between Christmas and Epiphany during the twelve days of Christmas. It is the only story we have about the childhood of Jesus, so it would be nice to tell right after his birth or on the Sunday after Epiphany. But it is great story and can be used at any time during Ordinary Time. In this story, Jesus is lost and ends up at the temple. Jerusalem at Passover would be like New York City after the New Year's Eve celebration in Times Square. Mary and Joseph must have been distraught at losing their child. But Jesus knew where to go . . . to the temple. It was a safe place for him and a place where everyone listened to him and realized how special he was.

The Sacred Circle Time Focus: We will focus on how special Jesus was as a child and how special each child is.

Sacred Circle Time Basic Format

Sacred Circle basket and contents:

- Sacred space cloth
- Symbols for Creator (globe), Christ (cross), and Holy Spirit (bell or chimes)
- Small, unbreakable bottle to hold water or oil for the blessing
- A journal page (one per child)
- Crayons and/or markers
- A Bible bookmarked at Luke 2:41-52
- Focused objects from the Bible story: Several blank pieces of paper and crayons or makers

The Lesson

Gathering

Sit down and place the sacred basket in front of you.

Pause so that the children notice it and begin to come closer.

Invite them to form a circle.

Sit quietly until they settle in and are quiet.

Say: "It is time for Sacred Circle Time. I am so glad that you are here today. I love learning our stories and experiencing God with you."

Creating the Sacred Space

Say: "First, we create our sacred space."

Slowly lay out the sacred cloth.

Slowly lift the globe (symbol of God, the Creator) and hold it at the eye level of the children. Say: "This is our symbol for God, the Creator." Carefully lay it on the sacred cloth. *(Pause.)*

Slowly lift the cross (symbol of God, the Son). Say: "This is our symbol for God, the Son." Carefully lay it on the sacred cloth. (*Pause.*)

Slowly lift the bell (symbol of God, the Holy Spirit). Say: "This is our symbol of God, the Holy Spirit." Carefully lay it on the sacred cloth. (*Pause.*)

Point to each symbol and say: "So we have God, the Creator; God, the Son; and God, the Holy Spirit. (*Pause.*) Our sacred space is ready. We are ready to begin our Sacred Circle Time together."

God, the Creator (A Time to Wonder)

Use the paper to slowly draw something. Let the children try to guess what you are drawing as you go along. (Do not worry if you are not a good artist. Children have so much grace toward us, and they will not care.) Draw a few things.

God, the Son (Telling the Story)

Say: "Our story today is found in (*open the Bible*) Luke, chapter two, verses 41-52. It is story about Jesus. I am going to draw him for you. He had a head, just like you do. (*Draw the head.*) He had a body, just like you do. (*Draw the body.*) He had arms, just like you do and hands, just like you do. (*Draw the arms and hands*). He had legs and feet, just like you do. (*Draw the legs and feet*). And in this story he was a child, just as you are children.

"His mommy, Mary, and his daddy, Joseph, had gone to a city for a very important festival called the Passover. Lots and lots of people went there; and when it came time to leave, Jesus was missing. His mommy and daddy could not find him. How do you think they felt? (*Let the children answer.*)

"They looked everywhere for Jesus, and they finally found him in the temple. The temple is like a big church. And he was sitting with some teachers, and they were asking him questions. And do you know what they thought about Jesus? They thought he was very smart. (*Draw a brain inside the head.*) And they thought he was very loving and kind. (*Draw a heart inside the chest.*) They thought Jesus was amazing!

"Hummm. . . . . let's see, you have a head (*point to the head*), and a body (*point to the body*), and arms and hands (*point to the arms and hands*), and legs and feet (*point to the legs and feet*); and you are very smart (*point to the brain*); and you are kind and loving (*point to the heart*). The teachers in the story thought Jesus was amazing. And do you know what I think? I am your teacher, and I think you are amazing!"

God, the Holy Spirit (Quiet and Prayer Time)

Say: "It is now time to pray. I am going to invite each of you, one at a time, to stand up. As you stand, I will pray for you."

Pray: "God, I pray that you bless (*name of child*), who is an amazing, wonderful child. Amen."

Say: "Jesus was amazing, and he had a loving heart. You are also amazing children with loving hearts."

(If using the extended Sacred Circle Time, stop here)

A Time of Blessing

Explain that the symbol for today is an outline of a person because Jesus is amazing, and the children are amazing. Bless the children where they request, being sure to look them directly in their eyes.

Say: "Thank you for experiencing God with me today. You are a blessing!"

Closing Time

Slowly put each Trinity symbol away.

Say: "And now we are finished with our Sacred Circle Time. We put away our symbol for God, the Creator. We put away our symbol for God, the Son. And we put away our symbol for God, the Holy Spirit."

Then quietly and gently put the sacred cloth away.

Conclude: "And we are all done with our Sacred Circle time. You did a great job. Yay!" Clap and celebrate a job well done.

Extended Format

(*10 minutes*) Begin with free-play time. Greet the children warmly and let them get used to the space. Have something in the free-play space for them to play with. Rotate each week:

Week One: Paper and crayons, markers, or paint.

Week Two: Clay, wire, pipe cleaners and beads, and tools to work the clay.

Week Three: Things to build with: blocks, Legos®, cans, boxes, or flat stones.

Week Four: Things that make noise.

(*3 minutes*) Transition Time. Let the children know that it is almost Sacred Circle Time. Say: "It is almost our Sacred Circle Time. I cannot wait to have sacred time with you today. Will you start to finish up? Then come join me for our special, holy time together."

Sit down in the Sacred Circle Time space and place your sacred basket in front of you.

(*10 minutes*) **Sacred Circle Time** (*Basic Format*)—Use the Sacred Circle Basic Format, but do not include the blessing or closing.

(*10 minutes*) **Trinity Stations**

Explain the Trinity Stations procedure for new children and for those who might forget from time to time.

Walk with the children to the Trinity Stations and show them what they can do in the stations, but do not let them start until they have seen all three stations.

Tell the children that after the Trinity Stations, they will spend five minutes in quiet time thinking about the story and the activities they have completed. They will then return to the Sacred Circle Time space to draw pictures and talk about their activities.

Station One: God, the Creator (Wonder) Station

Walk with the children to this station and show them what they can do here. In addition to the suggested supplies (page 469), you might want to add some magnifying mirrors so the children can see how amazing they are.

Station Two: God, the Son (Story) Station.

Walk with the children to this station and show them what they can do here. In addition to the suggested supplies (page 469), you might want to include some prayer shawls and let the children dress up as the teachers at the temple.

Station Three: God, the Holy Spirit (Prayer) Station

Walk with the children to this station and show them what they can do here. In addition to the suggested supplies (page 469), you might want to add mirrors so that they can look and see how amazing they are.

Begin Quiet Time

Instruct the children to begin five minutes of quiet time to think about the Bible story. Explain that after the time has elapsed, you will invite them, one at a time, to the Sacred Circle Time space to draw what they did or thought about.

(2-minute transition time) Place paper, crayons, and other material in the circle. Invite the children, one at a time, to come and draw what they did, thought about, or experienced.

(10 minutes) **Journal and Share Time**

Let them draw and journal as they gather. When most of the children have finished, let them begin to share. Remind the children that listening to one another is important.

Say: "Thank you for spending time with me in the Trinity Stations. I cannot wait to find out what you experienced today. Who would like to share?" (Give each child time to talk, and you should talk as well.)

Place their activities in individual folders; or if they are to take the folders home, place them behind them so they will not be distracted. This will keep you from having to correct the children's behavior.

A Time of Blessing

Explain that the symbol for today is an outline of a person because Jesus is amazing, and the children are amazing. Bless the children where they request, being sure to look them directly in their eyes.

Say: "Thank you for experiencing God with me today. You are a blessing!"

Closing Time

Slowly put each Trinity symbol away.

Say: "And now we are finished with our Sacred Circle Time. We put away our symbol for God, the Creator. We put away our symbol for God, the Son. And we put away our symbol for God, the Holy Spirit."

Then quietly and gently put the sacred cloth away.

Conclude: "And we are all done with our Sacred Circle time. You did a great job. Yay!" Clap and celebrate a job well done.

Ordinary Time 25

Story: Jesus Calms the Storm

Text: Mark 4:35-41, NRSV

On that day, when evening had come, he said to them, "Let us go across to the other side." And leaving the crowd behind, they took him with them in the boat, just as he was. Other boats were with him. A great windstorm arose, and the waves beat into the boat, so that the boat was already being swamped. But he was in the stern, asleep on the cushion; and they woke him up and said to him, "Teacher, do you not care that we are perishing?" He woke up and rebuked the wind, and said to the sea, "Peace! Be still!" Then the wind ceased, and there was a dead calm. He said to them, "Why are you afraid? Have you still no faith?" And they were filled with great awe and said to one another, "Who then is this, that even the wind and the sea obey him?"

About the text: We would all like to think of childhood as a carefree time, but in reality, most children will experience some kind of trauma or grief before they reach their teen years. While the children may not be aware that they will have "storms" in their lives, this story demonstrates the power and willingness of Jesus to be with us during the storms of life.

The Sacred Circle Time Focus: We will focus on Jesus as the one who is with us during stormy times.

Sacred Circle Time Basic Format

Sacred Circle basket and contents:

- Sacred space cloth
- Symbols for Creator (globe), Christ (cross), and Holy Spirit (bell or chimes)
- Small, unbreakable bottle to hold water or oil for the blessing
- A journal page (one per child)
- Crayons and/or markers
- A Bible bookmarked at Mark 4:35-41
- Focused objects from the Bible story: A 2-liter clear plastic pop bottle filled about half way with water

The Lesson

Gathering

Sit down and place the sacred basket in front of you.

Pause so that the children notice it and begin to come closer.

Invite them to form a circle.

Sit quietly until they settle in and are quiet.

Say: "It is time for Sacred Circle Time. I am so glad that you are here today. I love learning our stories and experiencing God with you."

Creating the Sacred Space

Say: "First, we create our sacred space."

Slowly lay out the sacred cloth.

Slowly lift the globe (symbol of God, the Creator) and hold it at the eye level of the children. Say: "This is our symbol for God, the Creator." Carefully lay it on the sacred cloth. (Pause.)

Slowly lift the cross (symbol of God, the Son). Say: "This is our symbol for God, the Son." Carefully lay it on the sacred cloth. (*Pause.*)

Slowly lift the bell (symbol of God, the Holy Spirit). Say: "This is our symbol of God, the Holy Spirit." Carefully lay it on the sacred cloth. (*Pause.*)

Point to each symbol and say: "So we have God, the Creator; God, the Son; and God, the Holy Spirit. (*Pause.*) Our sacred space is ready. We are ready to begin our Sacred Circle Time together."

God, the Creator (A Time to Wonder)

Show the bottle of water to the children. Shake it, then watch it get still. Swish the water around inside. Slowly let the water move from end to end.

God, the Son (Telling the Story)

Say: "In our story today, which is in (*open the Bible*) Mark, chapter four, verses 35-41, we hear about Jesus and his disciples, who were his twelve special friends. They went on a boat in the middle of the Sea of Galilee. (*Show them the water bottle and pretend it is the Sea of Galilee.*) Jesus was tired, so he lay down to take a nap. And after he went to sleep, a big storm came up, and the water began to sway. (*Start to move the bottle gently side to side.*) The storm got worse. Before long, the water was like this. (*Shake the bottle so that the water inside is wild. Keep shaking it.*) And the disciples, the twelve special friends of Jesus, were afraid, so they woke Jesus up and said, 'Wake up!! The boat might tip over because this storm is so bad!' And Jesus woke up and said, 'You don't have anything to be afraid of when I am here. Stop, storm, stop!' (*Stop shaking the bottle.*) And everything was still. They did not have anything to fear because Jesus was with them."

God, the Holy Spirit (Quiet and Prayer Time)

Say: "It is now time to pray. I want you to be very still like the water was after Jesus told the storm to stop. Let me show you. (*Shake the bottle and then stop.*) I want you to be this still. Now sit quietly and feel the peace of Jesus." (*Give them a few seconds of silence.*)

Pray: "God, thank you for the peace of Jesus. We know that we do not need to be afraid when he is with us. Amen."

(*If using the extended Sacred Circle Time, stop here.*)

A Time of Blessing

Explain that the symbol for today is a cross because we do not need to be afraid when Jesus is with us. Bless the children where they request, being sure to look them directly in their eyes.

Say: "Thank you for experiencing God with me today. You are a blessing!"

Extended Format

(*10 minutes*) Begin with free-play time. Greet the children warmly and let them get used to the space. Have something in the free-play space for them to play with. Rotate each week:

Week One: Paper and crayons, markers, or paint.
Week Two: Clay, wire, pipe cleaners and beads, and tools to work the clay.
Week Three: Things to build with: blocks, Legos®, cans, boxes, or flat stones.
Week Four: Things that make noise.

(*3 minutes*) Transition Time. Let the children know that it is almost Sacred Circle Time. Say: "It is almost our Sacred Circle Time. I cannot wait to have sacred time with you today. Will you start to finish up? Then come join me for our special, holy time together."

Sit down in the Sacred Circle Time space and place your sacred basket in front of you.

(*10 minutes*) **Sacred Circle Time** (*Basic Format*)—Use the Sacred Circle Basic Format, but do not include the blessing or closing.

(*10 minutes*) **Trinity Stations**

Explain the Trinity Stations procedure for new children and for those who might forget from time to time.

Walk with the children to the Trinity Stations and show them what they can do in the stations, but do not let them start until they have seen all three stations.

Tell the children that after the Trinity Stations, they will spend five minutes in quiet time thinking about the story and the activities they have completed. They will then return to the Sacred Circle Time space to draw pictures and talk about their activities.

Station One: God, the Creator (Wonder) Station

Walk with the children to this station and show them what they can do here. In addition to the suggested supplies (page 469), you might want to add some two-liter pop bottles with different amounts of water in each so that the children can compare what happens in the bottles with the different amounts of water when they shake them.

Station Two: God, the Son (Story) Station

Walk with the children to this station and show them what they can do here. In addition to the suggested supplies (page 469), you might want to include a large box for the children to make a boat or a sheet for them to use to make waves and calm.

Station Three: God, the Holy Spirit (Prayer) Station

Walk with the children to this station and show them what they can do here. In addition to the suggested supplies (page 469), you might want to add some bottles filled with water for the children to use to contemplate the stillness after the storm.

Begin Quiet Time

Instruct the children to begin five minutes of quiet time to think about the Bible story. Explain that after the time has elapsed, you will invite them, one at a time, to the Sacred Circle Time space to draw what they did or thought about.

(2-minute transition time) Place paper, crayons, and other material in the circle. Invite the children, one at a time, to come and draw what they did, thought about, or experienced.

(10 minutes) Journal and Share Time

Let them draw and journal as they gather. When most of the children have finished, let them begin to share. Remind the children that listening to one another is important.

Say: "Thank you for spending time with me in the Trinity Stations. I cannot wait to find out what you experienced today. Who would like to share?"

Place their activities in individual folders. (Give each child time to talk, and you should talk as well.)

10 minutes (snack or toy time)

A Time of Blessing

Explain that the symbol for today is a cross because we do not need to be afraid when Jesus is with us. Bless the children where they request, being sure to look them directly in their eyes.

Say: "Thank you for experiencing God with me today. You are a blessing!"

Closing Time

Slowly put each Trinity symbol away.

Say: "And now we are finished with our Sacred Circle Time. We put away our symbol for God, the Creator. We put away our symbol for God, the Son. And we put away our symbol for God, the Holy Spirit."

Then quietly and gently put the sacred cloth away.

Conclude: "And we are all done with our Sacred Circle time. You did a great job. Yay!" Clap and celebrate a job well done.

Ordinary Time 26

Story: Jesus Washes the Disciples' Feet

Text: John 13:1-7, NRSV

Now before the festival of the Passover, Jesus knew that his hour had come to depart from this world and go to the Father. Having loved his own who were in the world, he loved them to the end. The devil had already put it into the heart of Judas son of Simon Iscariot to betray him. And during supper Jesus, knowing that the Father had given all things into his hands, and that he had come from God and was going to God, got up from the table, took off his outer robe, and tied a towel around himself. Then he poured water into a basin and began to wash the disciples' feet and to wipe them with the towel that was tied around him. He came to Simon Peter, who said to him, "Lord, are you going to wash my feet?" Jesus answered, "You do not know now what I am doing, but later you will understand."

About the text: This is one of the most intimate moments in the Bible, when the master washes the feet of those he loved so dearly. Bath time for children is also an intimate time with their parents: a time of joy and bonding. This story will help them equate footwashing with an act of great love, much like what they experience at bath time.

The Sacred Circle Time Focus: We will focus on how much Jesus loved his disciples.

Sacred Circle Time Basic Format

Sacred Circle basket and contents:

- Sacred space cloth
- Symbols for Creator (globe), Christ (cross), and Holy Spirit (bell or chimes)
- Small, unbreakable bottle to hold water or oil for the blessing
- A journal page (one per child)
- Crayons and/or markers
- A Bible bookmarked at John 13:1-7
- Focused objects from the Bible story: A pitcher filled with warm water, a large bowl, and a towel for the children to dry their hands

The Lesson

Gathering

Sit down and place the sacred basket in front of you.

Pause so that the children notice it and begin to come closer.

Invite them to form a circle.

Sit quietly until they settle in and are quiet.

Say: "It is time for Sacred Circle Time. I am so glad that you are here today. I love learning our stories and experiencing God with you."

Creating the Sacred Space

Say: "First, we create our sacred space."

Slowly lay out the sacred cloth.

Slowly lift the globe (symbol of God, the Creator) and hold it at the eye level of the children. Say: "This is our symbol for God, the Creator." Carefully lay it on the sacred cloth. (Pause.)

Slowly lift the cross (symbol of God, the Son). Say: "This is our symbol for God, the Son." Carefully lay it on the sacred cloth. (Pause.)

Slowly lift the bell (symbol of God, the Holy Spirit). Say: "This is our symbol of God, the Holy Spirit." Carefully lay it on the sacred cloth. (*Pause.*)

Point to each symbol and say: "So we have God, the Creator; God, the Son; and God, the Holy Spirit. (*Pause.*) Our sacred space is ready. We are ready to begin our Sacred Circle Time together."

God, the Creator (A Time to Wonder)

Say: "Did you know that you are each very special to me? You are! And I want to show you just how special you are to me. What could I do so that you would know how special you are to me?" (*Let them think of things such as buy toys, give hugs, etc.*)

"Those are all great ideas, but I am going to show you how special you are to me with this pitcher of water, this bowl, and a towel."

Invite the children, one at a time, to come over to the bowl. Pour some water over their hands and then, lovingly, dry them. While you dry their hands, tell them, by name, that they are very special!

After each child has had a turn, sit quietly for a moment and then say: "You are each very special to me."

God, the Son (Telling the Story)

Say: "In our story today, which is found in (*open the Bible*) John, chapter 13, verses 1-7, Jesus is having a very special dinner with his twelve closest friends, the disciples. They had been walking all day, and their feet were tired and dirty. And Jesus wanted them to know how special they were to him. So he took a basin of water (*lift the basin*), and he went to each of his disciples, and he washed each person's feet. And as their feet were washed, they realized how special they were to him."

God, the Holy Spirit (Quiet and Prayer Time)

Say: "It is now time to pray. Let's be still for a few moments and think about how special we are to Jesus." (*Give them a few seconds of silence. During the silence, cup your hands and pour small amounts of water into the bowl over and over.*)

Pray: "God, thank you for son Jesus who loves us so very much. In the name of Christ, we pray. Amen."

(If using the extended Sacred Circle Time, stop here.)

A Time of Blessing

Explain that the symbol for today is a heart because Jesus loves us so much. Bless the children where they request, being sure to look them directly in their eyes.

Say: "Thank you for experiencing God with me today. You are a blessing!"

Extended Format

(*10 minutes*) Begin with free-play time. Greet the children warmly and let them get used to the space. Have something in the free-play space for them to play with. Rotate each week:

Week One: Paper and crayons, markers, or paint.

Week Two: Clay, wire, pipe cleaners and beads, and tools to work the clay.

Week Three: Things to build with: blocks, Legos®, cans, boxes, or flat stones.

Week Four: Things that make noise.

(*3 minutes*) Transition Time. Let the children know that it is almost Sacred Circle Time. Say: "It is almost our Sacred Circle Time. I cannot wait to have sacred time with you today. Will you start to finish up? Then come join me for our special, holy time together."

Sit down in the Sacred Circle Time space and place your sacred basket in front of you.

(*10 minutes*) **Sacred Circle Time** (*Basic Format*)—Use the Sacred Circle Basic Format, but do not include the blessing or closing.

(*10 minutes*) **Trinity Stations**

Explain the Trinity Stations procedure for new children and for those who might forget from time to time.

Walk with the children to the Trinity Stations and show them what they can do in the stations, but do not let them start until they have seen all three stations.

Tell the children that after the Trinity Stations, they will spend five minutes in quiet time thinking about the story and the activities they have completed. They will then return to the Sacred Circle Time space to draw pictures and talk about their activities.

Station One: God, the Creator (Wonder) Station

Walk with the children to this station and show them what they can do here. In addition to the suggested supplies (page 469), you might want to add some water, cups, and things to measure and pour water.

Station Two: God, the Son (Story) Station

Walk with the children to this station and show them what they can do here. In addition to the suggested supplies (page 469), you might want to have a small pitcher, bowl, and towel. You do not have to include water, but it might be nice.

Station Three: God, the Holy Spirit (Prayer) Station

Walk with the children to this station and show them what they can do here. In addition to the suggested supplies (page 469), you might want to include some pictures of Jesus washing the feet of the disciples.

Begin Quiet Time

Instruct the children to begin five minutes of quiet time to think about the Bible story. Explain that after the time has elapsed, you will invite them, one at a time, to the Sacred Circle Time space to draw what they did or thought about.

(2-minute transition time) Place paper, crayons, and other material in the circle. Invite the children, one at a time, to come and draw what they did, thought about, or experienced.

(10 minutes) **Journal and Share Time**

Let them draw and journal as they gather. When most of the children have finished, let them begin to share. Remind the children that listening to one another is important.

Say: "Thank you for spending time with me in the Trinity Stations. I cannot wait to find out what you experienced today. Who would like to share?" (Give each child time to talk, and you should talk as well.)

Place their activities in individual folders; or if they are to take the folders home, place them behind them so they will not be distracted. This will keep you from having to correct the children's behavior.

10 minutes (snack or toy time)

A Time of Blessing

Explain that the symbol for today is a heart because Jesus loves us so much. Bless the children where they request, being sure to look them directly in their eyes.

Say: "Thank you for experiencing God with me today. You are a blessing!"

Closing Time

Slowly put each Trinity symbol away.

Say: "And now we are finished with our Sacred Circle Time. We put away our symbol for God, the Creator. We put away our symbol for God, the Son. And we put away our symbol for God, the Holy Spirit."

Then quietly and gently put the sacred cloth away.

Conclude: "And we are all done with our Sacred Circle time. You did a great job. Yay!" Clap and celebrate a job well done.

Ordinary Time 27

Story: Jesus Serves the Last Supper

Text: Matthew 26:26-29, NRSV

> While they were eating, Jesus took a loaf of bread, and after blessing it he broke it, gave it to the disciples, and said, "Take, eat; this is my body." Then he took a cup, and after giving thanks he gave it to them, saying, "Drink from it, all of you; for this is my blood of the covenant, which is poured out for many for the forgiveness of sins. I tell you, I will never again drink of this fruit of the vine until that day when I drink it new with you in my Father's kingdom."

About the text: The Last Supper is a great gift given by Christ to the church . . . his body and blood. Young children cannot understand, at this age, the significance of the symbolism of this meal, but they can understand that is a special meal. And young children often associate being fed with being cared for and loved. We will not serve Communion. We will simply help the children begin to understand the holiness and significance of this sacred meal.

The Sacred Circle Time Focus: We will focus on this meal being one of great love.

Sacred Circle Time Basic Format

Sacred Circle basket and contents:

- Sacred space cloth
- Symbols for Creator (globe), Christ (cross), and Holy Spirit (bell or chimes)
- Small, unbreakable bottle to hold water or oil for the blessing
- A journal page (one per child)
- Crayons and/or markers
- A Bible bookmarked at Matthew 26:26-29
- Focused objects from the Bible story: A slice of bread, a heart-shaped cookie cutter, a plate, a cup (or chalice) with one paper heart for each child placed in it

The Lesson

Gathering

Sit down and place the sacred basket in front of you.

Pause so that the children notice it and begin to come closer.

Invite them to form a circle.

Sit quietly until they settle in and are quiet.

Say: "It is time for Sacred Circle Time. I am so glad that you are here today. I love learning our stories and experiencing God with you."

Creating the Sacred Space

Say: "First, we create our sacred space."

Slowly lay out the sacred cloth.

Slowly lift the globe (symbol of God, the Creator) and hold it at the eye level of the children. Say: "This is our symbol for God, the Creator." Carefully lay it on the sacred cloth. (Pause.)

Slowly lift the cross (symbol of God, the Son). Say: "This is our symbol for God, the Son." Carefully lay it on the sacred cloth. (*Pause.*)

Slowly lift the bell (symbol of God, the Holy Spirit). Say: "This is our symbol of God, the Holy Spirit." Carefully lay it on the sacred cloth. (*Pause.*)

Point to each symbol and say: "So we have God, the Creator; God, the Son; and God, the Holy Spirit. (*Pause.*) Our sacred space is ready. We are ready to begin our Sacred Circle Time together."

God, the Creator (A Time to Wonder)

Ask: "How many of you have a favorite food? Don't tell me, I want you to show me using my special plate! (*Show the children the empty plate.*) Here is how my special plate works. I think of my favorite food; and it appears on my plate, and I eat it. Let me show you. My favorite food is watermelon, and there it is on my plate. You don't see it? (*They will say no.*) Oh, you have to use your imagination to see the food. We are using our imaginations today. So, let's try it again. My favorite food is watermelon, and there it is. (*Pretend to pick it up and eat it.*) Now, I am going to pass my special plate to each of you, and I want you to tell us what your favorite food is and then pretend to eat it." (*Pass the plate and let everyone have a turn. This will be fun. Enjoy and let them be silly.*)

God, the Son (Telling the Story)

Say: "Our story today, which is found in (*open the Bible*) Matthew, chapter 26, verses 26-29, talks about some special bread. Jesus and his twelve close friends, the disciples, were eating dinner together. And after they got through eating, Jesus stood up and took bread (*hold up one slice of the bread*) and broke it (*cut it with the heart-shaped cookie cutter*) and gave it to the disciples, his friends. And something amazing happened when Jesus gave them that bread. It turned to his love! (*Show them the bread is now shaped like a heart.*) And as he gave them the special bread, they knew that Jesus loved them very much. And then Jesus said, "If you ever miss me, eat this special bread and you will know how much I love you."

456

"And then Jesus took a cup of juice and gave it to the disciples, and guess what? The juice turned into his love as well. (*Show them that the cup is filled with hearts.*) Jesus loved the disciples, his special friends, very much; and he gave them a special meal of love to eat when they missed him. We still eat this meal in church when we eat together, Holy Communion. Everyone in the church gets to eat the bread made of love and drink the juice made of love. It is a very special meal. Jesus asked us to eat this special meal and remember how much Jesus loves us all!"

God, the Holy Spirit (Quiet and Prayer Time)

Say: "It is now time to pray. For the prayer, I am going to pass this cup to each of you. You may reach inside and find a little reminder that Jesus loves you very much. (*Pass the cup and let each child pull out a heart.*)

"Let's sit silently now and think about how much Jesus loves us and about the special meal, called Holy Communion, that he gave us." (*Give them a few seconds of silence.*)

Pray: "God, thank you for Holy Communion. Thank you for the bread and juice made of your love. In the name of Christ, we pray. Amen."

(If using the extended Sacred Circle Time, stop here.)

A Time of Blessing

Explain that the symbol for today is a heart because Jesus loves us so much. Bless the children where they request, being sure to look them directly in their eyes.

Say: "Thank you for experiencing God with me today. You are a blessing!"

Extended Format

(*10 minutes*) Begin with free-play time. Greet the children warmly and let them get used to the space. Have something in the free-play space for them to play with. Rotate each week:

Week One: Paper and crayons, markers, or paint.

Week Two: Clay, wire, pipe cleaners and beads, and tools to work the clay.

Week Three: Things to build with: blocks, Legos®, cans, boxes, or flat stones.

Week Four: Things that make noise.

(*3 minutes*) Transition Time. Let the children know that it is almost Sacred Circle Time. Say: "It is almost our Sacred Circle Time. I cannot wait to have sacred time with you today. Will you start to finish up? Then come join me for our special, holy time together."

Sit down in the Sacred Circle Time space and place your sacred basket in front of you.

(*10 minutes*) **Sacred Circle Time** (*Basic Format*)—Use the Sacred Circle Basic Format, but do not include the blessing or closing.

(*10 minutes*) **Trinity Stations**

Explain the Trinity Stations procedure for new children and for those who might forget from time to time.

Walk with the children to the Trinity Stations and show them what they can do in the stations, but do not let them start until they have seen all three stations.

Tell the children that after the Trinity Stations, they will spend five minutes in quiet time thinking about the story and the activities they have completed. They will then return to the Sacred Circle Time space to draw pictures and talk about their activities.

Station One: God, the Creator (Wonder) Station

Walk with the children to this station and show them what they can do here. In addition to the suggested supplies (page 469), you might want to provide the ingredients to make simple dough and let the children knead it and feel it.

Station Two: God, the Son (Story) Station

Walk with the children to this station and show them what they can do here. In addition to the suggested supplies (page 469), you might want to include candles, a table setting, bread, and cups so that children can act out the Last Supper.

Station Three: God, the Holy Spirit (Prayer) Station

Walk with the children to this station and show them what they can do here. In addition to the suggested supplies (page 469), you might want to include the heart-shaped cookie cutter and other heart-shaped objects and pencils to trace with while the children contemplate the love of God.

Begin Quiet Time

Instruct the children to begin five minutes of quiet time to think about the Bible story. Explain that after the time has elapsed, you will invite them, one at a time, to the Sacred Circle Time space to draw what they did or thought about.

(*2-minute transition time*) Place paper, crayons, and other material in the circle. Invite the children, one at a time, to come and draw what they did, thought about, or experienced.

(*10 minutes*) Journal and Share Time

Let them draw and journal as they gather. When most of the children have finished, let them begin to share. Remind the children that listening to one another is important.

Say: "Thank you for spending time with me in the Trinity Stations. I cannot wait to find out what you experienced today. Who would like to share?" (Give each child time to talk, and you should talk as well.)

Place their activities in individual folders; or if they are to take the folders home, place them behind them so they will not be distracted. This will keep you from having to correct the children's behavior.

10 minutes (snack or toy time)

A Time of Blessing

Explain that the symbol for today is a heart because Jesus loves us so much. Bless the children where they request, being sure to look them directly in their eyes.

Say: "Thank you for experiencing God with me today. You are a blessing!"

Closing Time

Slowly put each Trinity symbol away.

Say: "And now we are finished with our Sacred Circle Time. We put away our symbol for God, the Creator. We put away our symbol for God, the Son. And we put away our symbol for God, the Holy Spirit."

Then quietly and gently put the sacred cloth away.

Conclude: "And we are all done with our Sacred Circle time. You did a great job. Yay!" Clap and celebrate a job well done.

Ordinary Time 28

Story: Paul and the Disciples Spread the Good News

Text: Matthew 28:16-20, NRSV

Now the eleven disciples went to Galilee, to the mountain to which Jesus had directed them. When they saw him, they worshiped him; but some doubted. And Jesus came and said to them, "All authority in heaven and on earth has been given to me. Go therefore and make disciples of all nations, baptizing them in the name of the Father and of the Son and of the Holy Spirit, and teaching them to obey everything that I have commanded you. And remember, I am with you always, to the end of the age."

About the text: The ascension and the Resurrection are not the same event. When Jesus rose from the grave, it was the Resurrection. But after he was resurrected, he was still on earth. Forty days after his Resurrection, Jesus gathered his followers and gave them the Great Commission: to make disciples of all nations. This gave them permission to take the gospel beyond Israel and to the world. And they were faithful to this command. Once he gave them the Great Commission, he bid them farewell, promised to send the Holy Spirit, and ascended into heaven. The Great Commission still speaks to us today as we share the good news of Jesus with others.

The Sacred Circle Time Focus: We will celebrate that Christians all over the world love Jesus.

Sacred Circle Time Basic Format

Sacred Circle basket and contents:

- Sacred space cloth
- Symbols for Creator (globe), Christ (cross), and Holy Spirit (bell or chimes)
- Small, unbreakable bottle to hold water or oil for the blessing
- A journal page (one per child)
- Crayons and/or markers
- A Bible bookmarked at Matthew 28:16-20
- Focused objects from the Bible story: A globe or map of the world, a ball of yarn

The Lesson

Gathering

Sit down and place the sacred basket in front of you.

Pause so that the children notice it and begin to come closer.

Invite them to form a circle.

Sit quietly until they settle in and are quiet.

Say: "It is time for Sacred Circle Time. I am so glad that you are here today. I love learning our stories and experiencing God with you."

Creating the Sacred Space

Say: "First, we create our sacred space."

Slowly lay out the sacred cloth.

Slowly lift the globe (symbol of God, the Creator) and hold it at the eye level of the children. Say: "This is our symbol for God, the Creator." Carefully lay it on the sacred cloth. (*Pause.*)

Slowly lift the cross (symbol of God, the Son). Say: "This is our symbol for God, the Son." Carefully lay it on the sacred cloth. (*Pause.*)

Slowly lift the bell (symbol of God, the Holy Spirit). Say: "This is our symbol of God, the Holy Spirit." Carefully lay it on the sacred cloth. (*Pause.*)

Point to each symbol and say: "So we have God, the Creator; God, the Son; and God, the Holy Spirit. (*Pause.*) Our sacred space is ready. We are ready to begin our Sacred Circle Time together."

God, the Creator (A Time to Wonder)

Show the children the globe and tell them that this is the whole world. Then show them where they live on the globe. Show them where Jesus lived in Israel. Let them look at the different countries. Tell them the names of some countries, and have them notice how some are large and some are small. Show them where the oceans are and where land is.

God, the Son (Telling the Story)

Say: "Our story today, which is found in (*open the Bible*) Matthew, chapter 28, verses 16-20, begins here in Israel (*point on the globe*), where Jesus and his disciples, his twelve close friends, lived. Jesus was in Israel with his disciples, but the time had come for Jesus to leave earth and go to live with God. So he gathered his friends and said, 'I am going to go live in heaven with God now. I have taught you many things, and now I want you to teach other people what I taught you. In fact, I want you to go all over the world and tell people that God loves them!'"

"And so, after Jesus went to heaven, his disciples, his friends, started telling people all over the world about Jesus. They went so far! They didn't go this far. (*Measure out about 12 inches of the yarn.*) They didn't go this far. (*Measure about a yard of the yarn.*) They went this far (*take the yarn and stretch it as far as you can*), telling people all over the world about Jesus. And then a man named Paul came along, and he started telling people all over the world about Jesus. Before long, he traveled all over the world. (*Stand up and start stretching the yarn all over the room.*) And other people who loved Jesus started telling people about God. And before long, the whole world knew about

Jesus. And today, because those people shared God's love with others, people from all over the world know about Jesus and how much he loves them."

God, the Holy Spirit (Quiet and Prayer Time)

Say: "It is now time to pray. I am going to slowly turn the globe in a circle. As I do, I want you to think of all the countries and places all over the world where the people love Jesus." (*Turn the globe a few times while they sit in silence.*)

Pray: "God, thank you for the whole world and for all the people, all over the world, who love you. In the name of Christ, we pray. Amen."

(If using the extended Sacred Circle Time, stop here.)

A Time of Blessing

Explain that the symbol for today is a world because people all over the world love God, and God loves all the people of the world. Bless the children where they request, being sure to look them directly in their eyes.

Say: "Thank you for experiencing God with me today. You are a blessing!"

Extended Format

(*10 minutes*) Begin with free-play time. Greet the children warmly and let them get used to the space. Have something in the free-play space for them to play with. Rotate each week:

Week One: Paper and crayons, markers, or paint.
Week Two: Clay, wire, pipe cleaners and beads, and tools to work the clay.
Week Three: Things to build with: blocks, Legos®, cans, boxes, or flat stones.
Week Four: Things that make noise.

(*3 minutes*) Transition Time. Let the children know that it is almost Sacred Circle Time.

Say: "It is almost our Sacred Circle Time. I cannot wait to have sacred time with you today. Will you start to finish up? Then come join me for our special, holy time together."

Sit down in the Sacred Circle Time space and place your sacred basket in front of you.

(*10 minutes*) **Sacred Circle Time** (*Basic Format*)—Use the Sacred Circle Basic Format, but do not include the blessing or closing.

(*10 minutes*) **Trinity Stations**

Explain the Trinity Stations procedure for new children and for those who might forget from time to time.

Walk with the children to the Trinity Stations and show them what they can do in the stations, but do not let them start until they have seen all three stations.

Tell the children that after the Trinity Stations, they will spend five minutes in quiet time thinking about the story and the activities they have completed. They will then return to the Sacred Circle Time space to draw pictures and talk about their activities.

Station One: God, the Creator (Wonder) Station

Walk with the children to this station and show them what they can do here. In addition to the suggested supplies (page 469), you might want to add a globe and some maps of the world.

Station Two: God, the Son (Story) Station

Walk with the children to this station and show them what they can do here. In addition to the suggested supplies (page 469), you might want to include some maps and toy cars to show how people take the good news all over the world. Or you might want to bring some costumes or hats of people from around the world for the children to try on.

Station Three: God, the Holy Spirit (Prayer) Station

Walk with the children to this station and show them what they can do here. In addition to the suggested supplies (page 469), you might want to have a globe of the world and/or pictures of people from all over the world for the children to look at as they pray.

Begin Quiet Time

Instruct the children to begin five minutes of quiet time to think about the Bible story. Explain that after the time has elapsed, you will invite them, one at a time, to the Sacred Circle Time space to draw what they did or thought about.

(2-minute transition time) Place paper, crayons, and other material in the circle. Invite the children, one at a time, to come and draw what they did, thought about, or experienced.

(*10 minutes*) **Journal and Share Time**

Let them draw and journal as they gather. When most of the children have finished, let them begin to share. Remind the children that listening to one another is important.

Say: "Thank you for spending time with me in the Trinity Stations. I cannot wait to find out what you experienced today. Who would like to share?" (Give each child time to talk, and you should talk as well.)

Place their activities in individual folders; or if they are to take the folders home, place them behind them so they will not be distracted. This will keep you from having to correct the children's behavior.

10 minutes (snack or toy time)

A Time of Blessing

Explain that the symbol for today is a world because people all over the world love God and God loves all the people of the world. Bless the children where they request, being sure to look them directly in their eyes.

Say: "Thank you for experiencing God with me today. You are a blessing!"

Closing Time

Slowly put each Trinity symbol away.

Say: "And now we are finished with our Sacred Circle Time. We put away our symbol for God, the Creator. We put away our symbol for God, the Son. And we put away our symbol for God, the Holy Spirit."

Then quietly and gently put the sacred cloth away.

Conclude: "And we are all done with our Sacred Circle time. You did a great job. Yay!" Clap and celebrate a job well done.

APPENDIX 1:
SACRED CIRCLE TIME SUPPLIES

Supplies You Will Need for Both Formats

The Sacred Circle basket

Sacred space cloth

Symbols for Creator (globe), Christ (cross), and Holy Spirit (bell or chimes)

A Bible marked to the passage you will be studying

Small, unbreakable bottle to hold water or oil for the blessing

A journal page (one per child)

Crayons and/or markers

The Additional Trinity Station Supplies

Suggested supplies are listed below. Additional suggestions will be made with each lesson. However, use your imagination and the things you already have to create these spaces. The importance of these stations is not what supplies are in them, but rather that the supplies can be used to invite the children to reflect through touch, exploration, and play. This is how young children reflect and process. The more options they have, the better.

God, the Creator (Wonder) Station

- A bowl of water and small cups
- Beans and or seeds in a large plastic container
- Clay and sand
- Spices in small containers to smell
- Magnifying glass
- Mirror
- Plants and leaves
- Crystal prisms

God, the Son (Story) Station

- Children's Bibles
- Bibles with pictures
- Lego® sets
- Blocks
- Dolls dressed up as Bible characters
- Puppets
- Costumes and cloth to create costumes
- Simple props such as broom, table, chairs, rocking horse, old boxes of different sizes

God, the Holy Spirit (Prayer) Station

FOR QUIET REFLECTION:

- Electric candles
- Crosses of all sizes and types
- Icons
- Pictures
- A mirror
- Material and boxes to create altars

FOR ART AND MUSICAL PRAYER:

- Paper
- Crayons
- Scissors
- Magazines
- Glue
- Markers
- Sequins, buttons, etc. for decorating
- CD player and several selections of music
- Rubber bands and boxes
- Tubes for blowing
- Simple stringed instruments or chimes or bells
- Buckets for drumming

APPENDIX 2:
BLANK SAMPLE FOR YOU TO USE

Once you get the idea of Sacred Circle Time, you are welcome to use this blank format to create your own holy times with the children. May God bless you and the children in your lives!

Date or Occasion of Lesson: _____

Story: _____

Text: _____

(*Print text here*)

About the text:

(*Knowing the background and context for the story is helpful. Write a few sentences about the text here.*)

_____

_____

_____

_____

Sacred Circle Time Focus:

(What is the one main focus for the story?)

_____

Sacred Circle Time Basic Format

Sacred Circle basket and contents:

- Sacred space cloth
- Symbols for Creator (globe), Christ (cross), and Holy Spirit (bell or chimes)
- Small, unbreakable bottle to hold water or oil for the blessing
- A journal page (one per child)
- Crayons and/or markers
- Bible bookmarked at the Bible passage

Focused objects from the Bible story: _____

(These objects should ideally come from the story and be used both as the wonder object and as a focal point for the story.)

The Lesson

Gathering

Begin by sitting down and placing the sacred basket in front of you.

Pause so that the children notice it and begin to come closer.

Invite them to form a circle.

Sit quietly until they settle in and are quiet.

Say: "It is time for Sacred Circle Time. I am so glad that you are here today. I love learning our stories and experiencing God with you."

Creating the Sacred Space

Say: "First, we create our sacred space."

Slowly lay out the sacred cloth.

Slowly lift the globe (symbol of God, the Creator) and hold it at the eye level of the children.

Say: "This is our symbol for God, the Creator."

Carefully lay it on the sacred cloth. *(Pause.)*

Slowly lift the cross (symbol of God, the Son).

Say: "This is our symbol for God, the Son."

Carefully lay it on the sacred cloth. (*Pause.*)

Slowly lift the bell (symbol of God, the Holy Spirit).

Say: "This is our symbol of God, the Holy Spirit." (*Pause.*)

Point to each symbol and say: "So we have God, the Creator; God, the Son; and God, the Holy Spirit. (*Pause.*) Our sacred space is ready. We are ready to begin our Sacred Circle Time together."

God, the Creator (A Time to Wonder)

Use your object as a time of wonder. Remember, this is a time to enjoy, listen, and engage with the children. There are no correct or wrong answers.

God, the Son (Telling the Story)

Tell the story. Remember to slow down and focus on the story, repeat yourself often, and tell the story as simply as you can, much like you would read a simple children's book to children.

God, the Holy Spirit (Quiet and Prayer Time)

Say: "It is now time to pray." Explain what the prayer will be.

Pray the prayer. Remember that word prayers are not always best. The children can use their bodies and their hands, sing songs, be silent, and so on.

Pray: "God, (Use a simple one-line closing for the prayer time.) In the name of Christ, we pray. Amen."

A Time of Blessing

The symbol for the story today is (*name the symbol*) because (*connect the symbol back with the story*).

Ask: "Where would you like your blessing today?" (*Let them tell you.*)

(*Make the symbol and look the children in their eyes.*)

Say: "Thank you for being here today and spending time experiencing God with me. You are a blessing!"

Extended Format

(*10 minutes*) Begin with free-play time. Greet the children warmly and let them get used to the space. Have something in the free-play space for them to play with. Rotate each week:

Week One: Paper and crayons, markers, or paint.

Week Two: Clay, wire, pipe cleaners and beads, and tools to work the clay.

Week Three: Things to build with: blocks, Legos®, cans, boxes, or flat stones.

Week Four: Things that make noise.

(*3 minutes*) Transition Time. Let the children know that it is almost Sacred Circle Time. Say: "It is almost our Sacred Circle Time. I cannot wait to have sacred time with you today. Will you start to finish up? Then come join me for our special, holy time together."

Sit down in the Sacred Circle Time space and place your sacred basket in front of you.

(*10 minutes*) **Sacred Circle Time** (*Basic Format*)—Use the Sacred Circle Basic Format, but do not include the blessing or closing.

(*10 minutes*) **Trinity Stations**

Explain the Trinity Stations procedure for new children and for those who might forget from time to time.

Walk with the children to the Trinity Stations and show them what they can do there, but do not let them start until they have seen all three stations.

Tell the children that after the Trinity Stations, they will spend five minutes in quiet time thinking about the story and the activities they have completed. They will then return to the Sacred Circle Time space to draw pictures and talk about their activities.

Station One: God, the Creator (Wonder) Station

(*Walk with the children to this station and show them what they can do here.*) In addition to the suggested supplies, you might want to add _____ (*something that comes from the story that they can use to touch, build or create*).

Station Two: God, the Son (Story) Station

(*Walk with the children to this station and show them what they can do here.*) In addition to the suggested supplies, you might want to add _____ (*something that comes from the story that helps them to act the story out and pretend to be characters in the story.*)

Station Three: God, the Holy Spirit (Prayer) Station

(*Walk with the children to this station and show them what they can do here.*) In addition to the suggested supplies, you might want to add _____ (*something that comes from the story to use in a reflective prayer time. It can be creative or a tool to help the children be still. Remember to vary this so that they can use all of their senses during their prayer times.*)

Begin Quiet Time

Say: "Let's begin five minutes of thinking about (*recap the story briefly*).

And then, after the time is over, I will invite you one at a time, to come to the Sacred Circle Time space and draw what you did or thought about, so we can all share together."

(*2-minute transition time*) Place paper, crayons, and other material in the circle. Invite the children, one at a time, to come and draw what they did, thought about, or experienced.

(*10 minutes*) **Journal and Share Time**

Let them draw and journal as they gather. When most of the children have finished, let them begin to share. Stress that listening is important.

Say: "Thank you for spending time with me in the Trinity Stations. I cannot wait to find out what you experienced today. Who would like to share?" (Give each child time to speak, and you should also speak.)

Place their activities in individual folders; or if they are to take them home, place them behind them so they will not be distracted. This will keep you from having to correct any one.

10 minutes (snack or toy time)

A Time of Blessing

The symbol for the story today is (*name the symbol*) because (*connect the symbol back with the story*).

Ask: "Where would you like your blessing today?" (*Let them tell you.*)

(Make the symbol and look the children in their eyes.)

Say: "Thank you for being here today and spending time experiencing God with me. You are a blessing!"

Slowly put each Trinity symbol away.

Say: "And now we are finished with our Sacred Circle Time. We put away our symbol for God, the Creator. We put away our symbol for God, the Son. And we put away our symbol for God, the Holy Spirit.

Then quietly and gently put the sacred cloth away.

Conclude: "And we are all done with our Sacred Circle time. You did a great job. Yay!" Clap and celebrate a job well done.

APPENDIX 3:
SUGGESTED SACRED CIRCLE SET UP

Basic Sacred Circle Time

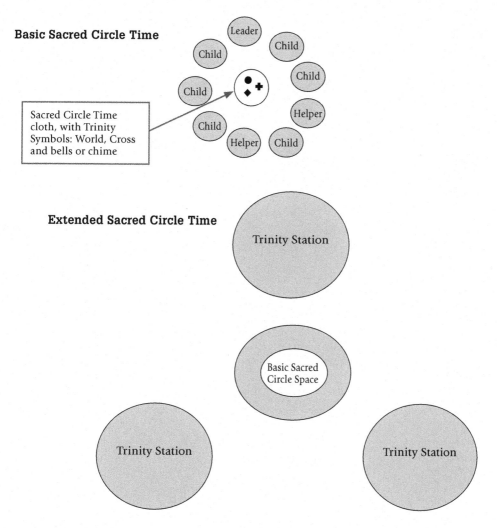

Sacred Circle Time cloth, with Trinity Symbols: World, Cross and bells or chime

Extended Sacred Circle Time

Trinity Station

Basic Sacred Circle Space

Trinity Station

Trinity Station

APPENDIX 4:
SCRIPTURE INDEX

OLD TESTAMENT

Genesis

Exodus

NEW TESTAMENT

Matthew

Mark

Luke

John

Acts

CPSIA information can be obtained
at www.ICGtesting.com
Printed in the USA
LVOW02s0401070217
523398LV00002B/3/P